Frommer's®

Spanish Phrasebook & Culture Guide

European Edition

1st Edition

WILEY

Wiley Publishing, Inc.

Published by:

Wiley Publishing, Inc.

111 River St.
Hoboken, NJ 07030-5774

ISBN-13: 978-0-471-79297-0
ISBN-10: 0-471-79297-7

Series Editor: Maureen Clarke
Travel Content by Peter Stone
Travel Content Editor: Michael Spring
Editorial Assistant: Melinda Quintero
Photo Editor: Richard H. Fox
Cover design by Fritz Metsch

Interior Design, Content Development, Translation, Copyediting, Proofreading,
Production, and Layout by:
Publication Services, Inc., 1802 South Duncan Road, Champaign, IL 61822
Linguists: Laura F. Temes, Nanette Monet, & Justin Serrano

For information on our other products and services or to obtain technical support,
please contact our Customer Care Department within the U.S. at 800/762-2974, outside the U.S. at 317/572-3993 or fax 317/572-4002.
Wiley also publishes its books in a variety of electronic formats. Some content that
appears in print may not be available in electronic formats.

Manufactured in the United States of America

5 4 3 2 1

Contents

An Invitation to the Reader

In researching this book, we discovered many wonderful sayings and terms useful to travelers in Spain. We're sure you'll find others. Please tell us about them, so we can share the information with your fellow travelers in upcoming editions. If you were disappointed with an aspect of this book, we'd like to know that, too. Please write to:

Frommer's Spanish Phrasebook & Culture Guide,
European Edition, 1st Edition
Wiley Publishing, Inc.
111 River St. • Hoboken, NJ 07030-5774

An Additional Note

The packager, editors, and publisher cannot be held responsible for the experiences of readers while traveling. Your safety is important to us, however, so we encourage you to stay alert and be aware of your surroundings. Keep a close eye on cameras, purses, and wallets, all favorite targets of thieves and pickpockets.

Frommers.com

Now that you have the language for a great trip, visit our website at **www.frommers.com** for travel information on more than 3,000 destinations. With features updated regularly, we give you instant access to the most current trip-planning information available. At Frommers.com, you'll also find the best prices on airfares, accommodations, and car rentals—and you can even book travel online through our travel booking partners. At Frommers.com, you'll also find:

- Online updates to our most popular guidebooks
- Vacation sweepstakes and contest giveaways
- Newsletter highlighting the hottest travel trends
- Online travel message boards with featured travel discussions

INTRODUCTION: HOW TO USE THIS BOOK

As a Romance language, Spanish is closely related to Latin, French, Italian, Portuguese, and Romanian. But not one of these European tongues is used with half the frequency of Spanish—with more than 332 million speakers world-wide, including more than 23 million in the United States. Variations spoken by Mexicans, Ecuadorians, Puerto Ricans, and other Latino ethnic groups are considerable, but we have used European Spanish (Castilian) throughout this book.

Our intention is not to teach you Spanish; we figure you'll find an audio program for that. Our aim is to provide a portable travel tool that's easy to use. With most phrasebooks, you practically have to memorize the contents before you know where to look for a term on the spot. This phrasebook is designed for fingertip referencing, to help you find the language you need fast.

Part of this book organizes terms by chapters, as in a Frommer's guide—getting a room, getting a good meal, etc. Within those sections, we tried to organize phrases according to how frequently readers are likely to use them. But let's say you're in a cab and received the wrong change, and don't know where to look in the money chapter. With Frommer's PhraseFinder, you can quickly look up "change" in the dictionary, and learn how to say "Sorry, but this isn't the right change." Then you can follow the cross reference for numbers, and specify how much you're missing.

What will make this book most practical? What will make it easiest to use? These are the questions we asked ourselves as we assembled these travel terms.

Our immediate goal was to create a phrasebook as indispensable as your passport. But our far-ranging objective is to enrich your experience of travel. And with that we offer the following wish: *¡Que tenga un buen viaje!*

CHAPTER ONE

SURVIVAL SPANISH

If you tire of toting around this phrasebook, tear out this chapter. You should be able to navigate your destination with only the terms found in the next 35 pages.

BASIC GREETINGS

For a full list of greetings, see p125.

Hello.	**Hola.**
	OH-lah
How are you?	**¿Cómo está?**
	KOH-moh ehs-TAH
I'm fine, thanks.	**Estoy bien, gracias.**
	ehs-TOY BYEHN, GRAH-thyahs
And you?	**¿Y usted?**
	ee oos-TEHD
My name is ____.	**Me llamo ____.**
	meh YAH-mo
And yours?	**¿Y usted?**
	ee oos-TEHD
It's a pleasure to meet you.	**Es un placer conocerle.**
	EHS oon plah-THEHR koh-noh-THEHR-leh
Please.	**Por favor.**
	pohr fah-VOHR
Thank you.	**Gracias.**
	GRAH-thyahs
Yes.	**Sí.**
	see
No.	**No.**
	noh
Okay.	**Vale.**
	vah-leh
	De acuerdo.
	deh ah-KWEHR-doh

1

No problem.	**No hay problema.**
	noh aye proh-BLEH-mah
I'm sorry, I don't understand.	**Lo siento, no entiendo.**
	loh SYEHN-toh no ehn-TYEHN-doh
Would you speak slower, please?	**¿Puede hablar un poco más despacio?**
	PWEH-deh ah-BLAHR oon POH-koh mahs deh-SPA-thee-oh
Would you speak louder, please?	**¿Puede hablar un poco más alto?**
	PWEH-deh ah-BLAHR oon POH-koh mahs AHL-toh
Do you speak English?	**¿Usted habla inglés?**
	oos-TEHD AH-blah eeng-GLEHS
Do you speak any other languages?	**¿Usted habla otro idioma?**
	oos-TEHD AH-blah OH-troh ee-DYOH-ma
I speak ____ better than Spanish.	**Yo hablo ____ mejor que español.**
	yoh AH-bloh ____ meh-HOHR keh ehs-pah-NYOL

For languages, see English / Spanish dictionary.

Would you spell that?	**¿Puede deletrear lo?**
	PWEH-de deh-leh-treh-AHR loh
Would you please repeat that?	**¿Puede repetir, por favor?**
	PWEH-deh rreh-peh-TEER pohr fah-VOHR
Would you point that out in this dictionary?	**¿Puede señalarlo en este diccionario?**
	PWEH-deh seh-nyah-LAHR-loh ehn EHS-deh deek-thyoh-NAHR-yoh

THE KEY QUESTIONS

With the right hand gestures, you can get a lot of mileage from the following list of single-word questions and answers.

Who?	**¿Quién? ¿Quiénes?**
	KYEHN? KYEH-nehs?

What?	**¿Qué?**
	keh
When?	**¿Cuándo?**
	KWAHN-doh
Where?	**¿Dónde?**
	DOHN-deh
To where?	**¿Adónde?**
	ah-DOHN-deh
Why?	**¿Por qué?**
	pohr-KEH
How?	**¿Cómo?**
	KOH-moh
Which?	**¿Cuál?**
	KWAHL
How many? / How much?	**¿Cuánto? ¿Cuántos?**
	KWAHN-toh, KWAHN-tohs

THE ANSWERS: WHO

For full coverage of pronouns, see p21.

I	**yo**
	yoh
you	**usted / tú**
	oos-TEHD, too
him	**él**
	ehl
her	**ella**
	EH-yah
us	**nosotros**
	noh-SOH-trohs
you (plural)	**vosotros**
	voh-SOH-trohs
them	**ellos / ellas**
	EH-yohs, EH-yahs

THE ANSWERS: WHEN

For full coverage of time, see p12.

now	**ahora**
	ah-OH-rah
later	**después**
	dehs-PWEHS
in a minute	**en un minuto**
	ehn oon mee-NOO-toh
today	**hoy**
	oy
tomorrow	**mañana**
	mah-NYAH-nah
yesterday	**ayer**
	ah-YEHR
in a week	**en una semana**
	ehn OO-nah seh-MAH-nah
next week	**la próxima semana**
	lah PROHK-see-mah seh-MAH-nah
last week	**la semana pasada**
	lah seh-MAH-nah pah-SAH-dah
next month	**el próximo mes**
	ehl PROHK-see-moh MEHS
At _____	**A las _____**
	ah lahs
ten o'clock this morning.	**diez en punto esta mañana.**
	DYETH ehn POON-toh EHS-tah mah-NYAH-nah
two o'clock this afternoon.	**dos en punto esta tarde.**
	dohs ehn POON-toh EHS-tah TAHR-deh
seven o'clock this evening.	**siete en punto esta noche.**
	SYEH-teh ehn POON-toh EHS-ahOH-cheh

For full coverage of numbers, see p7.

THE ANSWERS: WHERE

here	**aquí**
	ah-KEE
there	**allí**
	ah-EE
near	**cerca**
	THEHR-kah
closer	**más cerca**
	mahs THEHR-kah
closest	**lo más cerca**
	loh MAHS THEHR-kah
far	**lejos**
	LEH-hohs
farther	**más lejos**
	mahs LEH-hohs
farthest	**lo más lejos**
	loh MAHS LEH-hohs
across from	**enfrente de**
	ehn-FRHEN-teh deh
next to	**al lado de**
	ahl LAH-doh deh
behind	**detrás de**
	deh-TRAHS deh
straight ahead	**adelante / todo recto**
	ah-deh-LAHN-teh / TOH-doh
	REHK-toh
left	**la izquierda**
	lah ees-KYEHR-dah
right	**la derecha**
	lah deh-REH-chah
up	**arriba**
	ah-RREE-bah
down	**abajo**
	ah-BAH-hoh
lower	**más abajo**
	mahs ah-BAH-hoh

higher	**más arriba**
	mahs ah-RREE-bah
forward	**hacia delante**
	AH-thyah deh-LAHN-teh
back	**hacia atrás**
	AH-thyah ah-TRAHS
around	**alrededor**
	ahl-reh-deh-DOHR
across the street	**al cruzar la calle**
	ahl kroo-THAHR lah KAH-yeh
down the street	**calle abajo**
	KAH-yeh ah-BAH-hoh
on the corner	**en la esquina**
	ehn lah ehs-KEE-nah
kitty-corner	**la esquina diagonal**
	lah ehs-KEE-nah dee-ah-goh-NAHL
____ blocks from here	**a ____ manzanas de aquí**
	ah ____ mahn-THAH-nahs deh ah-KEE

For a full list of numbers, see the next page

THE ANSWERS: WHICH

this one	**éste / ésta**
	EH-steh / EH-stah
that (that one, close by)	**ese / esa**
	EH-seh / EH-sah
(that one, in the distance)	**aquel / aquella**
	ah-KEHL / ah-KEH-yah
these	**éstos / éstas**
	EHS-tohs / EHS-tahs
those (those there, close by)	**ésos / ésas**
	EH-sohs / EH-sahs

NUMBERS & COUNTING

one	**uno** *OO-noh*	seventeen	**diecisiete** *dyeh-theeh-SYEH-teh*
two	**dos** *dohs*	eighteen	**dieciocho** *dyeh-THYOH-choh*
three	**tres** *trehs*	nineteen	**diecinueve** *dyeh-theeh-NWEH-veh*
four	**cuatro** *KWAH-troh*	twenty	**veinte** *VEH-een-teh*
five	**cinco** *THEEN-koh*	twenty-one	**veintiuno** *veh-een-TYOO-noh*
six	**seis** *SEH-ees*	thirty	**treinta** *TREH-een-tah*
seven	**siete** *SYEH-teh*	forty	**cuarenta** *kwah-REN-teh*
eight	**ocho** *OH-cho*	fifty	**cincuenta** *theen-KWEHN-tah*
nine	**nueve** *NWEH-veh*	sixty	**sesenta** *seh-SEHN-tah*
ten	**diez** *dyeth*	seventy	**setenta** *seh-TEHN-tah*
eleven	**once** *OHN-theh*	eighty	**ochenta** *o-CHEHN-tah*
twelve	**doce** *DOH-theh*	ninety	**noventa** *noh-VEHN-tah*
thirteen	**trece** *TREH-theh*	one hundred	**cien** *thyehn*
fourteen	**catorce** *kah-TOHR-theh*	two hundred	**doscientos** *doh-THYEHN-tohs*
fifteen	**quince** *KEEN-theh*	one thousand	**mil** *meel*
sixteen	**dieciséis** *dyeh-theeh-SEH-ees*		

FRACTIONS & DECIMALS

one eighth	**un octavo**
	oon ohk-TAH-voh
one quarter	**un cuarto**
	oon KWAHR-toh
one third	**un tercio**
	oon TEHR-thyoh
one half	**medio**
	MEH-dyoh
two thirds	**dos tercios**
	dohs TEHR-thyohs
three quarters	**tres cuartos**
	trehs KWAHR-tohs
double	**doble**
	DOH-bleh
triple	**triple**
	TREE-pleh
one tenth	**un décimo**
	oon DEH-theeh-moh
one hundredth	**un centésimo**
	oon thehn-TEH-see-moh
one thousandth	**un milésimo**
	oon mee-LEH-see-moh

MATH

addition	**la suma**
	SOO-mah
2 +1	**dos más uno**
	dohs mahs OO-noh
subtraction	**la resta**
	RREHS-tah
2 - 1	**dos menos uno**
	dohs MEH-nohs OO-noh

multiplication	**la multiplicación** *mool-tee-plee-kah-THYOHN*
2 × 3	**dos por tres** *dohs pohr trehs*
division	**la división** *dee-vee-SYOHN*
6 ÷ 3	**seis dividido entre tres** *SEH-ees dee-vee-DEE-doh EHN-treh TREHS*

ORDINAL NUMBERS

first	**primero -a** *pree-MEH-roh / pree-MEH-rah*
second	**segundo -a** *seh-GOON-doh / seh-GOON-dah*
third	**tercero -a** *tehr-THEH-roh / tehr-THEH-rah*
fourth	**cuarto -a** *KWAHR-toh / KWAHR-tah*
fifth	**quinto -a** *KEEN-toh / KEEN-tah*
sixth	**sexto -a** *SEHK-sto / SEHK-stah*
seventh	**séptimo -a** *SEHP-tee-moh / SEHP-tee-mah*
eighth	**octavo -a** *ohk-TAH-voh / ohk-TAH-vah*
ninth	**noveno -a** *noh-VEH-noh / noh-VEH-nah*
tenth	**décimo -a** *DEH-thee-moh / DEH-thee-mah*
last	**último -a** *OOL-tee-mo / OOL-tee-mah*

MEASUREMENTS

Measurements will usually be metric, though you may need a
few American measurement terms.

inch	**la pulgada**
	lah pool-GAH-dah
foot	**el pie**
	ehl PYEH
mile	**la milla**
	lah MEE-yah
millimeter	**el milímetro**
	ehl mee-lee-MEH-troh
centimeter	**el centímetro**
	ehl thehn-tee-MEH-troh
meter	**el metro**
	ehl MEH-troh
kilometer	**el kilómetro**
	ehl kee-LOH-meh-troh
hectare	**la hectárea**
	lah hehk-TAH-reh-ahs
squared	**cuadrado -a**
	kwah-DRAH-doh / kwah-DRAH-dah
short	**corto -a**
	KOHR-toh / KOHR-tah
long	**largo -a**
	LAHR-goh / LAHR-gah

VOLUME

milliliters	**mililitros**
	mee-lee-LEE-trohs
liter	**litro**
	LEE-troh
kilo	**kilo**
	Kee-loh
ounce	**onza**
	OHN-thah

cup	**taza**
	TAH-thah
pint	**pinta**
	PEEN-tah
quart	**cuarto (de galón)**
	KWAHR-toh deh gah-LOHN
gallon	**galón**
	gah-LOHN

QUANTITY

some	**algún -a / algunos -as**
	ahl-GOON / ahl-GOO-nah /
	ahl-GOO-nohs / ahl-GOO-nahs
none	**nada / ninguno -a / ningunos -as**
	NAH-dah / neeng-GOO-noh /
	neeng-GOO-nah / neeng-GOO-
	nohs / neeng-GOO-nahs
all	**todo -a / todos -as**
	TOH-doh / TOH-dah / TOH-dohs /
	TOH-dahs
many / much	**mucho -a / muchos -as**
	MOO-cho / MOO-cha / MOO-
	chohs / MOO-chas
a little bit (can be used for quantity or for time)	**un poco / una poca**
	oon POH-koh / oo-nah POH-kah
dozen	**docena**
	doh-THEH-na

SIZE

small	**pequeño -a**
	peh-KEH-nyoh / peh-KEH-nyah
the smallest (literally "the most small")	**el / la / lo más pequeño -a**
	ehl / lah / loh mahs peh-KEH-
	nyoh / peh-KEH-nyah

medium	**mediano -a**
	meh-DYAH-no / meh-DYAH-na
big	**grande**
	GRAHN-deh
fat	**gordo -a**
	GOHR-doh / GOHR-dah
wide	**ancho -a**
	AHN-cho / AHN-cha
narrow	**angosto -a**
	ahng-GOH-stoh / ahng-GOH-stah

TIME

Time in Spanish is referred to, literally, by the hour. What time is it? translates literally as "What hour is it? / What hours are they?"

For full coverage of number terms, see p7.

HOURS OF THE DAY

What time is it?	**¿Qué hora es?**
	keh OH-ra ehs
At what time?	**¿A qué hora?**
	ah KEH OH-rah
For how long?	**¿Por cuánto tiempo?**
	pohr KWAHN-toh TYEHM-poh

A little tip

By adding a diminutive suffix -ito / -ita, -ico / -ica, or a combination of the two, you can make anything smaller or shorter. These endings replace the original -o and -a.

| advice, tip | **consejo** (*kohn-THEH-hoh*) |
| a little tip | **consejito** (*kohn-theh-HEE-toh*) |

It's one o'clock.	**Es la una en punto.** *ehs lah OO-nah ehn POON-toh*
It's two o'clock.	**Son las dos en punto.** *sohn lahs DOHS ehn POON-toh*
It's two thirty.	**Son las dos y media.** *sohn lahs DOHS ee MEH-dyah*
It's two fifteen.	**Son las dos y cuarto.** *sohn lahs DOHS ee KWAHR-toh*
It's a quarter to three.	**Son las tres menos cuarto.** *sohn las TREHS MEH-nohs KWAHR-toh*
It's noon.	**Es mediodía.** *ehs MEH-dyoh DEE-ah*
It's midnight.	**Es medianoche.** *ehs meh-dyah-NOH-cheh*
It's early.	**Es temprano.** *ehs tehm-PRAH-noh*
It's late.	**Es tarde.** *ehs TAHR-deh*
in the morning	**de la mañana** *deh lah mah-NYAH-nah*
in the afternoon	**de la tarde** *deh lah TAHR-deh*
at night	**de la noche** *deh lah NOH-cheh*
dawn	**la madrugada** *lah mah-droo-GAH-dah*

DAYS OF THE WEEK

Sunday	**el domingo**
	ehl doh-MEENG-go
Monday	**el lunes**
	ehl LOO-nehs
Tuesday	**el martes**
	ehl MAHR-tehs
Wednesday	**el miércoles**
	ehl MYEHR-koh-lehs
Thursday	**el jueves**
	ehl HWEH-vehs
Friday	**el viernes**
	ehl VYEHR-nehs
Saturday	**el sábado**
	ehl SAH-bah-doh
today	**hoy**
	oy
tomorrow	**mañana**
	mah-NYAH-nah
yesterday	**ayer**
	ah-YEHR
the day before yesterday	**anteayer**
	ahn-teh-ah-YEHR
one week	**una semana**
	OO-nah seh-MAH-nah
next week	**la próxima semana**
	lah PROHK-see-mah seh-MAH-nah
last week	**la semana pasada**
	lah seh-MAH-nah pah-SAH-dah

MONTHS OF THE YEAR

January	**enero**
	eh-NEH-roh
February	**febrero**
	feh-BREH-roh

March	**marzo**
	MAHR-thoh
April	**abril**
	ah-BREEL
May	**mayo**
	MAH-yoh
June	**junio**
	HOO-nee-oh
July	**julio**
	HOO-lee-oh
August	**agosto**
	ah-GOHS-toh
September	**septiembre**
	sehp-TYEHM-breh
October	**octubre**
	ohk-TOO-breh
November	**noviembre**
	noh-VYEHM-breh
December	**diciembre**
	dee-THYEHM-breh
next month	**el mes entrante**
	ehl MEHS ehn-TRAHN-teh
	el próximo mes
	ehl PROHK-see-moh MEHS
last month	**el mes pasado**
	ehl MEHS pah-SAH-doh

SEASONS OF THE YEAR

spring	**la primavera**
	lah pree-mah-VEH-rah
summer	**el verano**
	ehl veh-RAH-noh
autumn	**el otoño**
	ehl oh-TOH-nyoh
winter	**el invierno**
	ehl een-VYEHR-noh

Falsos Amigos

If you try winging it with Spanglish, beware of false cognates, known as *falsos amigos*, "false friends"—Spanish words that sound like English ones, but with different meanings. Here are some of the most commonly confused terms.

bomba	pump / tank / bomb
explosivo	bomb
arma	weapon
brazo	arm
constipado -a	congested
estreñido -a	constipated
embarazada	pregnant
avergonzado -a	embarrassed
injuria	insult
herida	injury
parientes	relatives
padres	parents
largo	long
grande	large
actual	now, current
verdadero -a	actual
asistir	to attend
ayudar	to assist
sopa	soup
jabón	soap
ropa	clothing
ropa vieja (lit. old clothes)	delicious Cuban dish of stewed, shredded beef
cuerda	rope

SPANISH GRAMMAR BASICS

Classified as a Romance language, descended from the Latin spoken when Spain was part of the Roman Empire, Castilian Spanish is a linguistic amalgamation closely related to Latin, French, Italian, Portuguese, and Romanian. Spanish was strongly affected by the Arabic of Spain's Moorish conquerors, who occupied the country from A.D. 711 to 1492. When Spain conquered what is today Latin America, it imposed its language on millions of Native Americans, from the Caribbean to Tierra del Fuego. But the indigenous languages they spoke, in turn, affected the local spoken Spanish, accounting for some of the rich diversity of the language worldwide.

THE ALPHABET

Spanish is a straightforward language with a simple alphabet. If foreign letters (k and w) are counted, the alphabet has 27 letters (ñ, in addition to the English alphabet).

Spanish also has two double letters: ll (elle), pronounced like y in English "yes," and rr (erre), pronounced like an English r trilled by vibrating the end of the tongue against the hard palate, just above the upper teeth. There is also ch, as in chipmunk.

Letter	Name	Pronunciation of Letter Name
a	a	*ah*
b	be	*beh*
c	ce	*theh*
d	de	*deh*
e	e	*eh*
f	efe	*EH-feh*
g	ge	*heh*
h	hache	*AH-cheh*
i	i	*ee*
j	jota	*HOH-tah*
k	ka	*kah*
l	ele	*EH-leh*

Letter	Name	Pronunciation of Letter Name
m	eme	*EH-meh*
n	ene	*EH-neh*
ñ	eñe	*EH-nyeh*
o	o	*oh*
p	pe	*peh*
q	cu	*koo*
r	ere	*EH-reh*
s	ese	*EH-seh*
t	te	*teh*
u	u	*oo*
v	ve, uve	*veh*
w	doble uve	*DOH-bleh OO-veh*
x	equis	*EH-kees*
y	i griega	*ee GRYEH-gah*
z	zeta	*THEH-tah*

PRONUNCIATION GUIDE

Vowels

a	ah as the a in father: abajo *(ah BAH hoh)*
au	ow as in cow: automático *(ow-to-MAH-tee-koh)*
ay	aye as in "All in favor, say aye": hay *(aye)*
e	eh to rhyme with the e in nestle: espera *(ehs PEH rah)*
i	ee as in feed: pasillo *(pah SEE yoh)*
o	oh as in boat: modismo *(moh DEES moh)*
oy	oy as in boy: hoy *(oy)*
u	oo as in the word coo: buscar *(boos KAHR)*

Consonants

b	as in bean, but softer with less explosion than in English: buscar *(boos-KAHR)*
c	before e and i as English initial s; ce is pronounced as theh: necesito *(neh theh SEE toh)*; ci is pronounced as first three letters in think: cinco *(THEEN-koh)*; before a, o, u as English k, but softer with less explosion: caballero *(kah bah YEH roh)*; consejo *(kohn THEH hoh)*; Cuba *(KOO bah)*

cu	in combination with a, e, i, o pronounced like the qu in quick: cuándo (KWAHN doh); cuestión (kwehs TYOHN)
d	as the d in day, but softer with less explosion than in English. Some final ds can be pronounced as the th in the: usted (oo STEHTH). If you pronounce Spanish d like the English d, you will be understood: ciudad (thee-oo-DAHD); de (deh)
f	as in fox: favor (fah-VOHR)
g	before e and i as English h; ge is pronounced like he in hen: emergencia (eh-mehr-HEHN-thy-ah); gi is pronounced like English he: puerta giratoria (PWEHR-tah hee-rah-TOHR-yah) before a, o, u as initial hard g in English as in gate: llegar (yeh GAHR); tengo (TEHN-goh); seguridad (seh-goo-ree-DAHD)
h	silent; hizo (EE-thoh), hasta (AHS-tah); hi before a vowel is pronounced like English y: hielo (YEH-loh)
j	as English h in hot: equipaje (eh-kee-PAH-heh)
k	as in English: kilómetro (kee-LOH-meh-troh)
l	as in English: ala (AH-lah)
ll	as in English million: calle (KAHL-yeh)
m	as in English: aeromozo (eh-roh-MOH-thoh)
n	as in English: negocios (neh-GOH-thyohs)
ñ	as ny in canyon: cañón (kahn-YOHN)
p	as in English but softer: pasaporte (pah-sah-POHR-teh)
q	qu is pronounced as k: máquina (MAH-kee-nah)
r	as in English but more clipped: puerta (PWEHR-tah)
rr	as a trilled r sound, vibrating the end of the tongue against the area just above the top teeth: perro (PEH-rroh). A single r that starts a word is pronounced like the double r: rayos X (RRAH-yohs EH-kees)
s	as in English: salida (sah-LEE-dah)
t	as in English but softer: tranvía (trahn-VEE-ah)
v	as in English: vuelo (VWEH-loh)
w	as in English: waflera (wah-FLEH-rah)

x	like English x: próximo *(PROHK-see-moh)*; in some old names and some names of Native American origin, like h: Don Quixote *(dohn kee HOH teh)*, México *(MEH-hee-koh)* spelled with j in Spain; before a consonant, like s: Taxco *(TAHS-koh)*
y	as in English: yo *(yoh)*; by itself, as the ee sound in bead: y *(ee)*
z	like th in English think: aterrizaje *(ah-teh-rree-THAH-heh)*

Castilian Pronunciation

Most residents of Northern Spain use the so-called Castilian "lisp." *Ce*, *ci*, and *z* followed by a vowel are pronounced like the *th* in "thud." (When *c* is followed by *a*, *o*, or *u*, it is pronounced like English *k*.)

WORD PRONUNCIATION

Syllables in words are also accented in a standard pattern. Generally, the last syllable is stressed except when a word ends in a vowel, n, or s; then the stress falls on the second to last syllable. If a word varies from this pattern, an accent mark is shown. Examples:

Ending in r

comer   *koh-MEHR*

Ending in a

comida   *koh-MEE-dah*

Ending in s

comemos   *koh-MEH-mohs*

Ending in n but with an accent mark

comilón   *koh-mee-LOHN*

GENDER, ADJECTIVES, MODIFIERS

Each noun takes a masculine or feminine gender, most often accompanied by a masculine or feminine definite article (el or la). Definite articles ("the"), indefinite articles ("a," "an"), and related adjectives must also be masculine or feminine, singular or plural, depending on the noun they're modifying.

The Definite Article ("The")

	Masculine	Feminine
Singular	*el* perro (the dog)	*la* mesa (the table)
Plural	*los* perros (the dogs)	*las* mesas (the tables)

The Indefinite Article ("A" or "An")

	Masculine	Feminine
Singular	*un* perro (a dog)	*una* mesa (a table)
Plural	*unos* perros (some dogs)	*unas* mesas (some tables)

PERSONAL PRONOUNS

AMAR: "To Love"

I love.	*Yo amo.*	AH-moh
You (singular familiar) **love.**	*Tú amas.*	AH-mahs
He / She loves. You (singular, formal) **love.**	*Él / Ella / Ud. ama.*	AH-mah
We love.	*Nosotros -as amamos.*	ah-MAH-mohs
You (plural, familiar) **love.**	*Vosotros -as amáis.*	ah-MAH-ees
They / You (plural, formal) **love.**	*Ellos / Ellas / Uds. aman.*	AH-mahn

> ### Hey, You!
>
> Spanish has two words for "you"—tú, spoken among friends and relatives, and Usted (abbreviated Ud. or Vd.), used among strangers or as a sign of respect toward elders and authority figures. When speaking with a stranger, expect to use Usted, unless you are invited to do otherwise. The second-person familiar plural form (vosotros) is used in Spain.

REGULAR VERB CONJUGATIONS

Spanish verb infinitives end in AR (hablar, to speak), ER (comer, to eat), or IR (asistir, to attend). Most verbs (known as "regular verbs") are conjugated according to those endings. To conjugate the present tense of regular verbs, simply drop the AR, ER, or IR and add the following endings:

Present Tense

AR Verbs   HABLAR "To Speak"

I speak.	Yo hablo.	AH-bloh
You (singular familiar) speak.	Tú hablas.	AH-blahs
He / She speaks. You (singular formal) speak.	Él / Ella / Ud. habla.	AH-blah
We speak.	Nosotros -as hablamos.	ah-BLAH-mohs
You (plural familiar) speak.	Vosotros -as habláis.	ah-BLAH-ees
They / You (plural formal) speak.	Ellos / Ellas / Uds. hablan.	AH-blahn

ER Verbs — COMER "To Eat"

ER Verbs	COMER "To Eat"	
I eat.	Yo como.	KOH-moh
You (singular familiar) eat.	Tú comes.	KOH-mehs
He / She eats. You (singular formal) **eat.**	Él / Ella / Ud. come.	KOH-meh
We eat.	Nosotros -as comemos.	koh-MEH-mohs
You (plural familiar) eat.	Vosotros -as coméis.	koh-MEH-ees
They / You (plural formal) **eat.**	Ellos / Ellas / Uds. comen.	KOH-mehn

IR Verbs — ASISTIR "To Attend"

IR Verbs	ASISTIR "To Attend"	
I attend.	Yo asisto.	ah-SEES-toh
You (singular familiar) **attend.**	Tú asistes.	ah-SEES-tehs
He / She attends. You (singular formal) **attend.**	Él / Ella / Ud. asiste.	ah-SEES-teh
We attend.	Nosotros -as asistimos.	ah-sees-TEE-mohs
You (plural familiar) **attend.**	Vosotros -as asistís.	ah-sees-TEES
They / You (plural formal) **attend.**	Ellos / Ellas / Uds. asisten.	ah-SEES-tehn

Simple Past Tense

These are the simple past tense conjugations for regular verbs.

AR Verbs **HABLAR "To Speak"**

I spoke.	Yo hablé.	ah-BLEH
You (singular familiar) spoke.	Tú hablaste.	ah-BLAHS-teh
He / She/ You (singular formal) spoke.	Él / Ella / Ud. habló.	ah-BLOH
We spoke.	Nosotros -as hablamos.	ah-BLAH-mohs
You (plural familiar) spoke.	Vosotros -as hablasteis.	ah-BLAHS-teh-ees
They / You (plural formal) spoke.	Ellos / Ellas / Uds. hablaron.	ah-BLAH-rohn

ER Verbs **COMER "To Eat"**

I ate.	Yo comí.	koh-MEE
You (singular familiar) ate.	Tú comiste.	koh-MEES-teh
He / She / You singular formal) ate.	Él / Ella / Ud. comió.	koh-mee-OH
We ate.	Nosotros -as comimos.	koh-MEE-mohs
You (plural familiar) ate.	Vosotros -as comisteis.	koh-MEES-teh-ees
They / You (plural formal) ate.	Ellos / Ellas / Uds. comieron.	koh-MYEH-rohn

IR Verbs	ASISTIR "To Attend"	
I attended.	Yo asist*í*.	ah-sees-TEE
You (singular familiar) **attended.**	Tú asist*iste*.	ah-sees-TEES-teh
He / She / You (singular formal) **attended.**	Él / Ella / Ud. asist*ió*.	ah-sees-TYOH
We attended.	Nosotros -as asist*imos*.	ah-sees-TEE-mohs
You plural familiar) **attended.**	Vosotros -as asist*isteis*.	ah-sees-TEES-teh-ees
They / You (plural formal) **attended.**	Ellos / Ellas / Uds. asist*ieron*.	ah-sees-TYEH-rohn

The Future

For novice Spanish speakers, the easiest way to express the future is to conjugate the irregular verb IR (to go) + a + any infinitive ("I am going to speak," "you are going to speak," etc.).

I am going to speak.	Yo *voy a* hablar.	voy ah ah-BLAHR
You (singular familiar) **are going to speak.**	Tú *vas a* hablar.	vahs ah ah-BLAHR
He / She is going to speak. You (singular formal) **are going to speak.**	Él / Ella / Ud. *va a* hablar.	vah ah ah-BLAHR
We are going to speak.	Nosotros -as *vamos a* hablar.	VAH-mohs ah ah-BLAHR

| You (plural familiar) are going to speak. | Vosotros -as *vais a* hablar. | VAH-ees ah ah-BLAHR |
| They / You (plural formal) are going to speak. | Ellos / Ellas / Uds. *van a* hablar. | vahn ah ah-BLAHR |

TO BE OR NOT TO BE (ESTAR & SER)

There are two forms of "being" in Spanish. One is for physical location or temporary conditions (estar), and the other is for fixed qualities or conditions (ser).

I am here.
(temporary, estar)

Yo estoy aquí.

I am from the United States.
(fixed, ser)

Yo soy de los Estados Unidos.

Norman is bored.
(temporary, estar)

Norman está aburrido.

Norman is boring.
(quality, ser)

Norman es aburrido.

The TV is old.
(quality, ser)

La televisión es vieja.

The TV is broken.
(condition, estar)

La televisión está rota.

Present Tense

Estar "To Be" (conditional)

I am.	Yo estoy.	ehs-TOY
You (singular, familiar) **are.**	Tú estás.	ehs-TAHS
He / She is. **You** (singular formal) **are.**	Él / Ella / Ud. está.	ehs-TAH
We are.	Nosotros -as estamos.	ehs-TAH-mohs
You (plural familiar) **are.**	Vosotros -as estáis.	ehs-TAH-ees
They / You (plural formal) **are.**	Ellos / Ellas / Uds. están.	ehs-TAHN

Simple Past Tense

Estar "To Be" (conditional)

I was.	Yo estuve.	ehs-TOO-veh
You were.	Tú estuviste.	ehs-too-VEES-teh
He / She was. **You** (formal) **were.**	Él / Ella / Ud. estuvo.	ehs-TOO-voh
We were.	Nosotros -as estuvimos.	ehs-too-VEE-mohs
You were.	Vosotros -as estuvisteis.	ehs-too-VEES-teh-ees
They / You (plural formal) **were.**	Ellos / Ellas / Uds. estuvieron.	ehs-too-VYEH-rohn

Present Tense

	Ser "To be" (permanent)	
I am.	Yo *soy*.	soy
You (singular familiar) **are.**	Tú *eres*.	EH-rehs
He/ She is. You (singular formal) **are.**	Él / Ella / Ud. *es*.	ehs
We are.	Nosotros -as *somos*.	SOH-mohs
You (plural familiar) **are.**	Vosotros -as *sois*.	SOH-ees
They / You (plural formal) **are.**	Ellos / Ellas / Uds. *son*.	sohn

Simple Past Tense

	Ser "To be" (permanent)	
I was.	Yo *fui*.	FOO-ee
You (singular familiar) **were.**	Tú *fuiste*.	foo-EES-teh
He/ She was. You (singular formal) **were.**	Él / Ella / Ud. *fue*.	FOO-eh
We were.	Nosotros -as *fuimos*.	foo-EE-mohs
You (plural familiar) **were.**	Vosotros -as *fuisteis*.	foo-EES-teh-ees
They / You (plural formal) **were.**	Ellos / Ellas / Uds. *fueron*	foo-EH-rohn

IRREGULAR VERBS

Spanish has numerous irregular verbs that stray from the standard AR, ER, and IR conjugations. Rather than bog you down with too much grammar, we're providing the present tense conjugations for the most commonly used irregular verbs.

TENER "To Have" (possess)

I have.	Yo *te*ngo.	TEHNG-goh
You (singular familiar) **have.**	Tú *ti*enes.	TYEH-nehs
He / She has. **You** (singular formal) **have.**	Él / Ella / Ud. *ti*ene.	TYEH-neh
We have.	Nosotros -as *te*nemos.	TYEH-neh
You (plural familiar) **have.**	Vosotros -as *te*néis.	teh-NEH-mohs
They / You (plural formal) **have.**	Ellos / Ellas / Uds. *ti*enen.	TYEH-nehn

---

Tener

Tener means "to have," but it's also used to describe conditions such as hunger, body pain, and age. For example:

Tengo hambre. I'm hungry.
(Literally: I have hunger.)
Tengo dolor de cabeza. I have a headache.
Tengo diez años. I am ten years old.
(Literally: I have ten years.)

HACER "To Do, To Make"

I make.	Yo hago.	AH-goh
You (singular familiar) make.	Tú haces.	AH-thehs
He / She makes. You (singular formal) make.	Él / Ella / Ud. hace.	AH-theh
We make.	Nosotros -as hacemos.	ah-THEH-mohs
You (plural familiar) make.	Vosotros -as hacéis.	ah-THEH-ees
They / You (plural formal) make.	Ellos / Ellas / Uds. hacen.	AH-thehn

COMENZAR "To Begin"

I begin.	Yo comienzo.	koh-MYEHN-thoh
You (singular familiar) begin.	Tú comienzas.	koh-MYEHN-thahs
He / She begins. You (singular formal) begin.	Él / Ella / Ud. comienza.	koh-MYEHN-thah
We begin.	Nosotros -as comenzamos	koh-mehn-THAH-mos
You (plural familiar) begin.	Vosotros -as comenzais.	koh-MEHN-thays
They / You plural formal) being.	Ellos / Ellas / Uds. comienzen.	koh-MYEHN-thahn

QUERER "To Want"

I want.	Yo qu*ie*ro.	KYEH-roh
You (singular familiar) **want.**	Tú qu*ie*res.	KYEH-rehs
He / She wants. You (singular formal) **want.**	Él / Ella / Ud. qu*ie*re.	KYEH-reh
We want.	Nosotros -as quer*e*mos	keh-REH-mohs
You (plural familiar) **want.**	Vosotros -as quer*éis*.	keh-REH-ees
They / You plural formal **want.**	Ellos / Ellas / Uds. qu*ie*ren.	KYEH-rehn

PODER "To Be Able"

I can. (I)	Yo p*ue*do.	PWEH-doh
You (singular familiar) **can.**	Tú p*ue*des.	PWEH-dehs
He / She can. You singular formal) **can.**	Él / Ella / Ud. p*ue*de.	PWEH-deh
We can.	Nosotros -as pod*e*mos.	poh-DEH-mohs
You (plural familiar) **can.**	Vosotros -as pod*éis*.	poh-DEH-ees
They / You (plural formal) **can.**	Ellos / Ellas / Uds. p*ue*den.	PWEH-dehn

HABER "To Have" (with past participle)		
I have.	Yo he.	eh
You (singular familiar) have.	Tú has.	ahs
He / She has. You (singular formal) have.	Él / Ella / Ud. ha.	ah
We have.	Nosotros -as hemos.	EH-mohs
You (plural familiar) have.	Vosotros -as habéis.	ah-BEH-ees
They / You plural formal have.	Ellos / Ellas / Uds. han.	ahn

PEDIR "To Ask"		
I ask.	Yo pido.	PEE-doh
You (singular familiar) ask.	Tú pides.	PEE-dehs
He / She asks. You (singular formal) ask.	Él / Ella / Ud. pide.	PEE-deh
We ask.	Nosotros -as pedimos.	peh-DEE-mohs
You (plural familiar) ask.	Vosotros -as pedís.	PEH-dees
They / You (plural formal) ask.	Ellos / Ellas / Uds. piden.	PEE-dehn

> **Note:** Verbs that end in **-cer** such as **conocer** change the **c** to **zc** before an ending that begins with **o** or **a**.

CONOCER "To Know" (someone)

I know.	Yo cono**zc**o.	koh-NOHTH-koh
You (singular familiar) **know.**	Tú conoce**s**.	koh-NOH-thehs
He / She knows. You (singular formal) **know.**	Él / Ella / Ud. conoce.	koh-NOH-theh
We know.	Nosotros -as conoce**mos**.	koh-noh-THEH-mohs
You (plural familiar) **know.**	Vosotros -as conocé**is**.	koh-noh-THEH-ees
They / You (plural formal) **know.**	Ellos / Ellas / Uds. conoce**n**.	koh-NOH-thehn

SABER "To Know" (something)

I know.	Yo sé.	seh
You (singular familiar) **know.**	Tú sabe**s**.	SAH-behs
He/ She knows. You (singular formal) **know.**	Él / Ella / Ud. sabe.	SAH-beh
We know.	Nosotros -as sabe**mos**.	sah-BEH-mohs
You (plural familiar) **know.**	Vosotros -as sabé**is**.	sah-BEH-ees
They / You (plural formal) **know.**	Ellos / Ellas / Uds. sabe**n**.	SAH-behn

Gustar

Spanish doesn't have a verb that literally means "to like." Instead, they use *gustar*, which means to please. So rather than say I like chocolate, you say:

Me gusta el chocolate. I like chocolate.
(Literally: Chocolate is pleasing to me.)

When what is liked is plural, the verb is plural:

Me gustan las tortillas. I like tortillas.
(Literally: Tortillas are pleasing to me.)

The person doing the liking is represented by an indirect object pronoun placed in front of the verb, as illustrated below.

	GUSTAR "To Like"
I like the tortilla.	*Me* gusta la tortilla.
You (informal singular) **like the tortilla.**	*Te* gusta la tortilla.
He / She likes the tortilla. You (formal singular) **like the tortilla.**	*Le* gusta la tortilla.
We like the tortilla.	*Nos* gusta la tortilla.
You (informal plural) **like the tortilla.**	*Os* gusta la tortilla.
They / You (formal plural) **like the tortilla.**	*Les* gusta la tortilla.

JUGAR "To Play"

I play.	Yo j*ueg*o.	HWEH-goh
You (singular familiar) **play.**	Tú j*uega*s.	HWEH-gahs
He / She plays. You (singular formal) **play.**	Él / Ella / Ud. j*uega*.	HWEH-gah
We play.	Nosotros -as jug*amos*.	hoo-GAH-mohs
You (plural familiar) **play**	Vosotros -as jug*áis*.	hoo-OAYS
They / You (plural formal) **play.**	Ellos / Ellas / Uds. j*uega*n.	HWEH-gahn

REFLEXIVE VERBS

Spanish has many reflexive verbs (when subject and object both refer to the same person or thing). The following common verbs are used reflexively: vestirse (to dress oneself), quedarse (to stay), bañarse (to bathe oneself), and levantarse (to wake up).

VESTIRSE "To Dress"

I get dressed.	Yo me v*isto*.	meh VEES-toh
You (singular familiar) **get dressed.**	Tú te v*iste*s.	teh VEES-tehs
He / She gets dressed. You (singular formal) **get dressed.**	Él / Ella / Ud. se v*iste*.	seh VEES-teh
We get dressed.	Nosotros -as nos vest*imos*.	nohs vehs-TEE-mohs
You (plural familiar) **get dressed**	Vosotros -as os vest*ís*	ohs vehs-TEES
They / You (plural formal) **get dressed.**	Ellos / Ellas / Uds. se v*iste*n.	seh VEES-tehn

BASIC ETIQUETTE

While many aspects of social behavior are universal, each country has its own idiosyncrasies. Spain is no exception. Here are a few pointers to help you blend in more seamlessly.

Appointments & Punctuality   It's said that in Spain the only things that start on time are bullfights and theater performances. Accordingly, a 15- to 30-minute delay should be expected for social and even certain business appointments.

Business Cards   These are ideally two-sided, with Spanish printed on one side and English on the other. When you're presenting your card, it's best to place the card with the Spanish side facing upward.

Clothing & Attire   Dress is becoming increasingly informal among Spaniards in the workplace, even in banks, insurance offices, and the like. When it comes to formal international meetings, however, elegance, style, and conservative clothing are still much appreciated. Shorts and Hawaiian shirts are definitely not a good idea, and even in the hottest weather it's more acceptable to keep jackets on rather than doffing them.

Colloquial Expressions   *Encantado* (literally "enchanted") simply means "Nice to meet you." *Hasta luego* (literally, "until then!") really means "See you later." *De nada* means "Don't mention it" or "You're welcome" when replying to "Thank you."

In many bars, the waiter/barman will address a man as *caballero* (gentleman), which has a nice Don Quixote–esque ring to it. With females, it's more commonly *señora* or *señorita*.

Gestures   Most first-time introductions are made with a firm handshake and eye contact. With friends or close contacts, hugging and back-patting are common. It's usual for women to be kissed on both cheeks by men or women, even during a first meeting. It's less common for heterosexual men to kiss each other on both cheeks—as they do in France—but this often happens among close friends and members of the same family.

Spaniards often stand uncomfortably close and, to emphasize a point, will often hold your arm or shoulder when conversing with you. It's best not to move away when this happens, which could cause offense. When you're trying to attract someone's attention, turn your palm down and wave your fingers or hand. To signify "no," shake one finger slowly to and fro. Thumbs-up is not usually a sign for okay, and neither is making a circle with thumb and first finger (this is considered vulgar). If you pull down your eyelid it infers that you are "aware" of something. If you want to summon someone or simply attract their attention, wave to them with the palm of your hand facing down.

A typical toast consists, as at home, of simply raising a glass of whatever you're drinking. The only difference is that here you say *salud* (health) instead of "here's mud in your eye" (or whatever you say at home). Both arms raised rapidly and simultaneously can represent an expression of extreme impatience, either in a traffic jam or at a bad bullfight.

Gifts If you're invited to dine with Spanish people it's not customary to bring a bottle of wine as you might at home. A nicely wrapped gift, preferably showing a quality brand-name item, is more appreciated. So are chocolates, pastries, or flowers—though dahlias *(dalias)* and chrysanthemums *(crisantemos)* signify bereavement and are best avoided. Thirteen stems are considered unlucky.

Greetings Men shake hands, and women kiss—and are kissed—on both cheeks.

In Spain, as well as Italy, France, and Germany, a distinction is made between "you" spoken to familiars and "you" spoken to superiors or elders. In Spain, *tú* is used among close friends, families, and loved ones. With all other relationships, especially when you're conversing with someone for the first time, the formal *usted* or *ustedes* (abbreviations *Vd.* or *Vdes.*) are used. *¿Cómo está usted?* (plural: *¿Cómo están ustedes?*) is the standard formal greeting and *¿Cómo estás?* (plural: *¿Cómo estais?*) the informal greeting.

In a bar or cafe, forms of address may range from the very informal *jefe* (literally "boss") to the more flattering *caballero* (gentleman). There is no alternative here to the standard *señora* or *señorita* for females. *Tío* (literally, "uncle") is used as a familiar form of address among young people. The rough U.S. equivalent is "dude."

Social Interactions   Though Spaniards generally observe forms of courtesy as described above, they can also seem on occasions brusque in a way that may seem rude by other western standards. A man in an *estanco* (shop or occasionally a kiosk selling tobacco and stamps) will say bluntly *Da me un paquete de Ducados* ("Give me a packet of Ducados") with no "would you" or "please." The assistant may then toss the requested item to the buyer instead of handing it over politely, and the buyer consequently neglects to reply with a "thank you." No rudeness is intended on either part. It's simply the no-nonsense way they act in these circumstances. If you do say "thank you" then the automatic reply is *a usted,* which means literally "to you" and in reality is an appreciative "no, sir or madam, thank *you.*" People in a packed bar may push roughly past you without saying pardon or sorry. The same goes on the underground train (metro) or on a bus. It's also fairly common for persons to try cutting a line or queue. Instead of fights breaking out over this sort of thing, nobody usually pays any notice, as no offense is intended.

FUN FACTS

Driest Town   Almeria, at the easterly end of the Andalucían coastline, has minimal rain; the gulch-serrated inland moon-scape looks like California's Death Valley.

Hottest Town   Ecija, between Córdoba and Seville, beside the Guadalquivir River and only a few feet above sea level, is known as the *sartén,* or "frying pan," of Spain. This dazzling white town is fine to visit between fall and spring but best avoided in July and August, when temperatures rise above 120°F (49°C).

Coldest Town   Soria, in the province of Castilla-Leon, routinely tops the charts in winter, with its frostbite-inducing chill. (Close rivals include Teruel and Vitoria.)

Best Standard of Living   This is enjoyed in the **Basque Country,** whose administrative capital, **Vitoria,** was the first Spanish city to follow UNESCO guidelines for urban planning.

Largest City   This is, unsurprisingly, Spain's booming capital **Madrid**—where the population has exploded in just 2 decades from one to five million (nearly two million more than its closest rival, Barcelona). It's continuing to swell at a monumental rate, and some predict it could be a megalopolis in coming decades, rivaling Mexico City or Shanghai in size.

Craziest Fiesta   In **La Tomatina,** for 3 hours in the bludgeoning heat of high summer, everyone in the Valencian town of Buñol pelts each other with tomatoes until the whole pueblo looks like the scene of a horror movie gorefest.

CHAPTER TWO

GETTING THERE & GETTING AROUND

This section deals with every form of transportation. Whether you've just reached your destination by plane or you're renting a car to tour the countryside, you'll find the phrases you need in the next 30 pages.

AT THE AIRPORT

I am looking for ____	**Estoy buscando ____** *ehs-TOY boos-KAHN-doh*
a porter.	**un maletero.** *oon mah-lah-TEH-roh*
the check-in counter.	**el mostrador de facturación.** *ehl mohs-trah-DOHR deh* *fahk-too-rah-THYON*
the ticket counter.	**el mostrador de billetes.** *ehl mohs-trah-DOHR deh beel-* *YEH-tehs*
arrivals.	**las llegadas.** *lahs yeh-GAH-dahs*
departures.	**las salidas.** *lahs sah-LEE-dahs*
gate number ____.	**la puerta de embarque ____.** *lah PWEHR-tah de ehm-BAHR-keh*

For full coverage of numbers, see p7.

the waiting area.	**el área de espera.** *ehl AH-reh-ah deh ehs-PEH-rah*
the men's restroom.	**el baño para caballeros.** *ehl BAH-nyoh PAH-rah kah-bah-* *YEH-rohs*
the women's restroom.	**el baño para damas.** *ehl BAH-nyoh PAH-rah DAH-mahs*
the police station.	**la comisaría.** *lah koh-mee-sah-REE-ah*

a security guard.	**un guardia de seguridad.** *oon GWAHR-dyah deh seh-goo-ree-DAHD*
the smoking area.	**la zona para fumadores.** *lah THOH-nah PAH-rah foo-mah-DOH-res*
the information booth.	**el punto de información.** *ehl POON-toh deh een-for-mah-THYOHN*
a public telephone.	**un teléfono público.** *oon teh-LEH-foh-noh POO-blee-koh*
an ATM.	**un cajero automático.** *oon kah-HEH-roh ow-toh-MAH-tee-koh*
baggage claim.	**la recogida de equipajes.** *lah reh-koh-HEE-dah de eh-kee-PAH-hehs*
a luggage cart.	**un carrito para equipaje.** *oon kah-RREE-toh PAH-rah eh-kee-PAH-heh*
a currency exchange.	**un lugar de cambio de moneda.** *oon loo-GAHR deh KAHM-byoh deh moh-NEH-dah*
a café.	**un café.** *oon kah-FEH*
a restaurant.	**un restaurante.** *oon rehs-tow-RAHN-teh*
a bar.	**un bar.** *oon bahr*
a bookstore or newsstand.	**una librería o un quiosco.** *OO-nah lee-breh-REE-ah oh oon kee-OHS-koh*
a duty-free shop.	**una tienda libre de impuestos.** *OO-nah TYEHN-dah LEE-breh deh eem-PWEHS-tohs*

Is there Internet access here?	**¿Hay acceso a Internet aquí?** *aye ahk-SEH-soh ah een-tehr-NEHT ah-KEE*
I'd like to page someone.	**Quiero llamar a alguien por el altavoz.** *KYEH-roh yah-MAHR ah AHLG-yehn pohr ehl ahl-tah-VOHS*
Do you accept credit cards?	**¿Aceptan tarjetas de crédito?** *ah-THEP-tahn tahr-HEH-tahs deh KREH-dee-toh*

CHECKING IN

I would like a one-way ticket to ____.	**Me gustaría un billete de ida a ____.** *meh goos-tah-REE-ah oon beel-YEH-teh deh EE-dah ah*
I would like a round trip ticket to ____.	**Me gustaría un billete de ida y vuelta a ____.** *meh goos-tah-REE-ah oon beel-YEH-teh de EE-dah ee VWEHL-tah ah*
How much are the tickets?	**¿Cuánto cuestan los billetes?** *KWAHN-toh KWEHS-tahn lohs beel-YEH-tehs*
Do you have anything less expensive?	**¿Tiene algo más económico?** *TYEH-neh AHL-goh mahs eh-koh-NOH-mee-koh*
How long is the flight?	**¿Cuánto dura el vuelo?** *KWAHN-toh DOO-rah ehl VWEH-loh*
What time does flight ____ leave?	**¿A qué hora sale el vuelo ____?** *ah keh OH-rah SAH-leh ehl VWEH-loh*
What time does flight ____ arrive?	**¿A qué hora llega el vuelo ____?** *ah keh OH-rah YEH-gah ehl VWEH-loh*

For full coverage of number terms, see p7.
For full coverage of time, see p12.

Common Airport Signs

Llegadas	Arrivals
Salidas	Departures
Terminal	Terminal
Puerta de embarque	Gate
Mostrador de billetes	Ticketing
Aduana	Customs
Reclamo de equipaje	Baggage Claim
Empuje	Push
No fumar	No Smoking
Entrada	Entrance
Salida	Exit
Caballeros	Men's
Damas	Women's
Transporte publico	Shuttle Bus
Taxis	Taxis

GETTING THERE

Do I have a connecting flight?	**¿Tengo un vuelo de conexión?** *TEHNG-goh oon VWEH-loh deh koh-nehk-SYOHN*
Do I need to change planes?	**¿Necesito cambiar de avión?** *neh-seh-SEE-toh kahm-BYAHR deh ah-VYOHN*
My flight leaves at __:__.	**Mi vuelo sale a las ____:____.** *mee VWEH-loh SAH-leh ah lahs*
What time will the flight arrive?	**¿A qué hora llega el vuelo?** *ah keh OH-rah YEH-gah ehl VWEH-loh*
Is the flight on time?	**¿El vuelo está a tiempo?** *ehl VWEH-loh ehs-TAH ah TYEHM-poh*

For full coverage of numbers, see p7.

Is the flight delayed?	**¿El vuelo está retrasado?**
	ehl VWEH-loh ehs-TAH reh-trah-SAH-doh
From which terminal is flight _____ leaving?	**¿De qué terminal sale el vuelo _____?**
	deh keh tehr-mee-NAHL SAH-leh ehl VWEH-loh
From which gate is flight _____ leaving?	**¿De qué puerta de salida sale el vuelo _____?**
	deh keh PWEHR-tah deh sah-LEE-dah SAH-leh ehl VWEH-loh
How much time do I need for check-in?	**¿Cuánto tiempo necesito para facturar el equipaje?**
	KWAHN-toh TYEHM-poh neh-theh-SEE-toh PAH-rah fahk-too-RAHR ehl eh-kee-PAH-heh
Is there an express check-in line?	**¿Hay una cola para facturación rápida?**
	aye OO-nah KOH-lah pah-RAH fahk-too-rah-THYON RAH-pee-dah
Is there electronic check-in?	**¿Hay electrónica facturación?**
	ay eh-lehk-TROH-nee-kah fahk-too-rah-THYON

Seat Preferences

I would like _____ ticket(s) in _____

Me gustaría _____ asiento(s) en _____
meh goo-stah-REE-ah _____ ah-SYEN-toh -toh(s) ehn

first class.

primera clase.
pree-MEH-rah KLAH-seh

business class.

clase de negocios.
KLAH-seh deh neh-GOH-thyohs

economy class.

clase económica.
KLAH-seh eh-koh-NOH-mee-kah

I would like _____

Me gustaría _____
meh goos-tah-REE-ah

Please don't give me _____

Por favor no me dé _____
pohr fah-VOHR noh meh deh

a window seat.

un asiento de ventana.
oon ah-SYEHN-toh deh vehn-TAH-nah

an aisle seat.

un asiento de pasillo.
oon ah-SYEHN-toh deh pah-SEE-yoh

an emergency exit row seat.

un asiento en la fila de emergencia.
oon ah-SYEHN-toh ehn lah FEE-lah deh eh-mehr-HEHN-thyah

a seat by the restroom.

un asiento cerca de los baños.
oon ah-SYEHN-toh THEHR-kah deh lohs BAH-nyohs

a seat near the front.

un asiento en la parte delantera del avión.
oon ah-SYEHN-toh ehn lah PAHR-teh deh-lahn-TEH-rah dehl ah-VYOHN

a seat near the middle.

un asiento en el centro del avión.
oon ah-SYEHN-toh ehn ehl THEN-troh dehl ah-VYOHN

a seat near the back.	**un asiento en la parte trasera del avión.** *oon ah-SYEHN-toh ehn ehl PAHR-teh trah-SEH-rah dehl ah-VYOHN*
a bulkhead seat.	**un asiento detrás del tabique.** *oon ah-SYEHN-toh deh-TRAHS dehl tah-BEE-keh*
Is there a meal on the flight?	**¿Sirven comida en este vuelo?** *SEER-vehn koh-MEE-dah ehn EHS-teh VWEH-loh*
I'd like to order ____	**Quiero pedir ____** *KYEH-roh peh-DEER*
a vegetarian meal.	**una comida vegetariana.** *OO-nah koh-MEE-dah veh-heh-tah-RYAH-nah*
a kosher meal.	**una comida kósher.** *OO-nah koh-MEE-dah KOH-shehr*
a diabetic meal.	**una comida para diabéticos.** *OO-nah koh-MEE-dah PAH-rah dyah-BEH-tee-kohs*
I am traveling to ____.	**Viajo a ____.** *VYAH-hoh ah*
I am coming from ____.	**Vengo de ____.** *VEHN-goh deh*
I arrived from ____.	**Acabo de llegar de ____.** *ah-KAH-boh deh YEH-gahr deh*

For full coverage of country terms, see English / Spanish dictionary.

I'd like to change / cancel /confirm my reservation.	**Quiero cambiar / cancelar / confirmar mi reserva.** *KYEH-roh kahm-BYAHR / kahn-theh-LAHR / kohn-feer-MAHR mee reh-SEHR-vah*

| I have ____ bags to check. | **Tengo que facturar ____ maletas.** *TEHNG-goh keh fahk-too-RARH ____ mah-LEH-tahs* |

For full coverage of numbers, see p7.

Passengers with Special Needs

Is that wheelchair accessible?	**¿Eso es accesible para personas con impedimentos?** *EH-soh ehs ahk-theh-SEE-bleh PAH-rah pehr-SOH-nahs kohn eem-peh-dee-MEHN-tohs*
May I have a wheelchair / walker, please?	**¿Me puede dar una silla de ruedas / un andador, por favor?** *meh PWEH-deh dahr OO-nah SEE-yah deh RWEH-dahs / oon ahn-dah-DOHR pohr fah-VOHR*
I need some assistance boarding.	**Necesito que me ayuden a embarcar.** *neh-theh-SEE-toh keh meh ah-YOO-dehn ah ehm-bahr-KAHR*
I need to bring my service dog.	**Necesito traer a mi perro de servicio.** *neh-theh-SEE-toh trah-EHR ah mee PEH-rroh deh sehr-VEE-thyoh*
Do you have services for the hearing impaired?	**¿Tienen servicios para personas con discapacidad auditiva?** *TYEH-nehn sehr-VEE-thyohs PAH-rah pehr-SOH-nahs kohn dehs-kah-pah-thee-DAHD ow-dee-TEE-vah*
Do you have services for the visually impaired?	**¿Tienen servicios para personas con discapacidad visual?** *TYEH-nehn sehr-VEE-thyohs pah-rah pehr-SOH-nahs kohn dehs-kah-pah-thee-DAHD vee-SWAHL*

GETTING THERE

Trouble at Check-In

How long is the delay?	**¿Cuánto retraso lleva el vuelo?**
	KWAHN-toh reh-TRAH-soh YEH-vah ehl VWEH-loh
My flight was late.	**Mi vuelo llegó tarde.**
	mee VWEH-loh yeh-GOH TAHR-deh
I missed my flight.	**Perdí el vuelo.**
	pehr-DEE ehl VWEH-loh
When is the next flight?	**¿Cuándo sale el próximo vuelo?**
	KWAHN-doh SAH-leh ehl PROHK-see-moh VWEH-loh
May I have a meal voucher?	**¿Me puede dar un vale para comida?**
	meh PWEH-deh dahr oon VAH-leh pah-rah koh-MEE-dah
May I have a room voucher?	**¿Me puede dar un vale para hospedaje?**
	meh PWEH-deh dahr oon VAH-leh pah-rah ohs-peh-DAH-heh

AT CUSTOMS / SECURITY CHECKPOINTS

I'm traveling with a group.	**Estoy viajando con un grupo.**
	ehs-TOY vyah-HAHN-doh kohn oon GROO-poh
I'm on my own.	**Estoy viajando solo -a.**
	ehs-TOY vyah-HAHN-doh SOH-loh -lah
I'm traveling on business.	**Estoy viajando por negocios.**
	ehs-TOY vyah-HAHN-doh pohr neh-GOH-thyohs
I'm on vacation.	**Estoy de vacaciones.**
	ehs-TOY deh vah-kah-THYOH-nehs
I have nothing to declare.	**No tengo nada que declarar.**
	noh TEHNG-goh NAH-dah keh deh-klah-RAHR

I would like to declare ____.	**Quisiera declarar ____.**
	kee-SYEH-rah deh-klah-RAHR
I have some liquor.	**Traigo alcohol.**
	TRAY-goh ahl-koh-OHL
I have some cigars.	**Traigo cigarros.**
	TRAY-goh thee-GAH-rrohs
They are gifts.	**Son regalos.**
	sohn reh-GAH-lohs
They are for personal use.	**Son para uso personal.**
	sohn PAH-rah OO-soh pehr-soh-NAHL
That is my medicine.	**Esa es mi medicina.**
	EH-sah ehs mee meh-dee-THEE-nah
I have my prescription.	**Tengo a receta.**
	TEHNG-goh ah rreh-THEH-tah
My children are traveling on the same passport.	**Mis hijos viajan bajo el mismo pasaporte.**
	mees EE-hohs VYAN-hahn BAH-hoh ehl MEES-moh pah-sah-POHR-teh
I'd like a male / female to ____	**Prefiero que un hombre / una mujer ____**
	preh-FYEH-roh keh oon OHM-breh / OO-nah moo-HEHR
search my luggage.	**revise mi equipaje.**
	reh-VEE-seh mee eh-kee-PAH-heh
search me.	**haga el registro.**
	AH-gah ehl reh-HEE-stroh

Trouble at Security

Help me. I've lost ____	**Ayúdeme. He perdido ____**
	ah-YOO-dah-meh eh pehr-DEE-doh
my passport.	**el pasaporte.**
	ehl pah-sah-POHR-teh
my boarding pass.	**la tarjeta de embarque.**
	lah tahr-HEH-tah deh ehm-BAHR-keh

Listen Up: Security Lingo

Por favor, quítese los zapatos.	Please remove your shoes.
Quítese la chaqueta / el suéter.	Remove your jacket / sweater.
Quítese las joyas.	Remove your jewelry.
Coloque su equipaje sobre el cinturón.	Place your bags on the conveyor belt.
Por favor hágase a un lado.	Step to the side.
Debemos realizar una inspección manual.	We have to do a hand search.

my identification.	**el carné de identidad.**
	ehl KAHR-neh deh ee-dehn-tee-DAHD
my wallet.	**la cartera.**
	lah kahr-TEH-rah
my purse.	**el bolso.**
	ehl BOHL-soh
Someone stole my purse / wallet!	**¡Alguien me robó el bolso / la cartera!**
	ah-YOO-dah AHLG-yehn meh roh-BOH ehl BOHL-soh / lah kahr-TEH-rah

IN-FLIGHT

It's unlikely you'll need much Spanish on the plane, but these phrases will help if a bilingual flight attendant is unavailable or if you need to talk to a Spanish-speaking neighbor.

I think that's my seat.	**Creo que ese es mi asiento.**
	KREH-oh keh EH-seh ehs mee ah-SYEHN-toh

May I have ____	**¿Me puede dar ____**
	meh PWEH-deh dahr
water?	**agua?**
	AH-wah
sparkling water?	**agua con gas?**
	AH-wah kohn gahs
orange juice?	**zumo de naranja?**
	THOO-moh deh nah-RAHN-hah
soda?	**un refresco?**
	oon reh-FREHS-koh
diet soda?	**un refresco bajo en calorías?**
	oon reh-FREHS-koh BAH-hoh
	ehn kah-loh-REE-ahs
a beer?	**una cerveza?**
	OO-nah thehr-VEH-thah
wine?	**vino?**
	VEE-noh

For a complete list of drinks, see p100.

a pillow?	**una almohada?**
	OO-nah ahl-moh-AH-dah
a blanket?	**una manta?**
	OO-nah MAHN-tah
a hand wipe?	**una toallita húmeda?**
	OO-nah toh-ah-YEE-tah OO-meh-dah
headphones?	**cascos?**
	KAHS-kohs
a magazine or newspaper?	**una revista o un periódico?**
	OO-nah reh-VEES-tah oh oon pehr-YOH-dee-koh
When will the meal be served?	**¿Cuándo servirán la comida?**
	KWAHN-doh sehr-vee-RAHN lah koh-MEE-dah
How long until we land?	**¿Cuánto falta para llegar?**
	KWAHN-toh FAHL-tah pah-rah yeh-GAHR

GETTING THERE

May I move to another seat?	**¿Me puedo cambiar de asiento?** *meh PWEH-doh kahm-BYAHR deh ah-SYEHN-toh*
How do I turn the light on / off?	**¿Cómo enciendo / apago la luz?** *KOH-moh ehn-THYEN-doh / ah-PAH-goh lah looth*

Trouble In-Flight

These headphones are broken.	**Los cascos están rotos.** *lohs KAHS-kohs ehs-TAHN ROH-tohs*
I spilled.	**Se me ha derramado.** *seh meh ah deh-rrah-MAH-thoh*
My child spilled.	**A mi hijo se le ha derramado.** *ah mee EE-hoh seh leh ah deh-rrah-MAH-thoh*
My child is sick.	**Mi hijo -a está enfermo -a.** *mee EE-hoh -hah ehs-TAH ehn-FEHR-moh -mah*
I need an airsickness bag.	**Necesito una bolsa para mareos.** *neh-theh-SEE-toh OO-nah BOHL-sah pah-rah mah-REH-ohs*
I smell something strange.	**Huelo algo extraño.** *WEH-loh AHL-goh ehs-TRAH-nyoh*
That passenger is behaving suspiciously.	**Ese pasajero se está comportando sospechosamente.** *EH-seh pah-sah-HEH-roh seh ehs-TAH kohm-pohr-TAHN-doh sohs-peh-choh-sah-MEHN-teh*

BAGGAGE CLAIM

Where is baggage claim for flight ___?	**¿Dónde se recoge el equipaje para el vuelo ___?** *DOHN-deh seh rreh-KOH-heh ehl eh-kee-PAH-heh pah-rah ehl VWEH-loh*

Would you please help with my bags?	**¿Me puede ayudar con el equipaje?**
	meh PWEH-deh ah-yoo-DAHR kohn ehl eh-kee-PAH-heh
I am missing ____ bags.	**Me faltan ____ maletas.**
	meh FAHL-tahn ____ mah-LEH-tahs

For full coverage of numbers, see p7.

My bag ____	**Mi equipaje ____**
	mee eh-kee-PAH-heh
is lost.	**se ha perdido.**
	seh ah pehr-DEE-doh
is damaged.	**está dañado.**
	ehs-TAH dah-NYAH-doh
is stolen.	**ha sido robado.**
	ah SEE-doh roh-BAH-doh
is a suitcase.	**es una maleta.**
	ehs OO-nah mah-LEH-ta
is a briefcase.	**es un maletín.**
	ehs oon mah-leh-TEEN
is a carry-on.	**es equipaje de mano.**
	ehs eh-kee-PAH-heh deh MAH-noh
is a suit bag.	**es un portatrajes.**
	ehs oon pohr-tah-TRAH-hehs
is a trunk.	**es un baúl.**
	ees oon bah-OOL
is golf clubs.	**son palos de golf.**
	sohn PAH-lohs deh gohlf
is hard.	**es duro.**
	ehs DOO-roh
is made out of ____	**está hecho de ____**
	ehs-TAH EH-choh deh ____
canvas.	**lona.**
	LOH-nah
vinyl.	**vinilo.**
	vee-NEE-loh

leather.	**cuero.** *KWEH-roh*
hard plastic.	**plástico duro.** *PLAH-stee-koh DOO-roh*
aluminum.	**aluminio.** *ah-loo-MEE-nyoh*

For full coverage of color terms, see English / Spanish Dictionary.

RENTING A VEHICLE

Is there a car rental agency in the airport?	**¿Hay una compañía de alquiler de coches en el aeropuerto?** *aye OO-nah kohm-pah-NYEE-ah deh ahl-kee-LEHR deh KOH-chehs ehn ehl ah-eh-roh-PWEHR-toh*
I have a reservation.	**Tengo una reserva.** *TEHNG-goh OO-nah reh-SEHR-vah*

Vehicle Preferences

I would like to rent ____	**Me gustaría alquilar ____** *meh goo-stah-REE-ah ahl-kee-LAHR*
an economy car.	**un coche económico.** *oon KOH-cheh eh-koh-NOH-mee-koh*
a midsize car.	**un coche mediano.** *oon KOH-cheh meh-DYAH-noh*
a sedan	**un sedán.** *oon seh-DAHN*
a convertible.	**un descapotable.** *oon dehs-kah-poh-TAH-bleh*
a van.	**una furgoneta.** *OO-nah foor-goh-NEH-tah*
a sports car.	**un coche deportivo.** *oon KOH-cheh deh-pohr-TEE-voh*
a 4-wheel-drive vehicle.	**un vehículo de todo terreno.** *oon veh-EE-kuh-loh deh TOH-doh teh-RREH-noh*

a motorcycle.	**una motocicleta.** *OO-nah moh-toh-thee-KLEH-tah*
a scooter.	**una vespa.** *OO-nah VEHS-pah*
Do you have one with _____	**¿Tiene uno con _____** *TYEH-neh OO-noh kohn*
air conditioning?	**aire acondicionado?** *AYEE-reh ah-kohn-dee-thyoh- NAH-doh*
a sunroof?	**techo corredizo?** *TEH-choh koh-rreh-DEE-thoh*
a CD player?	**un reproductor de discos compactos / CD?** *oon reh-proh-dook-TOHR deh DEES-kohs kohm-PAHK-tohs / theh-DEH*
satellite radio?	**radio satelital?** *RAH-dyoh sah-teh-lee-TAHL*
satellite tracking?	**navegación por satélite?** *nah-veh-gah-THYOHN pohr sah- TEH-lee-teh*
an onboard map?	**un mapa a bordo?** *oon MAH-pah ah-BOHR-doh*
a DVD player?	**un reproductor de DVD?** *oon reh-proh-dook-TOHR deh deh-OO-vah-DEH*
child seats?	**asientos infantiles?** *ah-SYEHN-tohs een-fahn-TEE-lehs*
Do you have a _____	**¿Tiene un coche _____** *TYEH-neh oon KOH-cheh*
smaller car?	**más pequeño?** *mahs peh-KEH-nyoh*
bigger car?	**más grande?** *mahs GRAHN-deh*
cheaper car?	**más barato?** *mahs bah-RAH-toh*

Do you have a non-smoking car?	**¿Tiene un coche para no fumadores?**
	TYEH-neh oon KOH-cheh PAH-rah noh foo-mah-THOH-rehs
I need an automatic transmission.	**Necesito un coche con transmisión automática.**
	neh-theh-SEE-toh oon KOH-cheh kohn trahns-mee-SYOHN ow-toh-MAH-tee-kah
A standard transmission is okay.	**Con transmisión manual está bien.**
	kohn trahns-mee-SYOHN mah-NWAHL eh-STAH BYEHN
May I have an upgrade?	**¿Puede darme mejor categoría de vehículo?**
	PWEH-deh DAHR-meh meh-HOHR kah-teh-goh-REE-ah deh veh-EE-koo-loh

Money Matters

What's the daily / weekly /monthly rate?	**¿Cuál es la tarifa diaria / semanal / mensual?**
	kwahl ehs lah tah-REE-fah DYAHR-yah / seh-mah-NAHL / mehn-SWAHL
What is the mileage rate?	**¿Cuál es la tarifa por kilómetro?**
	kwahl ehs lah tah-REE-fah pohr kee-LOH-meh-troh
How much is insurance?	**¿Cuánto cuesta el seguro?**
	KWAHN-toh KWEHS-tah ehl seh-GOO-roh
Are there other fees?	**¿Hay cargos adicionales?**
	aye KAHR-gohs ah-dee-thyo-NAH-les
Is there a weekend rate?	**¿Tienen una tarifa de fin de semana?**
	TYEH-nehn OO-nah tah-REE-fah deh feen deh seh-MAH-nah

Technical Questions

What kind of fuel does it take?	**¿Qué tipo de gasolina usa?** *keh TEE-poh deh gah-soh-LEE-nah OO-sah*
Do you have the manual in English?	**¿Tiene el manual en inglés?** *TYEH-neh ehl mah-NWAHL ehn eeng-GLEHS*
Do you have a booklet in English with the local traffic laws?	**¿Tiene un folleto en inglés con las normas de tráfico locales?** *TYEH-neh oon foh-YEH-toh ehn eeng-GLEHS kohn lahs NOHR-mahs deh TRAH-fee-koh loh-KAH-lehs*

Car Troubles

The ____ doesn't work.	**El / La / Los / Las ____ no funciona -an.** *ehl / lah / lohs / lahs noh foon-THYOH-nah -nahn*

See diagram on p58 for car parts.

It is already dented.	**Ya está abollado.** *YAH ehs-TAH ah-boh-YAH-doh*
It is scratched.	**Está rayado.** *ehs-TAH rah-YAH-doh*
The windshield is cracked.	**El parabrisas está agrietado.** *ehl pah-rah-BREE-sahs ehs-TAH ahg-ryeh-TAH-doh*
The tires look low.	**Las ruedas se ven un poco desinfladas.** *lahs RWEH-thahs seh vehn oon POH-koh dehs-een-FLAH-dahs*
It has a flat tire.	**Tiene una rueda pinchada.** *TYEH-neh OO-nah RWEH-thah peen-CHAH-dah*
Whom do I call for service?	**¿A quién llamo para servicio de asistencia en carretera?** *ah KYEHN YAH-moh pah-rah sehr-VEE-thyoh deh ah-see-STEHN-thya ehn kah-rreh-TEH-rrah*

GETTING THERE

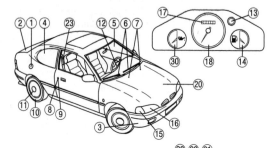

1. la tapa del depósito de gasolina
2. el portaequipaje
3. el parachoques
4. la ventana
5. el parabrisas
6. el limpiaparabrisas
7. el líquido lavaparabrisas
8. los seguros de las puertas
9. los seguros eléctricos
10. los neumáticos
11. las ruedas
12. la llave de contacto
13. la luz de advertencia
14. el indicador de combustible
15. las luces
16. los faros delanteros
17. el cuentakilómetros
18. el velocímetro
19. el silenciador de escape
20. el capó
21. el volante
22. el espejo retrovisor
23. el cinturón de seguridad
24. el motor
25. el acelerador
26. el embrague
27. los frenos
28. el freno de mano
29. la batería
30. el indicador de aceite
31. el radiador
32. la correa del ventilador

It won't start.	**No arranca.**
	noh ah-RRAHN-kah
It's out of gas.	**No tiene gasolina.**
	noh TYEH-neh gah-soh-LEE-nah
The Check Engine light is on.	**La luz de advertencia el motor está encendida.**
	lah looth dee ahd-vehr-TEHN-thyah ehl moh-TOHR ehs-TAH ehn-sehn-DEE-dah
The oil light is on.	**La luz del aceite está encendida.**
	lah looth dehl ah-THEH-ee-teh ehs-TAH ehn-thehn-DEE-dah
The brake light is on.	**La luz del freno está encendida.**
	lah looth dehl FREH-noh ehs-TAH ehn-thehn-DEE-dah
It runs rough.	**Noto que es un poco brusco al conducir.**
	NOH-toh keh ehs oon POH-koh BROOTH-koh ahl kohn-doo-THEER
The car is over-heating.	**El coche se recaliente.**
	ehl KOH-chah seh reh-kah-LYEHN-teh

Asking for Directions

Excuse me, please.	**Perdóneme.**
	pehr-DOH-neh-meh
How do I get to ____?	**¿Cómo llego a ____?**
	KOH-moh YEH-goh ah
Go straight.	**Siga todo derecho.**
	SEE-gah TOH-doh deh-REH-choh
Turn left.	**Gire a la izquierda.**
	GEE-reh ah lah eeth-KYEHR-dah
Continue right.	**Continúe a mano derecha.**
	kohn-tee-NOO-eh ah MAH-noh dee-REH-chah

It's on the right.	**Está a mano derecha.**
	ehs-TAH ah MAH-noh dee-REH-chah
Can you show me on the map?	**¿Puede enseñármelo en el mapa?**
	PWEH-deh ehn-sehn-YAHR-meh-loh ehn ehl MAH-pah
How far is it from here?	**¿A qué distancia está de aquí?**
	ah keh dee-STAHN-thyah eh-STAH deh ah-KEE
Is this the right road for ____?	**¿Es ésta la carretera correcta para llegar / ir a____?**
	ehs EHS-tah lah kah-rreh-TEH-rah koh-RREHK-tah PAH-rah yeh-GAHR / eer ah
I've lost my way.	**Estoy perdido -a.**
	ehs-TOY pehr-DEE-doh -dah
Would you repeat that?	**¿Me lo puede repetir?**
	meh loh PWEH-deh reh-peh-TEER
Thanks for your help.	**Gracias por su ayuda.**
	GRAH-thyahs pohr soo ah-YOO-dah

For full coverage of direction-related terms, see p5.

Road Signs

Límite de velocidad	Speed Limit
Alto / Stop	Stop
Ceda el paso	Yield
Peligro	Danger
Calle sin salida	No Exit
Calle / Vía de sentido único	One Way
Prohibida la entrada	Do Not Enter
Carretera cerrada	Road Closed
Peaje	Toll
Efectivo solamente	Cash Only
Prohibido aparcar	No Parking
Precio de aparcamiento	Parking Fee
Aparcamiento	Parking Garage

Sorry, Officer

What is the speed limit?	**¿Cuál es el límite de velocidad?**
	kwahl ehs ehl LEE-mee-teh deh veh-loh-thee-DAHD
I wasn't going that fast.	**No iba tan rápido.**
	noh EE-bah tahn RAH-pee-doh
How much is the fine?	**¿Cuánto es la multa?**
	KWAHN-toh ehs lah MOOL-tah
Where do I pay the fine?	**¿Dónde pago la multa?**
	DOHN-deh PAH-goh lah MOOL-tah
Do I have to go to court?	**¿Tengo que ir al juzgado?**
	TEHNG-goh keh eer ahl hoo-THKAH-doh
I had an accident.	**Tuve un accidente.**
	TOO-veh oon ahk-thee-DEHN-teh
The other driver hit me.	**El otro conductor chocó contra mí.**
	ehl OH-troh kohn-dook-TOHR choh-KOH KOHN-trah mee
I'm at fault.	**Ha sido mi culpa.**
	ah SEE-doh mee KOOL-pah

BY TAXI

Where is the taxi stand?	**¿Dónde está la parada de taxis?**
	DOHN-deh ehs-TAH lah pah-RAH-dah deh TAHK-sees
Is there a limo / bus / van for my hotel?	**¿Hay una limusina / un autobús / una furgoneta del hotel?**
	ay OO-nah lee-moo-SEE-nah / oon ow-toh-BOOS / OO-nah foor-goh-NEH-tah dehl oh-TEHL
I need to get to ____.	**Necesito ir a ____.**
	neh-theh-SEE-toh eer ah
How much will that cost?	**¿Cuánto costará?**
	KWAHN-toh kohs-tah-RAH
How long will it take?	**¿Cuánto tiempo tardará?**
	KWAHN-toh TYEHM-poh tahr-dahr-AH

Can you take me / us to the train / bus station?	**¿Puede llevarme / llevarnos a la estación de tren / autobús?** *PWEH-deh yeh-VAHR-meh / yeh-VAHR-nohs ah lah ehs-tah-THYOHN deh trehn / ow-toh-BOOS*
I am in a hurry.	**Tengo prisa.** *TEHNG-goh PREE-sah*
Slow down, please.	**Vaya más despacio, por favor.** *VAH-yah mahs deh-SPAH-thyoh pohr fah-VOHR*
Am I close enough to walk?	**¿Estoy lo suficientemente cerca como para caminar?** *ehs-TOY loh soo-fee-thyehn-teh-MEHN-teh THEHR-kah koh-moh pah-rah kah-mee-NAHR*
Let me out here.	**Déjeme salir aquí mismo.** *DEH-heh-meh sah-LEER ah-KEE MEES-moh*
That's not the correct change.	**Ese no es el cambio correcto.** *EH-seh noh ehs ehl KAM-byoh koh-REHK-toh*

Listen Up: Taxi Lingo

¡Súbase!	Get in!
Deje su equipaje. Yo me encargo.	Leave your luggage. I got it.
Son cien euros por maleta.	It's 100 euros for each bag.
¿Cuántos pasajeros?	How many passengers?
¿Tiene prisa?	Are you in a hurry?

BY TRAIN

How do I get to the train station?	¿Cómo llego a la estación de tren? *KOH-moh YEH-goh ah lah ehs-tah-THYOHN deh trehn*
Would you take me to the train station?	¿Puede llevarme a la estación de tren? *PWEH-deh yeh-VAHR-meh ah lah ehs-tah-THYOHN deh trehn*
How long is the trip to ____?	¿Cuanto tarda el viaje a ____? *KWAHN-toh TAHR-dah ehl VYAH-heh ah*
When is the next train?	¿Cuándo sale el próximo tren? *KWAHN-doh SAH-leh ehl PROHK-see-moh trehn*
Do you have a schedule / timetable?	¿Tiene un itinerario? *TYEH-neh oon ee-tee-neh-RAH-ryoh*
Do I have to change trains?	¿Tengo que cambiar de tren? *TEHNG-goh keh kahm-BYAHR deh trehn*
a one-way ticket	un billete de ida *oon beel-YEH-teh deh EE-dah*
a round-trip ticket	un billete de ida y vuelta *oon beel-YEH-teh deh EE-dah ee VWEHL-tah*
Which platform does it leave from?	¿De qué andén sale? *deh keh ahn-DEHN SAH-leh*
Is there a bar car?	¿Hay un vagón cantina? *aye oon vah-GOHN kahn-TEE-nah*
Is there a dining car?	¿Hay un vagón para cenar? *aye oon vah-GOHN pah-rah theh-NAHR*
Which car is my seat in?	¿En qué vagón está mi asiento? *ehn keh vah-GOHN ehs-TAH mee ah-SYEHN-toh*

Is this seat taken?	**¿Está ocupado este asiento?** *ehs-TAH oh-koo-PAH-doh EHS-teh ah-SYEHN-toh*
Where is the next stop?	**¿Cúal es la próxima parada?** *KWAHL ehs lah PROHK-see-mah pah-RAH-dah*
How many stops to _____?	**¿Cuántas paradas hay hasta llegar a _____?** *KWAHN-tahs pah-RAH-dahs ay AHS-tah yeh-GAHR ah*
What's the train number and destination?	**¿Cuál es el número del tren y su destino?** *kwahl ehs ehl NOO-meh-roh dehl trehn ee soo dehs-TEE-noh*

BY BUS

How do I get to the bus station?	**¿Cómo llego a la estación de autobuses?** *KOH-moh YEH-go ah lah ehs-tah- THYOHN deh ow-toh-BOO-sehs*
Would you take me to the bus station?	**¿Me puede llevar a la estación de autobuses?** *meh PWEH-deh yeh-VAHR ah lah ehs-tah-THYOHN deh ow-toh- BOO-sehs*
May I have a bus schedule?	**¿Me puede dar un itinerario?** *meh PWEH-deh dahr oon ee-tee- neh-RAH-ryoh*
Which bus goes to _____?	**¿Qúe autobús va hacia _____?** *keh ow-toh-BOOS vah AH-thyah*
Where does it leave from?	**¿De dónde sale?** *deh DOHN-deh SAH-leh*

How long does the trip take?	**¿Cuánto tarda el viaje?** *KWAHN-toh TAHR-dah ehl VYAH-heh*
How much is it?	**¿Cuánto cuesta?** *KWAHN-to KWEH-stah*
Is there an express bus?	**¿Hay un autobús exprés?** *ay oon ow-toh-BOOS ehs-PREHS*
Does it make local stops?	**¿Hace paradas locales?** *AH-theh pah-RAH-dahs loh-KAH-lehs*
Does it run at night?	**¿Hay servicio de autobús nocturno?** *ay sehr-VEE-thyoh de ow-toh-BOOS nohk-TOOR-noh*
When does the next bus leave?	**¿Cuándo parte el próximo autobús?** *KWAHN-doh PAHR-teh ehl PROHK-see-moh ow-toh-BOOS*
a one-way ticket	**un billete de ida** *oon beel-YEH-teh deh EE-dah*
a round-trip ticket	**un billete de ida y vuelta** *oon beel-YEH-teh deh EE-dah ee VWEHL-tah*
How long will the bus be stopped?	**¿Por cuánto tiempo va a parar el autobús?** *pohr KWAHN-toh TYEHM-poh vah ah pah-RAHR ehl ow-toh-BOOS*
Is there an air conditioned bus?	**¿Hay un autobús con aire acondicionado?** *aye oon ow-toh-BOOS kohn AYE-reh ah-kohn-dee-thyoh-NAH-doh*
Is this seat taken?	**¿Está ocupado este asiento?** *ehs-TAH oh-koo-PAH-doh EHS-teh ah-SYEHN-toh*
Where is the next stop?	**¿Cúal es la próxima parada?** *KWAHL ehs lah PROHK-see-mah pah-RAH-dah*

Please tell me when we reach ____.	**Por favor dígame cuando lleguemos a ____.**
	pohr fah-VOHR DEE-gah-meh KWAHN-doh yeh-GEH-mohs ah
Let me off here.	**Déjeme bajar aquí.**
	DEH-heh-meh bah-HAHR ah-KEE

BY BOAT OR SHIP

Would you take me to the port?	**¿Me puede llevar al puerto?**
	meh PWEH-deh yeh-VAHR ahl PWEHR-toh
When does the ship sail?	**¿Cuándo zarpa el barco?**
	KWAHN-doh THAHR-pah ehl BAHR-koh
How long is the trip?	**¿Cuánto tarda el trayecto?**
	kwahn-TOH tahr-dah ehl trah-YEHK-toh
Where are the life preservers?	**¿Dónde están los salvavidas?**
	DOHN-deh ehs-TAHN lohs sahl-vah-VEE-dahs
I would like a private cabin.	**Me gustaría un camarote privado.**
	meh goo-stah-REE-ah oon kah-mah-ROH-teh pree-VAH-doh
Is the trip rough?	**¿Es duro el viaje?**
	ehs DOO-roh ehl VYAH-heh
I feel seasick.	**Me siento mareado -a.**
	meh SYEHN-toh mah-reh-AH-doh -dah
I need some seasick pills.	**Necesito píldoras para el mareo.**
	neh-theh-SEE-toh PEEL-doh-rahs PAH-rah ehl mah-REH-oh
Where is the bathroom?	**¿Dónde está el baño?**
	DOHN-deh ehs-TAH ehl BAH-nyoh

Does the ship have a casino?	**¿El barco tiene casino?** *ehl BAHR-koh TYEH-neh kah-SEE-noh*
Will the ship stop at ports along the way?	**¿El barco se detendrá en puertos a lo largo del camino?** *ehl BAHR-koh seh deh-tehnd-RAH ehn PWEHR-tohs ah loh LAHR-goh dehl kah-MEE-noh*

BY SUBWAY

Where's the subway station?	**¿Dónde está la estación de metro?** *DOHN-deh ehs-TAH lah ehs-tah-THYOHN deh MEH-troh*
Where can I buy a ticket?	**¿Dónde puedo comprar un billete?** *DOHN-deh PWEH-doh kohm-PRAHR oon beel-YEH-teh*

SUBWAY TICKETS

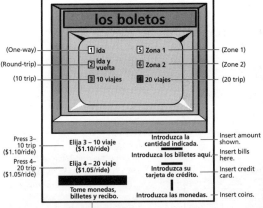

los boletos

(One-way) — **1 ida**
(Round-trip) — **2 ida y vuelta**
(10 trip) — **3 10 viajes**
5 Zona 1 — (Zone 1)
6 Zona 2 — (Zone 2)
20 viajes — (20 trip)

Press 3– 10 trip ($1.10/ride) — **Elija 3 – 10 viaje ($1.10/ride)**
Press 4– 20 trip ($1.05/ride) — **Elija 4 – 20 viaje ($1.05/ride)**

Introduzca la cantidad indicada. — Insert amount shown.
Introduzca los billetes aquí. — Insert bills here.
Introduzca su tarjeta de crédito. — Insert credit card.

Tome monedas, billetes y recibo.
(Take change, tickets, receipt)

Introduzca las monedas. — Insert coins.

Could I have a map of the subway?	**¿Puede darme un mapa del metro?** *PWEH-deh DAHR-meh oon MAH-pah dehl MEH-troh*
Which line should I take for ____?	**¿Qué línea debo tomar para ____?** *keh LEE-neh-ah DEH-boh toh-MAHR PAH-rah*
Is this the right line for ____?	**¿Es ésta la línea correcta para ____?** *ehs EHS-tah lah LEE-neh-ah koh-RREHK-tah PAH-rah*
Which stop is it for ____?	**¿Cuál es la parada para ____?** *kwahl ehs lah pah-RAH-dah PAH-rah*
How many stops is it to ____?	**¿Cuántas paradas faltan para ____?** *KWAHN-tahs pah-RAH-dahs FAHL-tahn PAH-rah*
Is the next stop ____?	**¿La próxima parada es ____?** *lah PROHK-see-mah pah-RAH-dah ehs*
Where are we?	**¿Dónde estamos?** *DOHN-deh ehs-TAH-mohs*
Where do I change to ____?	**¿Dónde cambio para ____?** *DOHN-deh KAHM-byoh PAH-rah*
What time is the last train to ____?	**¿A qué hora pasa el último tren a ____?** *ah keh OH-rah PAH-sah ehl OOL-tee-moh trehn ah*

TRAVELERS WITH SPECIAL NEEDS

Do you have wheelchair access?	**¿Tienen acceso para sillas de ruedas?** *TYEH-nehn ahk-THEH-soh PAH-rah SEE-yahs deh RWEH-dahs*
Do you have elevators? Where?	**¿Tienen ascensores? ¿Dónde?** *TYEH-nehn ah-then-SOH-rehs DOHN-deh*

Do you have ramps? Where?	**¿Tienen rampas? ¿Dónde?** *TYEH-nehn RRAHM-pahs DOHN-deh*
Are the restrooms wheelchair accessible?	**¿Los baños son accesibles para sillas de ruedas?** *lohs BAH-nyohs sohn ahk-theh-SEE-blehs pah-rah SEE-yahs deh RWEH-dahs*
Do you have audio assistance for the hearing impaired?	**¿Tienen asistencia auditiva para personas con discapacidad auditiva?** *TYEH-nehn ah-sees-TEHN-thyah ow-dee-TEE-vah PAH-rah pehr-SOH-nahs kohn dees-kah-pah-thee-DAHD ow-dee-TEE-vah*
I am deaf.	**Soy sordo -a.** *soy SOHR-doh -dah*
I am hearing impaired.	**Tengo discapacidad auditiva.** *TEHN-goh dees-kah-pah-thee-DAHD ow-dee-TEE-vah*
May I bring my service dog?	**¿Puedo traer a mi perro de servicio?** *PWEH-doh trah-EHR ah mee PEH-rroh deh sehr-VEE-thyoh*
I am blind.	**Soy ciego -a.** *soy thee-EH-goh -gah*
I need to charge my power chair.	**Necesito recargar mi silla de ruedas eléctricas.** *neh-theh-SEE-toh reh-kahr-GAHR mee SEE-yah deh RWEH-dahs eh-LEHK-tree-kahs*

BUS TRAVEL BETWEEN MAJOR TOWNS

In case you don't feel like driving, it's good to know that **long distance bus services** have improved immensely in recent years. The number of excellent highways crossing the country, coupled with high-speed services, means that buses rival trains for comfort, punctuality, and—above all—economy. The advantage over traveling by car is that you can sit back and enjoy the scenery. (If, that is, you can tear your gaze away from the Spanish-dubbed video movies shown on screens strategically positioned through the bus.)

Madrid is best-positioned for touring by bus. Its two main stations, **Méndez Álvaro** (Estación Sur; metro line 6; © **91-468-4200;** www.estaciondeautobuses.com) and **Avenida America** (metro lines 4, 7, and 6; © **91-745-6300**), cover southern and northern destinations, respectively. Méndez Álvaro covers destinations in Southern Spain such as Seville, Cádiz, and Córdoba, with the main coach operator **Alsa** (www.alsa.es). Avenida America covers northerly destinations such as Bilbao, San Sebastián, and Burgos; its main coach operator is **Continental-Auto** (www.continental-auto.es).

Barcelona's main bus station is **Barcelona Nord Estació d'Autobuses** (© **902-260-606;** www.barcelonanord.com). From here various bus companies cover cities and towns throughout Spain.

TRAVELING BY TRAIN

Twenty-first-century Spain's **rail services** are among the best in Europe. Long gone is that dated image of trains taking all day to cross half the country and—unless you booked a seat in the most exclusive first-class compartments—of having to sit on upright wooden seats sharing food and wine with your fellow travelers, with chickens on the rack and perhaps even a goat bleating under your seat.

Today's high-speed Talgo and AVEs are at least the equal of long-envied neighbor France's TGFs—and far ahead of the sluggish British Intercity services.

Prices are highly affordable. And when it comes to promptness, modernity, and downright sleek efficiency, the quality of service grows stronger every year. In the coming decade, even faster lines are scheduled to open—especially from **Madrid,** the well-located hub and capital of the country. From here, trains run to the north from **Chamartín** station (renovated in 2005) and to the south and Mediterranean coastal areas as far as Barcelona from **Atocha** station.

To book tickets online, in advance and from home, log on to **Rail Europe**'s website: www.raileurope.com. Their extensive website contains a powerful search engine to look up trains, prices, and stations for all of Europe. Also be sure to check out **Renfe,** Spain's national train line. Check online or call for ticket information and reservations (✆ **902-24-02-02;** www.renfe.es).

Travel Times on Major High-Speed Train Routes
High-Speed Train Services   (AVE, Alaris, and Talgo)
Madrid–Córdoba   AVE, 2 hours

Madrid–Seville   AVE, 2 hours 30 minutes (This is the only service that offers a full refund of your fare if the train is more than 10 minutes late.)

Madrid–Valencia   Alaris, 3 hours 10 minutes (By 2007 this is scheduled to be a stunning 1 hour 30 minutes!)

Madrid–Zaragoza   Talgo, 3 hours

Madrid–Málaga   Talgo, via Córdoba, 4 hours 15 minutes

Madrid–Barcelona   Talgo, via Zaragoza and Lérida/Lleida, 5 hours (By 2007 this should be reduced to a little over 3 hours.)

Future plans from Madrid include provision for a very fast 35-minute train service to **Toledo** and 1 hour 30 minute service to **Valladolid.**

GETTING THERE

Other High-Speed Train Routes
Seville–Córdoba   AVE, 30 minutes
Barcelona–Zaragoza   Talgo, 3 hours
Barcelona–Lérida/Lleida   Talgo, 2 hours

Travel Time on Major Train Routes at Average Speed
Madrid–Bilbao   4 hours
Madrid–Granada   4 hours
Madrid–Oviedo   4 hours
Madrid–Pamplona   4 hours
Madrid–Santiago de Compostela   6–7 hours
Madrid–Vigo   6–7 hours
Madrid–Lisbon (Portugal)   7 hours

Other Train Routes at Average Speed
Normal Services from Other Cities
Málaga–Granada   2 hours
Seville–Cádiz   1 hour
Seville–Málaga   2 hours
Barcelona–Gerona/Girona   40 minutes
Barcelona–Tarragona   1 hour
Barcelona–Valencia   3 hours
Bilbao–San Sebastián   1 hour
Bilbao–Oviedo   1 hour
San Sebastián–Biarritz (France)   1 hour
Valencia–Alicante/Alacant   1 hour 30 minutes

EUROPEAN BUDGET AIRLINES

The best **charter airline** operating **flights** among a wide range of Spanish and U.K. airports is **Easyjet.** You can only book online (www.easyjet.com). No seats are allocated, no in-flight refreshments provided, and no tickets issued—you just retain your e-mailed confirmation. Seating is also a case of first-come, first-served, though families with small children are given priority in the check-in queue. Service is disarmingly efficient and planes are usually on time. The fares are genuine bargains except at special holiday times such as Easter, Christmas, and July through August.

CANCELLED PLANS

If your flight is cancelled, don't submit to long lines at the ticket counter. Find the nearest phone and call the airline directly to reschedule. You'll be relaxing while other passengers are still standing in line.

CONVERSIONS

Feet/Meters   1m = 3.3 feet; 1 foot = .30m
To convert inches to centimeters, multiply by 2.54
To convert centimeters to inches, multiply by .39
To convert feet to meters, multiply by .30
To convert meters to feet, multiply by 3.28
To convert yards to meters, multiply by .91
To convert meters to yards, multiply by 1.0

Miles/Kilometers   1 mile = 1.6km; 1km = .62 miles
To convert miles to kilometers, multiply by 1.61
To convert kilometers to miles, multiply by .62

U.S. Gallons/Liters   1 U.S. gallon = 3.8 liters; 1 liter = .26 U.S. gallons
To convert U.S. gallons to liters, multiply by 3.80
To convert liters to U.S. gallons multiply by .26
To convert U.S. gallons to imperial gallons, multiply by .83
To convert imperial gallons to U.S. gallons, multiply by 1.20

GETTING THERE

CHAPTER THREE

LODGING

This chapter will help you find the right accommodations, at the right price, and the amenities you might need during your stay.

ROOM PREFERENCES

Please recommend ____	**Por favor recomiende ____**
	pohr fah-VOHR reh-koh-MYEHN-deh
a clean hostel.	**un hostal limpio.**
	oon ohs-TEHL LEEM-pyoh
a moderately priced hotel.	**un hotel de precio módico.**
	oon oh-TEHL deh PREH-syoh MOH-dee-koh
a moderately priced B&B.	**una hostería con cama y desayuno de precio módico.**
	OO-nah ohs-teh-REE-ah kohn KAH-mah ee deh-sah-YOO-noh deh PREH-thyoh MOH-dee-ko
a good hotel / motel.	**un buen hotel / motel.**
	oon bwehn oh-TEHL / moh-TEHL
Does the hotel have ____	**¿El hotel tiene ____**
	ehl oh-TEHL TYEH-neh
a pool?	**una piscina?**
	OO-nah pee-THEE-nah
a casino?	**un casino?**
	oon kah-SEE-noh
suites?	**suites?**
	soo-EE-tehs
a balcony?	**un balcón?**
	oon bahl-KOHN
a fitness center?	**un gimnasio?**
	oon heem-NAH-syoh
a spa?	**un balneario?**
	oon bahl-neh-AH-ryoh

74

a private beach?	una playa privada?
	OO-nah PLAH-yah pree-VAH-dah
a tennis court?	una cancha de tenis?
	OO-nah KAHN-chah deh
	TEH-nees
I would like a room for ____.	Quisiera una habitación para ____.
	kee-SYEH-rah OO-nah ah-bee-tah-THYOHN pah-rah

For full coverage of number terms, see p7.

I would like ____	Quisiera ____
	kee-SYEH-rah
a king-sized bed.	una cama matrimonial extragrande.
	OO-nah KAH-mah mah-tree-moh-nee-AHL ehk-strah-GRAHN-deh
a double bed.	una cama doble.
	OO-nah KAH-mah DOH-bleh
twin beds.	dos camas individuales.
	dohs KAH-mahs een-dee-vee-DWAHL-ehs
adjoining rooms.	habitaciones contiguas.
	ah-bee-tah-THYOH-nehs kohn-TEEH-wahs
a smoking room.	una habitación para fumadores.
	OO-nah ah-bee-tah-THYOHN PAH-rah foo-mah-DOH-rehs

LODGING

Listen Up: Reservations Lingo

No tenemos vacantes.	We have no vacancies.
¿Hasta cuándo se queda?	How long will you be staying?
¿Sección para fumadores o no fumadores?	Smoking or nonsmoking?

a nonsmoking room.	**una habitación para no fumadores.**
	OO-nah ah-bee-tah-THYOHN PAH-rah noh foo-mah-DOH-rehs
a private bathroom.	**un baño privado.**
	oon BAH-nyoh pree-VAH-doh
a shower.	**una ducha.**
	OO-nah DOO-cha
a bathtub.	**una bañera.**
	OO-nah bah-NYEH-rah
air conditioning.	**aire acondicionado.**
	AYE-reh ah-cohn-dee-thyoh-NAH-doh
televisión.	**un televisor.**
	oon teh-leh-vee-SOHR
cable.	**televisión por cable.**
	teh-leh-vee-SYOHN pohr KAH-bleh
satellite TV.	**televisión por satélite.**
	teh-leh-vee-SYOHN pohr sah-TEH-lee-teh
a telephone.	**un teléfono.**
	oon teh-LEH-foh-noh
Internet access.	**acceso a Internet.**
	ahk-THEH-soh ah een-tehr-NEHT
high-speed Internet access.	**acceso a Internet de alta velocidad.**
	ahk-THEH-soh ah een-tehr-NEHT deh AHL-tah veh-loh-thee-DAHD
a refrigerator.	**una nevera.**
	OO-nah neh-VEH-rah
a beach view.	**vistas a la playa.**
	VEES-tahs ah lah PLAH-yah
a city view.	**vistas a la ciudad.**
	VEES-tahs ah lah thee-oo-DAHD

a kitchenette.	**una cocina pequeña.** *OO-nah koh-THEE-nah* *peh-KEH-nyah*
a balcony.	**un balcón.** *oon bahl-KOHN*
a suite.	**una suite.** *OO-nah SWEE-teh*
a penthouse.	**un ático de lujo.** *oon AH-tee-koh deh LOO-ho*
I would like a room ____	**Quisiera una habitación ____** *kee-SYEH-rah OO-nah ah-bee-* *tah-THYOHN*
on the ground floor.	**en la planta baja.** *ehn lah PLAHN-tah BAH-hah*
near the elevator.	**cerca del ascensor.** *THEHR-kah dehl ah-thehn-SOHR*
near the stairs.	**cerca de las escaleras.** *THEHR-kah deh lahs ehs-kah-* *LEH-rahs*
near the pool.	**cerca de la piscina.** *THEHR-kah deh lah pee-* *THEE-nah*
away from the street.	**lejos de la calle.** *LEH-hohs deh lah KAH-yeh*
I would like a corner room.	**Quisiera una habitación que haga esquina.** *kee-SYEH-rah OO-na ah-bee-tah-* *THYOHN keh AH-gah ehs-KEE-nah*
Do you have ____	**¿Tiene ____** *TYEH-neh*
a crib?	**una cuna?** *OO-nah KOO-nah*
a foldout bed?	**una cama plegable?** *OO-nah KAH-mah pleh-* *GAH-bleh*

LODGING

FOR GUESTS WITH SPECIAL NEEDS

I need a room with ____	**Necesito una habitación con ____** *neh-theh-SEE-toh OO-nah ah-bee-tah-THYOHN kohn*
wheelchair access.	**acceso para silla de ruedas.** *ahk-THEH-soh pah-rah SEE-yah deh RWEH-dahs*
services for the visually impaired.	**servicios para personas con discapacidad visual.** *sehr-VEE-thyohs pah-rah pehr-SOH-nahs kohn dees-kah-pah-thee-DAHD vee-SWAHL*
services for the hearing impaired.	**servicios para personas con discapacidad auditiva.** *sehr-VEE-thyohs pah-rah pehr-SOH-nahs kohn dees-kah-pah-thee-DAHD ahoo-dee-TEE-vah*
I am traveling with a service dog.	**Estoy viajando con un perro de servicio.** *ehs-TOY vyah-HAHN-doh kohn oon PEH-rroh deh sehr-VEE-thyoh*

MONEY MATTERS

I would like to make a reservation.	**Me gustaría hacer una reserva.** *meh goos-tah-REE-ah ah-THEHR OO-nah reh-SEHR-vah*
How much per night?	**¿Cuánto cuesta por noche?** *KWAHN-toh KWEHS-tah pohr NOH-cheh*
Do you have a ____	**¿Tiene una tarifa _____** *TYEH-neh OO-nah tah-REE-fah*
weekly / monthly rate?	**semanal / mensual?** *seh-mah-NAHL / mehn-SWAHL*
a weekend rate?	**una tarifa de fin de semana?** *OO-nah tah-REE-fah deh feen deh seh-MAH-nah*

We will be staying for ____ days / weeks.	**¿Nos quedaremos por ____ días / semanas.** *nohs keh-dah-REH-mohs pohr ____ DEE-ahs / seh-MAH-nahs.*

For full coverage of number terms, see p7.

When is checkout time?	**¿Cuál es la hora de salida?** *kwahl ehs lah OH-rah deh sah-LEE-dah*

For full coverage of time-related terms, see p12.

Do you accept credit cards / travelers checks?	**¿Aceptan tarjetas de crédito / cheques de viaje?** *ah-THEHP-tahn tahr-HEH-tahs deh KREH-dee-toh / CHEH-kehs deh VYAH-heh*
May I see a room?	**¿Puedo ver una habitación?** *PWEH-doh vehr OO-nah ah-bee-tah-THYOHN*

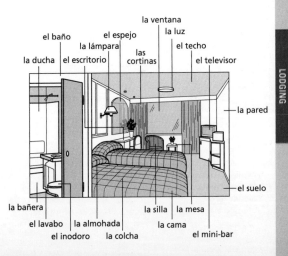

la ventana
la luz
el baño
el espejo
el techo
la lámpara
la ducha   el escritorio   las cortinas   el televisor
la pared
el suelo
la bañera
el lavabo   la almohada   la silla   la mesa
el inodoro   la colcha   la cama   el mini-bar

LODGING

How much are taxes?	**¿Cuántos son los impuestos?** *KWAHN-tohs sohn lohs eem-PWEHS-tohs*
Is there a service charge?	**¿Hay un cargo por servicio?** *aye oon KAHR-goh pohr sehr-VEE-thyoh*
I'd like to speak with the manager.	**Quisiera hablar con el gerente.** *kee-SYEH-rah ah-BLAHR kohn ehl heh-REHN-teh*

IN-ROOM AMENITIES

I'd like _____	**Quisiera _____** *kee-SYEH-rah*
to place an international call.	**hacer una llamada internacional.** *ah-THEHR OO-nah yah-MAH-dah een-tehr-nah-thyoh-NAHL*
to place a long-distance call.	**hacer una llamada de larga distancia.** *ah-SEHR OO-nah yah-MAH-dah deh LAHR-gah dees-TAHN-thyah*
directory assistance in English.	**asistencia en inglés.** *ah-sees-TEHN-thyah ehn een-GLEHS*

Instructions for dialing the hotel phone

Para llamar a otra habitación, marque el número de la habitación.	To call another room, dial the room number.
Para llamadas locales, marque primero el 9.	To make a local call, first dial 9.
Para la operadora, marque el 0.	To call the operator, dial 0.

room service.	**servicio de habitaciones.** *sehr-VEE-thyoh deh ah-bee-tah-THYOH-nehs*
maid service.	**servicio de limpieza.** *sehr-VEE-thyoh deh leem-PYEH-tha*
the front desk ATT operator.	**la operadora de ATT en recepción.** *lah oh-peh-rah-DOH-rah deh ah teh teh ehn reh-thehp-THYOHN*
Do you have room service?	**¿Tienen servicio de habitaciones?** *TYEH-nehn sehr-VEE-thyoh deh ah-bee-tah-THYOH-nehs*
When is the kitchen open?	**¿Cuándo abre la cocina?** *KWAHN-doh AH-breh lah koh-THEE-nah*
When is breakfast served?	**¿Cuándo se sirve el desayuno?** *KWAHN-doh seh SEER-veh ehl deh-sah-YOO-noh*

For full coverage of time-related terms, see p12.

Do you offer massages?	**¿El hotel tiene servicio de masajes?** *elh oh-TEHL TYEH-neh sehr-VEE-thyoh deh mah-SAH-hehs*
Do you have a lounge?	**¿Tienen un salón?** *TYEH-nehn oon sah-LOHN*
Do you have a business center?	**¿Tienen un centro de negocios?** *TYEH-nehn oon THEHN-troh deh neh-GOH-thyohs*
Do you serve breakfast?	**¿Sirven desayuno?** *SEER-vehn deh-sah-YOO-noh*
Do you have Wi-Fi?	**¿Tienen red inalámbrica?** *TYEH-nehn rehd ee-nah-LAHM-bree-kah*

May I have a newspaper in the morning?	**¿Puedo recibir el periódico por la mañana?** *PWEH-deh reh-see-BEER ehl pehr-YOH-dee-koh pohr lah mah-NYAH-nah*
Do you offer a tailor service?	**¿Tienen servicio de sastrería?** *TYEH-nehn ser-VEE-thyoh deh sahs-treh-REE-ah*
Do you offer laundry service?	**¿Tienen servicio de lavandería?** *TYEH-nehn ser-VEE-thyoh deh lah-vahn-deh-REE-ah*
Do you offer dry cleaning?	**¿Tienen servicio de limpieza en seco?** *TYEH-nehn ser-VEE-thyoh deh leem-PYEH-thah ehn SEH-koh*
May we have _____	**¿Podemos tener _____** *poh-DEH-mohs teh-NEHR*
clean sheets today?	**sábanas limpias hoy?** *SAH-bah-nahs LEEM-pee-ahs oy*
more towels?	**más toallas?** *mahs toh-AH-yahs*
more toilet paper?	**más papel higiénico?** *mahs pah-PEHL ee-HYEH-nee-koh*
extra pillows?	**más almohadas?** *mahs ahl-moh-AH-dahs*
Do you have an ice machine?	**¿Tienen una máquina de hielo?** *TYEH-nehn OO-nah MAH-kee-nah deh YEH-loh*

Did I receive any ____	**¿Recibí ____**
	reh-see-BEE
messages?	**algún mensaje?**
	ahl-GOON mehn-SAH-heh
mail?	**alguna correspondencia?**
	ahl-GOO-nah koh-rrehs-pohn-DEHN-thyah
faxes?	**algún fax?**
	ahl-GOON fahks
A spare key, please.	**Una llave adicional, por favor.**
	OO-nah YAH-veh ah-deeth-yoh-NAHL pohr fah-VOHR
More hangers, please.	**Más perchas, por favor.**
	mahs PEHR-chahs pohr fah-VOHR
I am allergic to down pillows	**Soy alérgico -a a las almohadas de plumas.**
	soy ah-LEHR-hee-koh I-kah ah lahs ahl-moh-AH-dahs deh PLOO-mahs
May I have a wake up call?	**¿Me podrían llamar por la mañana?**
	meh poh-DREE-ahn yah-MAHR pohr lah mah-NYAH-nah

For full coverage of how to tell time, see p12.

Do you have alarm clocks?	**¿Tiene un despertador?**
	TYEH-neh oon dehs-pehr-tah-DOHR
Is there a safe in the room?	**¿Hay caja fuerte en la habitación?**
	aye KAH-hah FWEHR-teh ehn lah ah-bee-tah-THYOHN
Does the room have a hair dryer?	**¿Tiene la habitación secador de pelo?**
	TYEH-neh lah ah-bee-tah-THYOHN seh-kah-DOHR deh PEH-loh

LODGING

HOTEL ROOM TROUBLE

May I speak with the manager?

¿Puedo hablar con el gerente?
PWEH-doh ah-BLAHR kohn ehl heh-REHN-teh

The ____ does not work.

____ no funciona.
noh foon-THYOH-nah

television

El televisor
ehl teh-leh-vee-SOHR

telephone

El teléfono
ehl teh-LEH-foh-noh

air conditioning

El aire acondicionado
ehl AYE-reh ah-kohn-dee-thyoh-NAH-doh

Internet access

El acceso a Internet
ehl ahk-SEH-soh ah een-tehr-NET

cable TV

El servicio de televisión por cable
ehl sehr-VEE-thyoh deh teh-leh-vee-SYOHN pohr KAH-blah

There is no hot water.

No hay agua caliente.
noh ay AH-wah kah-LYEHN-teh

The toilet is over-flowing!

¡El inodoro se está desbordando!
ehl ee-noh-DOH-roh seh ehs-TAH dehs-bohr-DAHN-doh

This room is too noisy.	**Esta habitación es muy ruidosa.** *EHS-tah ah-bee-tah-THYOHN ehs* *MOO-ee roo-ee-DOH-sah*
This room is too cold.	**En esta habitación hace mucho frío.** *ehn EHS-tah ah-bee-tah-THYOHN* *AH-theh MOO-choh FREE-oh*
This room is too warm.	**En esta habitación hace mucho** **calor.** *ehn EHS-tah ah-bee-tah-THYOHN* *AH-theh MOO-choh kah-LOHR*
This room has ____	**Esta habitación tiene ____** *EHS-tah ah-bee-tah-THYOHN* *TYEH-neh*
bugs.	**insectos.** *een-SEHK-tohs*
mice.	**ratones.** *rah-TOH-nehs*
I'd like a different room.	**Quiero otra habitación.** *KYEH-roh OH-trah ah-bee-tah-* *THYOHN*
Do you have a bigger room?	**¿Tiene una habitación más** **grande?** *TYEH-neh OO-nah ah-bee-tah-* *THYOHN mahs GRAHN-deh*
I locked myself out of my room.	**Me he quedado fuera sin llaves** **para entrar la habitación.** *meh EH keh-DAH-doh FWEH-rah* *seen YAH-vehs pah-rah ehn-TRAHR* *ehn lah ah-bee-tah-THYOHN*
Do you have any fans?	**¿Tiene abanicos?** *TYEH-ne ah-bah-NEE-kohs*
The sheets are not clean.	**Las sábanas no están limpias.** *lahs SAH-bah-nahs noh ehs-TAHN* *LEEM-pyahs*

LODGING

The towels are not clean.	**Las toallas no están limpias.**
	lahs to-AH-yahs noh ehs-TAHN
	LEEM-pyahs
The room is not clean.	**La habitación no está limpia.**
	lah ah-bee-tah-THYOHN noh ehs-
	TAH LEEM-pyah
The guests next door /	**Los huéspedes de al lado / arriba /**
above / below are being	**abajo son muy ruidosos.**
very loud.	*lohs WEHS-peh-dehs deh ahl LAH-*
	doh / ah-RREE-bah / ah-BAH-hoh
	sohn MOO-ee roo-ee-DOH-sohs

CHECKING OUT

I think this charge is a	**Creo que este cargo es un error.**
mistake.	*KREH-oh keh EHS-teh KAHR-goh*
	ehs oon eh-RROHR
Please explain this charge	**Por favor explíqueme a qué se**
to me.	**debe este cargo.**
	pohr fah-VOHR ehs-PLEE-keh-meh
	ah KEH seh DEH-beh EHS-teh
	KAHR-goh
Thank you, we enjoyed	**Gracias, disfrutamos nuestra**
our stay.	**estadía.**
	GRAH-thyahs dees-froo-TAH-mohs
	NWEHS-trah ehs-tah-DEE-ah
The service was excellent.	**El servicio fue excelente.**
	ehl sehr-VEE-thyoh fweh ehk-
	theh-LEHN-teh
The staff is very	**El personal es muy profesional y**
professional and	**cortés.**
courteous.	*ehl pehr-soh-NAHL ehs MOO-ee*
	proh-feh-syoh-NAHL ee kohr-TEHS
Would you please call	**¿Por favor, me puede llamar un**
a cab for me?	**taxi?**
	pohr fah-VOHR meh PWEH-deh
	yah-MAHR oon TAHK-see

Would someone please get my bags?	**¿Alguien puede ayudarme con el equipaje?** *AHLG-yehn PWEH-deh ah-yoo-DAHR-meh kohn ehl eh-kee-PAH-heh*

HAPPY CAMPING

I'd like a site for ____	**Quisiera un lugar para ____** *kee-SYEH-rah oon loo-GAHR pah-rah*
a tent.	**una tienda de campaña.** *OO-nah TYEHN-dah deh kahm-PAH-nyah*
a camper.	**una caravana.** *OO-nah kah-rah-VAH-nah*
Are there ____	**¿Hay ____** *ay*
bathrooms?	**baños?** *BAH-nyohs*
showers?	**duchas?** *DOOH-chahs*
Is there running water?	**¿Hay agua corriente?** *ay AH-wah koh-rree-EHN-teh*
Is the water drinkable?	**¿El agua es potable?** *ehl AH-wah ehs poh-TAH-bleh*
Where is the electrical hookup?	**¿Dónde está la conexión eléctrica?** *DOHN-deh ehs-TAH lah koh-nehk-SYOHN eh-LEHK-tree-kah*

GOVERNMENT LODGING RATES

Spain is one of many countries that rates accommodations from one to five stars, according to price and the presence or absence of a number of objective criteria—from private bathrooms to pools, elevators, air-conditioning, and other amenities. It's a good idea to check out these ratings, particularly when you sign up for an escorted tour or a land/air package that includes lodging in the price. But keep in mind that a high rating may not reflect such intangibles as character, charm, or comfort, and that an expensive five-star hotel with four restaurants may be less desirable than a more modest three-star hotel with no restaurant. It's best to let guidebook ratings help you make these fine distinctions. For what it's worth, here's how the government rating system works:

Five stars   **Very Expensive** $275 and up. Accommodation of the highest standard with luxury furnishings and a wide range of stylish amenities.

Four stars   **Expensive** $190 to $274. Very high standards. These and the five-star hotels often have sophisticated conference facilities.

Three stars   **Moderate** $120 to $189. Comfortable rooms with good service and amenities including a private bathroom. A safe middle choice in Spain that won't break the bank.

Two stars   **Inexpensive** $75 to $120. Comfortable but more basic, with adequate rooms and service; usually a private bathroom.

One star   **Budget**   Under $75. Basic but clean, sometimes with a shared bathroom on each floor.

DIFFERENT TYPES OF LODGING

Hostals are modest hotels with no porters. They have their own one- to three-star rating and are easily recognized by the blue plaque by the entry door bearing the sign Hs.

Hostal Residencias are similar, with the same star ratings. They either serve no meals or breakfast only, and they're recognizable by their exterior HsR sign.

Pensions, signposted with a P, are simple but adequate boarding houses. They're among the least expensive, but you'll probably have to take full or half board, which is breakfast plus lunch or dinner. They have no star ratings.

Casa de Huéspedes (Guest Houses) and **fondas (inns)** are usually located in basic but respectable establishments and are the cheapest of all. Their light blue plaques by the entrance display a CH or F sign, respectively. They have no star ratings.

Officially for youngsters, but open to all age groups, Spain's **youth hostels** total more than 200. Accommodations are in dormitories that usually impose an 11pm curfew. The central office of all youth hostels in Spain is **Albergues Juveniles** (Gran Vía 10, Madrid; Mon–Fri 9am–2pm; © **91-720-11-65** (some English spoken); fax 91-720-11-64; www.reaj.com).

HOTEL GROUPS & CHAINS

Spain's famous **paradors** are luxury hotels in converted castles, palaces, fortresses, convents, monasteries, and other historic buildings—many of them in spectacular locations across the country. Though state-run, they are tastefully and individually restored, with modern amenities and restaurants that specialize in regional dishes. For details, check **www.paradores-spain.com.**

The tourist boom in the past decade has led to a proliferation of very high-standard private hotel chains. The oldest of them is **HUSA,** founded in 1930. Its 170 hotels are located in more than 100 Spanish towns and cities. Check **www.husa.es.**

The largest and most prestigious group is **Sol Melia,** which has absorbed other companies such as HOTASA and Tryp, in the course of its expansion, and now has some 350 hotels in 30 countries. See the website **www.solmelia.com** for details.

Hesperia provides some of the country's most luxurious hostelries with some 49 hotels spread throughout Spain, the U.K., Belgium, and Venezuela. For details and reservations, go to www.hesperia.com or call ✆ **0870-225-4134.**

NH Hotels (www.nh-hotels.com) have accommodations in Madrid, Barcelona, Bilbao, Granada, and other Spanish towns. E-mail messages to nh@nh-hotels.com or ring ✆ **902-115-116** for reservations.

AC Hotels have a wide selection of hotels. Their flagship property is the colorful (and expensive) Avenida America Hotel in Madrid, each of whose floors was designed by a different architect. Visit **www.ac-hotels.es.**

HAI (Associated Independent Hotels; www.hai.es) is a smaller organization based in Madrid providing accommodations in the capital and other Spanish towns.

HOW TO GET THE BEST ROOMS & PRICES

- **Traveling with kids**   Find out if they stay free, or if there is a special rate. Also note that a suite may cost less than two separate rooms.

- **Dial direct**   When booking a room in a chain hotel, you'll often get a better deal by contacting the individual hotel rather than calling the chain's main number.

- **Book online**   Many hotels offer Internet-only discounts, available through the hotel's website or through an online booking engine, such as Expedia or Travelocity. If you book online, you may not be able to ask for certain preferences, such as a quiet room, so call or fax the hotel directly and let them know what you need.

- **Remember the law of supply and demand**   Resort hotels are most crowded and therefore most expensive on weekends, so discounts are more common for midweek stays. Business hotels in downtown locations are busiest during the week, so you can expect deals over the weekend. Many hotels have high-season and low-season prices; booking the day after high season ends (for example, in Sept for beachfront beds) can mean savings.

- **Look into group or long-stay discounts**   If you come as part of a large group, you should be able to negotiate a bargain rate. Likewise, if you're planning a long stay (at least 5 days), you might qualify for a discount. As a general rule, expect 1 free night after a 7-night stay.

- **Avoid hidden costs**   When you book a room, confirm whether the hotel charges for parking or provides airport transfers. Ask about taxes and service charges to avoid unpleasant surprises when you check out.

- **Book an "efficiency"**   A room with a kitchenette allows you to shop for groceries and cook your own meals.

ROOM RESERVATIONS & LAND/AIR PACKAGES

Investigate reservation services first. These outfits usually work as consolidators, buying up rooms in bulk, and then dealing them out to customers at a competitive rate. They offer deals that range from 10% to 50% off, but remember, the discounts apply to rack rates—inflated prices that people rarely pay. You may be better off dealing directly with a hotel, but if you don't like bargaining, a consolidator is a viable option. Here are a few:

Hotel Locators © 800/423-7846; www.hotellocators.com
Accommodations Express © 800/950-4685;
www.accommodationsexpress.com
Hotel Discounts © 800/715-7666; www.hoteldiscount.com
Quikbook © 800/789-9887; www.quikbook.com.

CHAPTER FOUR

DINING

This chapter includes a menu reader and the language you need to communicate in a range of dining establishments and food markets.

FINDING A RESTAURANT

Would you recommend a good ____ restaurant?

¿Me podría recomendar un buen restaurante ____
meh poh-DREE-ah reh-koh-mehn-DAHR oon bwehn reh-stow-RAHN-teh

local	**local?** *loh-KAHL*
Italian	**italiano?** *ee-tah-LYAH-noh*
French	**francés?** *frahn-SEHS*
German	**alemán?** *ah-leh-MAHN*
Spanish	**español?** *ehs-pah-NYOHL*
Chinese	**chino?** *CHEE-noh*
Japanese	**japonés?** *hah-poh-NEHS*
Asian	**asiático?** *ah-SYAH-tee-koh*
pizza	**de pizza?** *deh PEET-thah*
steakhouse	**asador?** *ah-sah-DOHR*

family	**familiar?**
	fah-mee-LYAHR
seafood	**de mariscos?**
	deh mah-REES-kohs
vegetarian	**vegetariano?**
	veh-heh-tah-RYAH-noh
buffet-style	**estilo buffet?**
	ehs-TEE-loh boo-FEH
Greek	**griego?**
	GRYEH-goh
budget	**económico?**
	eh-koh-NOH-mee-koh
Which is the best restaurant in town?	**¿Cuál es el mejor restaurante de la ciudad?**
	kwahl ehs ehl meh-HOHR reh-stoh-RAHN-teh deh lah theeh-OO-dahd
Is there a late-night restaurant nearby?	**¿Hay un restaurante cercano abierto hasta tarde en la noche?**
	aye oon reh-stoh-RAHN-teh THEHR-kah-noh ah-BYEHR-toh AHS-tah TAHR-deh ehn lah NOH-cheh
Is there a restaurant that serves breakfast nearby?	**¿Hay un restaurante cercano que sirva desayuno?**
	aye oon reh-stoh-RAHN-teh THEHR-ka-noh keh SEER-vah deh-sah-YOO-noh
Is it very expensive?	**¿Es muy caro?**
	ehs MOO-ee KAH-roh
Do I need a reservation?	**¿Necesito hacer una reserva?**
	neh-theh-SEE-toh ah-thehr OO-nah reh-SEHR-vah-
Do I have to dress up?	**¿Necesito vestirme elegante-mente?**
	neh-theh-SEE-toh veh-STEER-meh eh-leh-gahn-teh-MEHN-teh

Do they serve lunch?	**¿Sirven almuerzo?**
	SEER-vehn ahl-MWEHR-soh
What time do they open for dinner?	**¿A qué hora abren para cenar?**
	ah KEH OH-rah AHB-rehn PAH-rah theh-NAHR
For lunch?	**¿Para almorzar?**
	PAH-rah ahl-MOHR-thahr
What time do they close?	**¿A qué hora cierran?**
	ah KEH OH-rah THYEH-rrahn
Do you have a take out menu?	**¿Tienen un menú para llevar?**
	TYEH-nehn oon meh-NOO PAH-rah yeh-VAHR
Do you have a bar?	**¿Tienen un bar?**
	TYEH-nehn oon bahr
Is there a café nearby?	**¿Hay un café cerca?**
	aye oon kah-FEH THEHR-kah

GETTING SEATED

Are you still serving?	**¿Todavía están sirviendo?**
	toh-dah-VEE-ah ehs-TAHN seer-VYEHN-doh
How long is the wait?	**¿Cuánto tiempo hay que esperar?**
	kwahn-toh TYEHM-poh ay keh ehs-peh-RAHR
Do you have a nonsmoking section?	**¿Tienen una sección para no fumadores?**
	TYEH-nehn OO-nah sehk-THYOHN PAH-rah noh foo-mah-DOH-rehs
A table for ____, please.	**Una mesa para ____ , por favor.**
	OO-nah MEH-sah PAH-rah ____ , pohr fah-VOHR

For a full list of numbers, see p7.

Do you have a quiet, table?	**¿Tienen una mesa tranquila?**
	TYEH-nehn OO-nah MEH-sah trahn-KEE-lah

Listen Up: Restaurant Lingo

¿Sección para fumadores o
  no fumadores?
*sehk-THYOHN PAH-rah foo-
mah-DOH-rehs o noh foo-
mah-DOH-rehs*

Smoking or
  nonsmoking?

Necesita corbata y chaqueta.
*neh-theh-SEE-tah kohr-
BAH-tah ee chah-KEH-tah*

You'll need a tie and
jacket.

Lo siento, no se permite
  pantalones cortos.
*loh SYEHN-toh noh seh pehr-MEE-
tehn pahn-tah-LOH-nehs KOHR-tohs*

I'm sorry, no shorts
  are allowed.

¿Le puedo traer algo de beber?
*leh PWEH-doh trah-EHR
AHL-goh deh beh-BEHR*

May I bring you
  something to drink?

¿Le gustaría ver una
  carta de vinos?
*leh goos-tah-REE-ah vehr OO-
nah KAHR-tah deh VEE-nohs*

Would you like to see
  a wine list?

¿Le gustaría saber
  cuáles son nuestros
  platos especiales?
*leh goos-tah-REE-ah sah-BEHR
KWAH-lehs sohn NWEHS-trohs
PLAH-tohs ehs-peh-THYAH-lehs*

Would you like to
  hear our specials?

¿Está listo para pedir?
*ehs-TAH LEES-toh PAH-rah
peh-DEEHR*

Are you ready to
  order?

Lo siento. Su tarjeta de
  crédito ha sido rechazada.
*loh SYEHN-toh soo tahr-HEH-tah deh
KREH-dee-toh hah SEE-doh
reh-chah-THAH-dah*

I'm sorry. Your credit
  card was declined.

May we sit outside / inside please?	**¿Podemos sentarnos afuera / dentro por favor?** *poh-DEH-mohs sehn-TAHR-nohs ah-FWEH-rah / DEHN-troh pohr fah-VOHR*
May we sit at the counter?	**¿Podemos sentarnos en el mostrador?** *poh-DEH-mohs sehn-TAHR-nohs ehn ehl mohs-trah-DOHR*
A menu please?	**¿Un menú por favor?** *oon meh-NOO pohr fah-VOHR*

ORDERING

Do you have a special tonight?	**¿Tienen un especial esta noche?** *TYEH-nehn oon ehs-peh-THYAHL EHS-tah NOH-cheh*
What do you recommend?	**¿Qué recomienda usted?** *KEH reh-koh-MYEHN-dah oos-TEHD*
May I see a wine list?	**¿Puedo ver una carta de vinos?** *PWEH-doh vehr OO-nah KAHR-tah deh VEE-nohs*
Do you serve wine by the glass?	**¿Ustedes sirven vino por la copa?** *oos-TEH-dehs SEER-vehn VEE-noh pohr lah KOH-pah*
May I see a drink list?	**¿Puedo ver una lista de bebidas?** *PWEH-doh vehr OO-nah LEES-tah deh beh-BEE-dahs*
I would like it cooked ____	**Me gustaría ____** *meh goos-tah-REE-ah*
rare.	**poco hecho -a.** *POH-koh EH-choh -chah*
medium rare.	**en su punto.** *ehn soo POOHN-toh*
medium / medium well.	**medio hecho -a.** *MEH-dyoh EH-choh -chah*

well.	**bien hecho -a.**
	byehn EH-choh -chah
charred.	**muy bien hecho -a.**
	MOO-ee byehn EH-choh -chah
Do you have a ____ menu?	**¿Tiene un menú ____**
	TYEH-neh oon meh-NOO
diabetic	**para diabéticos?**
	PAH-rah dee-ah-BEH-tee-kohs
kosher	**kósher?**
	KOH-shehr
vegetarian	**vegetariano?**
	veh-heh-tah-RYAH-noh
children's	**para niños?**
	PAH-rah NEE-nyohs
What is in this dish?	**¿Qué hay en este plato?**
	keh aye ehn EHS-teh PLAH-toh
How is it prepared?	**¿Cómo está preparado?**
	KOH-moh eh-STAH preh-PAH-rah-do
What kind of oil is that cooked in?	**¿En qué tipo de aceite está cocido?**
	ehn keh TEE-poh deh ah-THEH-ee-teh eh-STAH koh-THEE-doh
Do you have any low-salt dishes?	**¿Tiene platos bajos en sal?**
	TYEH-neh PLAH-tohs BAH-hohs ehn sahl
On the side, please.	**Al lado, por favor.**
	ahl LAH-doh pohr fah-VOHR
May I make a substitution?	**¿Puedo hacer una sustitución?**
	PWEH-doh ah-SEHR OO-nah soos-tee-too-THYOHN
I'd like to try that.	**Me gustaría probar eso.**
	meh goos-tah-REE-ah proh-BAHR EH-soh

DINING

Is that fresh?	**¿Eso es fresco?**
	EH-so ehs FREHS-koh
Waiter!	**¡Camarero!**
	cah-mah-REH-roh
Extra butter, please.	**Déme mas mantequilla, por favor.**
	DEH-meh mahs mahn-teh-KEE-yah
	pohr fah-VOHR
No butter, thanks.	**Sin mantequilla, por favor.**
	seen mahn-teh-KEE-yah pohr fah-VOHR
No cream, thanks.	**Sin crema, por favor.**
	seen KREH-mah pohr fah-VOHR
Dressing on the side, please.	**El aderezo a un lado, por favor.**
	ehl ah-deh-REH-thoh ah oohn LAH-doh pohr fah-VOHR
No salt, please.	**Sin sal, por favor.**
	seen sahl pohr fah-VOHR
May I have some oil, please?	**¿Me puede dar un poco de aceite, por favor?**
	meh PWEH-deh dahr oon POH-koh deh ah-THEH-ee-teh pohr fah-VOHR
More bread, please.	**Más pan, por favor.**
	mahs pahn pohr fah-VOHR
I am lactose intolerant.	**Soy intolerante a la lactosa.**
	soy een-toh-loh-RAHN-teh ah lah lahk-TOH-sah
Would you recommend something without milk?	**¿Podría recomendar algo sin leche?**
	poh-DREE-ah reh-koh-mehn-DAHR AHL-goh seen LEH-cheh

I am allergic to ____	**Soy alérgico -a a ____**
	soy ah-LEHR-hee-koh -kah ah
seafood.	**al pescado y los mariscos.**
	ahl pay-SKAH-doh ee lohs mah-REES-kohs
shellfish.	**los crustáceos.**
	lohs kroos-TAH-theh-ohs
nuts.	**las nueces.**
	lahs-NWEH-thehs
peanuts.	**los cacahuetes**
	lohs kah-kah-WEH-tehs
Water ____, please.	**Agua ____, por favor.**
	AH-wah ____ pohr fah-VOHR
with ice	**con hielo**
	kohn YEH-loh
without ice	**sin hielo**
	seen YEH-loh
I'm sorry, I don't think this is what I ordered.	**Lo siento, creo que esto no es lo que pedí.**
	loh SYEHN-toh KREH-oh keh EHS-toh noh ehs loh keh peh-DEE
My meat is a little over / under cooked.	**La carne está poco hecha / demasiado hecha.**
	lah KAHR-neh ehs-TAH POH-koh EH-chah / day-mah-see-AH-doh EH-chah
My vegetables are a little over / under cooked.	**Las verduras están poco hechas / demasiado hechas.**
	lahs vehr-DUHR-ahs ehs-TAHN POH-koh EH-chahs / day-mah-see-AH-doh EH-chahs
There's a bug in my food!	**¡Hay un insecto en mi plato!**
	aye oon een-SEHK-toh ehn mee PLAH-toh

May I have more ___?	**¿Puede darme más ___?**
	PWEH-deh DAHR-meh mahs
A dessert menu, please.	**El menú de postres, por favor.**
	ehl meh-NOO deh POHS-trehs
	pohr fah-VOHR

DRINKS

alcoholic	**con alcohol**
	kohn ahl-koh-OHL
neat / straight	**sencillo**
	sehn-THEE-yoh
on the rocks	**con hielo**
	kohn YEH-loh
with (seltzer or soda)	**con sifón**
water	*kohn see-FOHN*
beer	**cerveza**
	thehr-VEH-thah
brandy	**brandy**
	BRAHN-dee
coffee	**café**
	kah-FEH
cappuccino	**cappuccino**
	kah-poo-THEE-noh
espresso	**café solo**
	kah-FEH SOH-loh
iced coffee	**café con hielo**
	kah-FEH kohn YEH-loh
cognac	**coñac**
	koh-NYAHK
fruit juice	**zumo de fruta**
	THUM-oh deh FROO-tah

For a full list of fruits, see p113.

gin	**ginebra**
	hee-NEH-brah
hot chocolate	**chocolate caliente**
	cho-koh-LAH-teh kah-LYEHN-teh

How Do You Take It?

Tomar means to take. But if a bartender asks, *¿Quiere tomar algo?*, he's not inviting you to steal his fancy corkscrew. He's asking what you'd like to drink.

lemonade	**limonada**
	lee-moh-NAH-dah
liqueur	**licor**
	lee-KOHR
milk	**leche**
	LEH-cheh
milkshake	**batido de leche**
	bah-TEE-doh deh LEH-cheh
nonalcoholic	**sin alcohol**
	seen ahl-koh-OHL
rum	**ron**
	rohn
tea	**té**
	teh
vodka	**vodka**
	VOHD-kah
wine	**vino**
	VEE-noh
dry white wine	**vino blanco seco**
	VEE-noh BLAHN-koh SEH-koh
full-bodied wine	**vino de mucho cuerpo**
	VEE-noh deh MOO-choh KWEHR-poh
house wine	**vino de la casa**
	VEE-noh deh lah KAH-sah
light-bodied wine	**vino ligero**
	VEE-noh lee-GAYR-oh
red wine	**vino tinto**
	VEE-noh TEEN-toh

rosé

vino rosado
VEE-noh roh-SAH-doh

sparkling sweet wine

vino dulce espumoso
VEE-noh DOOL-seh ehs-poom-OH-soh

sweet wine

vino dulce
VEE-noh DOOL-theh

SETTLING UP

I'm stuffed.

Estoy lleno -a.
ehs-TOY YEH-noh -nah

The meal was excellent.

La comida estuvo excelente.
lah koh-MEE-dah ehs-TOO-voh ehk-theh-LEHN-teh

There's a problem with my bill.

Hay un problema con la cuenta.
aye oon proh-BLEH-mah kohn lah KWEHN-tah

Is the tip included?

¿La propina está incluida?
lah proh-PEE-nah ehs-TAH een-kloo-EE-dah

My compliments to the chef!

¡Mi enhorabuena al chef!
meh ehn-orh-ah-BWEHN-ah ahl chehf

Check, please.

La cuenta, por favor.
lah KWEHN-tah pohr fah-VOHR

MENU READER

Spanish cuisine varies broadly from region to region, but we've tried to make our list of classic dishes as encompassing as possible.

APPETIZERS / TAPAS

aceitunas: olives
ah-theh-ee-TOO-nahs

aceitunas mixtas: mixed olives marinated with peppers, onion, and lemon
ah-theh-ee-TOO-nahs MEES-tahs

albóndigas: ground beef and pork meatballs
ahl-BOHN-dee-gohs

bacalao: dried salt cod
bah-kah-LAH-oh

boquerones en vinagre: fresh anchovies marinated in garlic and olive oil
boh-kehr-OHN-ehs ehn vee-NAH-greh

conejo: braised rabbit
koh-NEH-ho

croquetas: croquettes
kroh-KEH-tahs

gambas al ajillo: broiled shrimp (sautéed in garlic and oil)
GAHM-bahs ahl ah-HEE-yoh

jamón: ham
hah-MOHN

  jamón de bellota: free-range, acorn-fed ham
  hah-MOHN deh beh-YOH-tah

  jamón ibérico: aged Iberian ham
  hah-MOHN ee-BEH-ree-koh

  jamón serrano: dry-cured serrano ham
  hah-MOHN seh-RRAH-noh

langostinos a la plancha: grilled-on-shell jumbo shrimp with sea salt
lahn-goh-STEE-nohs ah lah PLAHN-chah

pan a la Catalana: toasted bread topped with garlic, tomato, and cilantro
pahn ah lah cah-tah-LAHN-ah

DINING

> ### Cheese!
>
> There are hundreds of cheeses in Spain. Each region has its own specialty cheese. Among the most famous are *queso Manchego, queso Mahón,* and *queso Cabrales.*

patatas panadera con salmorejo: fried slices of potato with a cold dip of tomato and garlic
pah-TAH-tahs pahn-ah-DEH-reh kohn sahl-moh-REH-hoh

pescados fritos: fried fish
pehs-KAH-dohs FREE-tohs

quesos: cheeses
KEH-sohs

  de leche de cabra: goat's milk
  deh LEH-cheh deh KAH-brah

  rallado: grated
  rah-YAH-doh

  requesón: cottage
  reh-keh-SOHN

  suave: mild
  soo-AH-veh

  queso cabrales: blue-veined Cabrales cheese
  KEH-soh kah-BRAH-lehs

tabla de quesos Españoles: combination of Spanish cheeses served with quince paste
TAH-blah deh KEH-sohs es-pah-NYOHL-ehs

tortilla española: omelet with potato
tohr-TEE-yah ehs-pah-NYOH-lah

SALADS

ensalada de lentejas aliñadas: lentil salad
ehn-sah-LAH-dah deh lehn-TEH-hahs ah-lee-NYAH-dahs

ensalada de arúgula: arugula salad
ehn-sah-LAH-dah deh ah-ROO-goo-lah

ensalada de berro: watercress salad
ehn-sah-LAH-dah deh BEH-rroh

ensalada de espinacas: spinach salad
ehn-sah-LAH-dah deh ehs-pee-NAH-kahs
ensalada de huerta: field green salad
ehn-sah-LAH-dah deh WEHR-tah
ensalada mixta: salad with lettuce, tomatoes, olives, tuna
ehn-sah-LAH-dah MEES-tah
ensalada de tomates: tomato salad
ehn-sah-LAH-dah deh toh-MAH-tehs
ensalada de verduras: green salad
ehn-sah-LAH-dah deh vehr-DOO-rahs
manojillo de la huerta: Mesclun salad
mah-noh-HEE-yoh deh lah WEHR-tah

Paella

Paella is a regional specialty dish. Each region in Spain
has its own version of this classic dish. Below are such
examples:
paella de carne: meat paella with chicken and sausage
pah-EH-yah deh KAHR-neh
paella de langosta: lobster and seafood paella
pah-EH-yah deh lahn-GOH-stah
paella marinera: seafood paella
pah-EH-yah mah-ree-NEH-rah
paella negra: black ink paella with shrimp, swordfish,
  squid, and squid ink
pah-EH-yah NEH-grah
paella Valenciana: paella rice with mixed seafood and
  chicken
pah-EH-yah vah-lehn-thee-AH-nah
arroz a banda: seafood paella
ah-RROHS ah BAHN-dah

SOUPS AND STEWS

caldo gallego: soup with salt pork, white beans, chorizo, ham, and turnip / collard greens
KAHL-doh gah-YEH-goh

crema de berros: watercress soup
KREH-mah deh BEH-rrohs

fabada asturiana: hearty white bean stew
fah-BAH-dah ah-stoo-RYAH-nah

gazpacho: cold vegetable soup
gahs-PAH-cho

menestra de verduras: hearty vegetable stew
meh-NEH-strah deh vehr-DOO-rahs

sopa de ajo: garlic soup
SOH-pah deh AH-hoh

sopa de manzana con sorbete de yogur: chilled apple soup with yogurt sorbet
SOH-pah deh mahn-THAH-nah kohn sohr-BEH-teh deh yoh-GOOR

SIDE / VEGETABLE DISHES

aguacate relleno: stuffed avocado
ah-wah-KAH-teh rreh-YEH-noh

berenjenas fritas con cabrales: fried eggplant with a cabrales cheese dip
beh-rehn-HEH-nahs FREE-tahs kohn cah-BRAH-lehs

berenjenas gratinadas: fresh eggplant baked with cheese, tomato, and herb
beh-rehn-HEH-nahs grah-tee-NAH-dahs

champiñones al ajillo: mushrooms sautéed in garlic and olive oil
cham-pee-NYON-ehs ahl ah-HEE-yoh

espinacas salteadas: sautéed spinach
ehs-pee-NAH-kahs sahl-teh-AH-dahs

patatas bravas: deep fried potatoes in a spicy sauce
pah-TAH-tahs BRAH-vahs

setas a la plancha: sautéed mushrooms
SEH-tahs ah lah PLAHN-chah

For a full list of vegetables, see p115.

SAUSAGES

butifarra: spiced pork breakfast sausage
boo-tee-FAH-rrah

chorizo: spicy, or sometimes sweet pork sausage
cho-REE-thoh

morcilla: blood sausage (can be sweet)
mohr-THEE-yah

salchichón: salami-style sausage
sahl-chee-CHOHN

BEEF

carrilleras de Ternera: braised veal cheeks
cah-rreel-YEH-rahs deh tehr-NEH-rah

chuleta de Ávila: veal chop
choo-LEH-tah deh AH-vee-lah

entrecot de buey: beef strip loin
ehn-TREH-koht deh bweh

falda de buey: beef flank steak
FAHL-dah deh bweh

guiso de carne con patatas: beef stew with potatoes
GEE-soh deh KAHR-neh kohn pah-TAH-tahs

lengua de ternera: veal tongue
LEHN-gwah deh tehr-NEHR-ah

mollejas de ternera: veal sweetbread
mohl-YEH-hahs deh tehr-NEH-rah

ORGAN MEATS

callos a la madrileña: tripe stew (typical of the Madrid region)
KAH-yohs ah lah mah-dree-LEH-nyah

WILD GAME

conejo al ajillo: garlic roasted rabbit
cohn-EH-hoh ahl ah-HEE-yoh

conejo guisado: braised rabbit
koh-NEH-hoh gee-SAH-doh

lomo de venado: venison loin
LOH-moh deh veh-NAH-doh

GOAT

cabrito asado: oven-roasted kid
kah-BREE-toh ah-SAH-doh

seco de chivo: goat stew in wine sauce
SEH-koh deh CHEE-voh

PORK

cochinillo / lechón asado: roast suckling pig
koh-chee-NEE-yoh / leh-CHOHN ah-SAH-doh

costillas de cerdo: pork ribs
kohs-TEE-yahs deh THEHR-doh

POULTRY

arroz con pollo: rice with chicken and vegetables
ah-RROHS kohn POH-yoh

brocheta de pollo: skewered chicken breast and red peppers
  marinated in spices
broh-CHEH-tah deh POH-yoh

codorniz crujiente: quail breast
koh-dohr-NEEZ kroo-HYEHN-teh

pollo a la brasa: spit-roasted chicken
POH-yoh ah lah BRAH-sah

pollo al jerez: chicken in sherry
POH-yoh ahl heh-REHS

pollo frito: fried chicken
POH-yoh FREE-toh

FISH AND SEAFOOD

bacalao guisado: cod marinated in herbs
bah-kah-LAH-oh gee-SAH-doh

camarones al ajillo: garlic shrimp stew
kah-mah-ROH-nehs ahl ah-HEE-yoh

zarzuela: mixed fish and seafood soup with tomatoes,
  saffron, garlic, and wine served over bread
thahr-THWEH-lah

For a full list of fish, see p112.

DESSERTS

arroz con leche / arroz con dulce: rice pudding
ah-RROHTH kohn LEH-cheh / ah-RROHTH kohn DOOL-theh

buñuelos: round, thin fritters dipped in sugar (may also be savory)
boon-yoo-EH-lohs

copita chocolate blanco: white chocolate mousse
coh-PEE-tah choh-koh-LAH-teh BLAHN-koh

empanadas: turnovers filled with meat, tuna, chicken and / or cheese, beans, potatoes
ehm-pah-NAH-dahs

flan: carmel custard
flahn

flan de queso: cheese flan
flahn deh KEH-soh

helado: ice cream
eh-LAH-doh

leche frita: fried milk custard
LEH-cheh FREE-tah

plato de fruta fresca: fresh fruit plate
PLAH-toh deh FROO-tah FREHS-kah

sorbetes de temporada: fresh fruit sorbets
sohr-BEH-tehs deh tehm-pohr-RAH-dah

tarta de Santiago: almond sponge cake, usually served warm
TAHR-tah deh sahn-tee-AH-goh

tocino de cielo: egg yolk custard
toh-THEE-noh deh THYEH-loh

Street Vendors

In the winter months, you may find street vendors selling *castañas* (roasted chestnuts) and *churros* (breakfast / dessert fritters). In the summer, it is common to see ice cream vendors throughout the large cities.

BUYING GROCERIES

In Spain, groceries can be bought at markets, neighborhood stores, or large supermarkets.

AT THE SUPERMARKET

Which aisle has ____	**¿En qué pasillo se encuentran ___** *ehn keh pah-SEE-yoh seh ehn-KWEHN-trahn?*
spices?	**las especias?** *lahs ehs-PEH-thyahs*
toiletries?	**los artículos de tocador?** *lohs ahr-TEE-koo-lohs deh toh-kah-DOHR*
paper plates and napkins?	**los platos de papel y las servilletas?** *lohs PLAH-tohs deh pah-PEHL ee lahs sehr-vee-YEH-tahs*
canned goods?	**los artículos en conserva?** *lohs ahr-TEE-koo-lohs ehn kohn-SEHR-vah*
snack food?	**los bocadillos?** *lohs boh-kah-DEE-yohs*
baby food?	**la comida para bebés?** *lah koh-MEE-dah PAH-rah beh-BEHS*
water?	**el agua?** *ehl AH-wah*
juice?	**el zumo?** *ehl thoo-moh*
bread?	**el pan?** *ehl pahn*
cheese?	**el queso?** *ehl KEH-soh*

fruit?	**la fruta?**
	lah FROO-tah
cookies?	**las galletas?**
	lahs gah-YEH-tahs

AT THE BUTCHER SHOP

Is the meat fresh?	**¿La carne es fresca?**
	lah KAHR-neh ehs FREHS-kah
Do you sell fresh _____	**¿Venden _____**
	VEHN-dehn
beef?	**carne de vacuno fresca?**
	KAHR-neh deh vah-KUH-noh
	FREHS-cah
pork?	**carne de cerdo fresca?**
	KAHR-neh deh THEHR-doh
	FREHS-kah
lamb?	**cordero fresco?**
	kohr-DEH-roh FREHS-koh
goat?	**carne de cabra fresca?**
	KAHR-neh deh KAH-brah
	FREHS-kah
I would like a cut of _____	**Quiero un corte de _____**
	KYEH-roh oon KOHR-teh deh
tenderloin.	**solomillo.**
	soh-loh-MEE-yoh
T-bone.	**chuletón.**
	choo-leh-TOHN
brisket.	**pecho.**
	PEH-cho
rump roast.	**rabadilla.**
	rah-bah-DEE-yah
chops.	**chuletas.**
	choo-LEH-tahs
filet.	**filete.**
	fee-LEH-teh

Thick / Thin cuts please.	**Cortes finos / gruesos por favor.**
	KOHR-tehs FEE-nohs / GRWEH-
	sohs pohr fah-VOHR
Please trim the fat.	**Por favor, córtele la grasa.**
	pohr fah-VOHR KOHR-teh-leh lah
	GRAH-sah
Do you have any sausage?	**¿Tiene salchichas?**
	TYEH-neh sahl-CHEE-chas
Is the _____ fresh?	**¿Es / Son fresco -a -os -as _____**
	ehs / sohn FREHS-koh -kah -kohs
	-kahs
fish	**el pescado?**
	ehl pehs-KAH-doh
seafood	**los mariscos?**
	lohs mah-REES-kohs
shrimp	**las gambas?**
	lahs GAHM-bahs
octopus	**el pulpo?**
	ehl POOL-poh
squid	**el calamar?**
	ehl kahl-ah-MAHR
sea bass	**el róbalo?**
	ehl ROH-bah-loh
flounder	**el lenguado?**
	ehl lehn-GWAH-doh
clams	**las almejas?**
	lahs ahl-MEH-hahs
oysters	**las ostras?**
	lahs OHS-trahs
shark	**el tiburón?**
	ehl tee-boo-ROHN

May I smell it?	**¿Puedo olerlo -a?** *PWEH-doh oh-LEHR-loh -lah*
Would you please ____	**¿Por favor, puede ____** *pohr fah-VOHR PWEH-deh*
filet it?	**cortarlo -a en filetes?** *kohr-TAHR-loh -lah ehn* *fee-LEH-tehs*
debone it?	**deshuesarlo -a?** *dehs-weh-SAHR-loh -lah*
remove the head and tail?	**quitarle la cabeza y el rabo?** *kee-TAHR-leh lah* *kah-BEH-thah ee ehl RAH-boh*

AT THE PRODUCE STAND / MARKET

Fruits

apple	**manzana** *mahn-THAH-nah*
apricot	**albaricoque** *ahl-bah-ree-KOH-keh*
banana	**plátano** *PLAH-tah-noh*
blackberry	**mora** *MOH-rah*
blueberry	**arándano azul** *ah-RAHN-dah-noh ah-SOOL*
cantaloupe	**melón** *meh-LOHN*
carambola, star fruit	**carambola** *kah-rahm-BOH-lah*
cherry	**cereza** *theh-REH-thah*
citron	**cidra** *THEE-drah*
coconut	**coco** *KOH-koh*

cranberry	**arándano rojo**
	ah-RAHN-dah-noh ROH-hoh
grapes (green, red)	**uvas (verdes, rojas)**
	OO-vahs (VEHR-dehs, RROH-hahs)
grapefruit	**pomelo**
	poh-MEH-loh
gooseberry	**grosella**
	groh-SEH-yah
guava	**guayaba**
	wah-YAH-bah
honeydew	**melón dulce**
	meh-LOHN DOOL-theh
kiwi	**kiwi**
	KEE-wee
lemon	**limón**
	lee-MOHN
lime	**lima**
	LEE-mah
mango	**mango**
	MAHNG-goh
melon	**melón**
	meh-LOHN
orange	**naranja**
	nah-RAHN-hah
palm fruit	**fruta de palma**
	FROO-tah deh PAHL-mah
papaya	**papaya**
	pah-PAH-yah
peach	**melocotón**
	meh-loh-koh-TOHN
pear	**pera**
	PEH-rah
pineapple	**piña**
	PEE-nyah

plum	**ciruela**
	theer-WEH-lah
strawberry	**fresa**
	FREH-sah
tamarind	**tamarindo**
	tah-mah-REEN-doh
tangerine	**mandarina**
	mahn-dah-REE-nah
watermelon	**sandía, melón de agua**
	sahn-DEE-ah, meh-LOHN deh
	AH-wah

Vegetables

artichoke	**alcachofa**
	ahl-kah-CHOH-fah
avocado	**aguacate**
	ah-wah-KAH-teh, PAHL-tah
bamboo shoots	**retoños de bambú**
	reh-TOH-nyohs deh bahm-BOO
beans	**judías**
	hoo-DEE-ahs
bean sprouts	**brotes de soja**
	BROH-tehs deh SOH-ha
broccoli	**brócoli**
	BROH-koh-lee
carrot	**zanahoria**
	thah-nah-OH-ryah
cauliflower	**coliflor**
	koh-lee-FLOHR
celery	**apio**
	AH-pyoh
corn	**maíz**
	mah-EES
cucumber	**pepino**
	peh-PEE-noh

eggplant	**berenjena**
	beh-rehn-HEH-nah
green beans	**judías verdes**
	hoo-DEE-ahs VEHR-dehs
lettuce	**lechuga**
	leh-CHOO-gah
mushrooms	**champiñones**
	cham-pee-NYON-ehs
ñame (white yam)	**ñame (batata blanca)**
	NYAH-meh (bah-TAH-tah
	BLAHN-kah)
olives	**aceitunas**
	ah-sehee-TOO-nahs
onion	**cebolla**
	theh-BOH-yah
peppers	**pimiento**
	pee-MYEHN-toh
bell	**cascabeles**
	kahs-kah-BEH-lehs
cayenne	**pimienta de Cayena**
	pee-MYEHN-tah deh
	kah-YEH-nah
hot	**picante**
	pee-KAHN-teh
mild	**suave**
	soo-AH-veh
plantain	**plátano verde, plantaina, llantén**
	PLAH-tah-noh VEHR-deh, plahn-
	TAHEE-nah, yahn-TEHN
regular	**regular**
	reh-goo-LAHR
ripe	**maduro**
	mah-DOO-roh
potato	**patata**
	pah-TAH-tah

sorrel	**acedera**
	ah-theh-DEH-rah
spinach	**espinaca**
	ehs-pee-NAH-kah
squash	**calabacín**
	kah-lah-bah-THEEN
sweet corn	**maíz dulce**
	mah-EES DOOL-theh
tomato	**tomate**
	toh-MAH-teh
yam	**batata**
	bah-TAH-tah

Fresh Herbs and Spices

allspice	**pimienta inglesa**
	pee-MYEHN-tah eeng-GLEH-sah
anise	**anís**
	AH-nees
basil	**albahaca**
	ahl-bah-AH-kah
bay leaf	**hoja de laurel seca**
	OH-hah deh low-REHL SEH-kah
black pepper	**pimienta negra**
	pee-MYEHN-tah NEH-grah
cacao	**cacao**
	kah-KAH-oh
dried	**seco**
	SEH-koh
fresh	**fresco**
	FREHS-koh
seed	**en semilla**
	ehn seh-MEE-yah
caraway	**alcaravea**
	ahl-kah-rah-VEH-ah
cilantro	**cilantro / culantro**
	see-LAHN-troh / kooh-LAHN-troh

clove	**clavo** *KLAH-voh*
coriander	**coriandro / cilantro** *koh-ree-AHN-droh / see-LAHN-troh*
cumin	**comino** *koh-MEE-noh*
dill	**eneldo** *eh-NEHL-doh*
garlic	**ajo** *AH-hoh*
marjoram	**mejorana** *meh-hoh-RAH-nah*
oregano	**orégano** *oh-REH-gah-noh*
paprika	**paprika** *pah-PREE-kah*
parsley	**perejil** *peh-reh-HEEL*
rosemary	**romero** *rroh-MEH-roh*
saffron	**azafrán** *ah-thah-FRAHN*
sage	**salvia** *SAHL-vyah*
salt	**sal** *sahl*
sugar	**azúcar** *ah-THOO-kahr*
thyme	**tomillo** *toh-MEE-yoh*

AT THE DELI

What kind of salad is that?	**¿Qué tipo de ensalada es ésa?**
	keh TEE-poh deh ehn-sah-LAH-dah ehs EH-sah
What type of cheese is that?	**¿Qué tipo de queso es ese?**
	keh TEE-poh deh KEH-soh ehs EH-seh
What type of bread is that?	**¿Qué tipo de pan es ese?**
	keh TEE-poh deh pahn ehs EH-seh
Some of that, please.	**Un poco de eso, por favor.**
	oon POH-koh deh EH-soh pohr fah-VOHR
Is the salad fresh?	**¿La ensalada está fresca?**
	lah ehn-sah-LAH-dah ehs-TAH FREHS-kah
I'd like _____	**Me gustaría _____**
	meh goo-stah-REE-ah
a sandwich.	**un sándwich.**
	oon SAHND-weech
a salad.	**una ensalada.**
	OO-nah ehn-sah-LAH-dah
tuna salad.	**ensalada de atún.**
	ehn-sah-LAH-dah deh ah-TOON
chicken salad.	**ensalada de pollo.**
	ehn-sah-LAH-dah deh POH-yoh
roast beef.	**rosbif.**
	rohs-BEEF
ham.	**jamón.**
	hah-MOHN
that cheese.	**ese queso.**
	EH-seh KEH-soh

cole slaw.	**ensalada de col.**
	ehn-sah-LAH-dah deh KOHL
a package of tofu.	**un paquete de tofu.**
	oon pah-KEH-teh deh TOH-foo
mustard.	**mostaza.**
	mohs-TAH-thah
mayonaisse.	**mayonesa.**
	mah-yoh-NEH-sah
a pickle.	**un pepinillo.**
	oon peh-pee-NEE-yoh
Is that smoked?	**¿Eso es ahumado?**
	EH-soh ehs ah-oo-MAH-doh
a pound (in kgs)	**medio kilo (500 grs.)**
	MEH-dyoh KEE-loh
a quarter-pound (in kgs)	**cien gramos (100 grs.)**
	thyehn GRAH-mohs
a half-pound (in kgs)	**un cuarto de kilo (250 grs.)**
	oon KWAHR-toh deh KEE-loh

VINTAGE WINE: REGIONS & TYPES

Rioja—in the northerly province of La Rioja, bordering the Basque Country—is Spain's most famous wine area, producing delicious *crianza* reds. Names to look out for are **Marqués de Riscal, Marqués de Murrieta, Beronia, Muga,** and **Viña Ardanza.**

Penedés is Cataluña's principal wine area, specializing in full-bodied reds and fruity whites, such as **Coronas** and **Viña Sol.** The country town of **Vilafranca del Penedés** specializes in quality **Cava**—the Catalan answer to Champagne. **Cordorniu** and **Freixenet** are the best.

Ribera del Duero, whose vineyards are near Valladolid beside the River Duero (or Douro, as it's known by the time it reaches Portugal), offers earthy, full-bodied reds that rival Rioja at their best. Most expensive (very) is **Vega Sicilia,** said to have been former dictator Franco's favorite tipple.

A more affordable name to look out for—at least with wines labelled *vino jóven* (or young wine), which means they're usually only a year old—is **Protos.**

Navarra, where the Basque country meets the Pyrenees, makes some very pleasant *rosados* (rosés) and robust reds such as **Gran Fuedo**—a more affordable alternative to the Riojas and Ribera del Dueros. Nearby **Somontano,** high in the Pyrenean province of Huesca, offers stylishly harsh reds designed to keep out the cold. **Carineña,** from the plains of Aragón near Zaragoza, is a no-nonsense red that improves in quality every year.

Albariño, in the southern part of Atlantic-facing Galicia, is one of Spain's most prestigious—and pricey—white wines. Delicate, aromatic, tangy, it goes down very well with fish dishes. Look for the demarcation **Rias Baixas.**

Valdepeñas, in the flat *meseta* of Castilla La Mancha between Madrid and Málaga, has vast vineyards that have produced bulk wine for centuries. It continues to produce workaday table wines as well as new quality vintages.

Jerez, near Cádiz in the sunny southwest corner of Andalucía, is the birthplace of sherry, which ranges from mellow *amontillados* and *olorosos* to dry *finos* and *secos.*

BEERS & SPECIALTY DRINKS: REGIONS & TYPES

In **Andalucía,** beers **San Miguel, Cruzcampo,** and **Alhambra** are brewed in the towns of Málaga, Sevilla, and Granada, respectively. **Coñac** is made in Jerez de la Frontera. **Manzanilla,** a very dry *fino,* comes from Sanlucar de Barrameda at the sandy mouth of the Guadalquivir River.

Coming from the province of Córdoba, **Montilla,** often unfairly regarded as a poor relation of *jerez seco,* is an underrated dry aperitif that goes quite well with olives. You'll find that **Málaga** is home to what's mellow, dark, and friendly—not just the locals, but also the deep-brown fortified wines, ideally drunk in winter. **Pedro Ximenez** is a draft-barrelled version.

In **Asturias,** *sidra* **(cider)** is the traditional drink, served fizzy or still. The latter version is *descansiado*—"poured" from arm's length height, from bottle to glass, to increase bubbles.

The **Balearic Islands** offer their own individual specialties. On **Ibiza,** the speciality is **Hierbas,** a yellow-green digestive made from local herbs, many of which are inserted into the bottle. **Mallorca** produces the medicinal-looking **Palo,** a delightful, jet-black liqueur made from figs. Some locals mix it with milk. Finally, **Minorca's Xoriguer Gin** is made from an original English recipe gathered during Britain's 18th-century rule. It's usually served with soda and a slice of lemon.

While visiting the **Basque Country,** you can whet your palette with **Pacharán,** a purple-hued, anis-flavored after-dinner drink made from sloe berries. It's best served with lots of ice. Then there is **Txacolí,** a low-alcohol, fizzy white wine in the San Sebastián area, where it's poured—like Asturian cider—from a great height into the glass; it's bubble-less in Guipuzcoa

(Bilbao). Acidy when drunk on its own, it goes perfectly with local fish dishes such as *bacalao pil pil* or *merluza vasca*.

Other regional delights include: **Cataluña's** three favorite sweet-strong liqueurs **Calisay, Cuarenta y Tres,** and **Aromas de Montserrat.** The after-dinner favorite of **Galicia** is *orujo,* an *aguardiente*—or raw spirit—similar to Italian grappa, which is made from grape stems and stalks. (Handle with care.) Home-brewed **Mahou beer** and fiery **anis** spirit (dry or sweet) from **Chinchón,** near Madrid, are the capital's top drinks. And finally, two interesting beers—**Aguila** and **Voll Damm**—are made in Valencia. A Sauternes-like heady sweet wine called **Casta Diva** comes from neighbouring Alicante.

CAFÉ

Coffee in Spain is much stronger than coffee back home—or anywhere in the world, except Italy. **Café Americano** is weaker, with hot water.

Café solo is black coffee served in a small cup or glass. **Café cortado** is the same with just a dash of milk. **Café con leche** is coffee with hot milk served in a cup or glass, whichever you prefer. In Madrid you may be asked if you want *leche caliente* (hot) or *templado* (lukewarm). In Málaga they have different names for strong and milky *cafés con leche: mitad* and *sombra,* respectively.

DINING TIMES & TIPPING

Meals start later in Spain than in most countries. It's the custom to consume lunch, the big meal of the day, from 2 to 4pm. After a recuperative siesta, Spaniards then enjoy tapas (tidbits of ham, cheese, fish, and so on) between 5 and 7pm. All this nibbling is followed by a light supper in a restaurant, usually from 9:30pm to as late as midnight. Many restaurants, however, start serving dinner at 8pm to accommodate visitors from other countries.

Meals include service and tax (7% or 12%, depending on the restaurant) but not drinks, which add to the tab considerably. In most cases service can seem perfunctory by U.S. standards. Waiters are matter-of-fact and don't usually return to the table to ask how things are. This can seem off-putting at first, but if you observe closely you'll see that Spanish waiters typically handle more tables than American waiters and they generally work quickly and more efficiently.

Follow the local custom and don't overtip. Theoretically, service is included in the price of the meal, but it's customary to leave an additional 10%.

DINING ESTABLISHMENTS

Restaurantes are standard places for three- or four-course lunches or dinners. If cost matters, order the *menú del día* (menu of the day) or *cubierto* (fixed price). Both fixed-price menus are based on what's fresh at the market that day, though often lacking the quality of more expensive a-la-carte dishes. Usually each will include a first course, such as fish soup or hors d'oeuvres, followed by a main dish, plus bread, dessert, and the wine of the house. You won't have a large choice. The *menú turístico* is a similar fixed-price menu, but for many it's too large, especially at lunch. Only those with big appetites will find it the best bargain.

Mesones (town inns) and *Tabernas* (taverns) are often centuries-old and therefore loaded with character, with original features such as alcoves and roof beams. Traditional Spanish cuisine is the standard fare here.

Tascas are similar but smaller, good for basic local food and wines. *Cellers* are a Catalan and Balearic specialty. The term means "wine cellar" in Catalan (*bodega* in Castilian Spanish), but in fact they're eating establishments of decent size, with plain but tasty local dishes on the menu.

CHAPTER FIVE

SOCIALIZING

Whether you're meeting people in a bar or a park, you'll find the language you need, in this chapter, to make new friends.

GREETINGS

Hello.	**Hola.**
	OH-lah
How are you?	**¿Cómo está?**
	KOH-moh ehs-TAH
Fine, thanks.	**Bien, gracias.**
	byehn GRAH-thyahs
And you?	**¿Y usted?**
	ee oos-TEHD
I'm exhausted from the trip.	**Estoy cansado -a del viaje.**
	ehs-TOY kahn-SAH-doh -dah dehl VYAH-heh
I have a headache.	**Tengo dolor de cabeza.**
	TEHNG-goh doh-LOHR deh kah-BEH-thah
I feel terrible.	**Me encuentro muy mal.**
	meh ehn-KWEHN-troh mwee mahl
I have a cold.	**Tengo un catarro.**
	TEHNG-goh oon kah-TAH-rroh
Good morning.	**Buenos días.**
	BWEH-nohs DEE-ahs
Good evening.	**Buenas noches.**
	BWEH-nahs NOH-chehs
Good afternoon.	**Buenas tardes.**
	BWEH-nahs TAHR-dehs
Good night.	**Buenas noches.**
	BWEH-nahs NOH-chehs

Listen Up: Common Greetings

Es un placer. *ehs oon plah-SEHR*	It's a pleasure.
Mucho gusto. *MOO-choh GOOS-toh*	Delighted.
A la orden. *ah lah OHR-dehn*	At your service. / As you wish.
Encantado -a. *ehn-kahn-TAH-do -dah*	Charmed.
Buenas. *BWEH-nahs*	Good day. (shortened)
Hola. *OH-lah*	Hello.
¿Qué tal? *keh TAHL*	How's it going?
¿Qué pasa? *keh PAH-sah*	What's going on?
¡Hasta luego! *VEHN-gah*	Bye! / See you later!
Adiós. *ah-DYOHS*	Goodbye.
Nos vemos. *nohs VEH-mohs*	See you later.

THE LANGUAGE BARRIER

I don't understand.	**No entiendo.** *noh ehn-TYEHN-doh*
Please speak more slowly.	**Por favor hable más despacio.** *pohr fah-VOHR AH-bleh mahs* *deh-SPAH-thyoh*
Please speak louder.	**Por favor hable más alto.** *pohr fah-VOHR AH-bleh mahs* *deh-SPAH-thyoh*

Do you speak English?	**¿Habla usted inglés?**
	AH-blah oos-TEHD eeng-GLEHS
I speak ____ better than Spanish.	**Yo hablo ____ mejor que español.**
	yoh AH-bloh ____ meh-HOHR keh ehs-pah-NYOHL
Please spell that.	**Por favor deletrée lo.**
	pohr fah-VOHR deh-leh-TREH-eh loh
Please repeat that.	**Por favor repita.**
	pohr fah-VOHR reh-PEE-tah
How do you say ____?	**¿Cómo se dice ____?**
	KOH-moh seh DEE-seh
Would you show me that in this dictionary?	**¿Me puede mostrar eso en el diccionario?**
	meh PWEH-deh mohs-TRAHR EH-soh ehn ehl deek-thyoh-NAH-ryoh

Curse Words

Here are some common curse words, used across Latin America and Spain.

mierda	shit
MYEHR-dah	
hijo de puta	son of a bitch (literally, son of a whore)
EE-hoh deh POO-tah	
carajo	damn
kah-RAH-hoh	
culo	ass
koo-LOH	
jodido	screwed up
hoh-DEE-doh	
cabrón	bastard
kah-BROHN	
follar	to fuck
foh-YAHR	

See p22, 23 for conjugation.

GETTING PERSONAL

People in Spain are generally friendly, but more formal than Americans. Remember to use the *usted* form of address, until given permission to employ the more familiar *tú*.

INTRODUCTIONS

What is your name?	**¿Cómo se / te llama (s)?** *KOH-moh seh / teh YAH-mah* *-mahs*
My name is ____.	**Me llamo ____.** *meh YAH-moh*
I'm very pleased to meet you.	**Es un placer conocerle / conocerte.** *ehs oon plah-SEHR koh-noh-* *THEHR-leh / koh-noh-THEHT-teh*
May I introduce my ____	**¿Puedo presentarle a mi ____ ?** *PWEH-doh preh-sehn-TAHR-leh* *ah mee*
How is / are your ____	**¿Cómo está su / están sus ____** *KOH-moh ehs-TAH soo / ehs-TAHN* *soos*
aunt / uncle?	**tía -o?** *TEE-ah -oh*
boss?	**jefe?** *HEH-feh*
boyfriend / girlfriend?	**novio -a?** *NOH-vyoh -vyah*
brother / sister?	**hermano -a?** *ehr-MAH-noh -nah*
child?	**hijo -a?** *EE-hoh -hah*
cousin?	**primo -a?** *PREE-moh -mah*
family?	**familia?** *fah-MEE-lyah*
father?	**padre?** *PAH-dreh*

fiancée / fiancé?	**prometido -a?**
	proh-meh-TEE-doh -dah
friend?	**amigo -a?**
	ah-MEE-goh -gah
grandparents?	**abuelos?**
	ah-BWEH-lohs
husband?	**marido?**
	mah-REE-doh
mother?	**madre?**
	MAH-dreh?
neighbor?	**vecino?**
	veh-THEE-noh
niece / nephew?	**sobrino -a?**
	soh-BREE-noh -nah
parents?	**padres?**
	PAH-drehs
partner?	**socio -a?**
	SOH-thyoh -thyah
wife?	**mujer?**
	moo-HEHR
Are you married?	**¿Está / Estás casado -a?**
	eh-STAH / eh-STAHS kah-SAH-doh -dah
Are you single?	**¿Es / Eres soltero -a?**
	ehs / EH-rehs sohl-TEH-roh -rah
I'm married.	**Estoy casado -a.**
	EH-stoy kah-SAH-doh -dah
I'm single.	**Estoy soltero -a.**
	EH-stoy sohl-TEH-roh -rah
I'm divorced.	**Estoy divorciado -a.**
	EH-stoy dee-vohr-THYAH-doh -dah
I'm a widow / widower.	**Soy viudo -a.**
	EH-stoy VYOO-doh -dah
We're separated.	**Estamos separados.**
	ehs-TAH-mohs seh-pah-RAH-dohs

Dos and Don'ts

Don't refer to your parents as *mis parientes*, which means relatives. Do call them *mis padres* (even though *el padre* alone means father).

I live with my boyfriend / girlfriend.	**Vivo con mi novio -a.** *VEE-voh kohn mee NOH-vyoh -vyah*
How old are you?	**¿Qué edad tiene / tienes?** *keh eh-DAHD TYEH-neh / TYEH-nehs*
How old are your children?	**¿Qué edad tienen sus hijos?** *keh eh-DAHD TYEH-nehn soos EE-hos*
Wow! That's very young.	**¡Caramba! Eso es muy joven.** *kah-RAHM-bah EH-soh ehs MOO-ee HOH-vehn*
No you're not! You're much younger.	**¡No lo es! Usted es / Tú eres mucho más joven.** *noh loh ehs oos-TEHD ehs / too EH-rehs MOO-choh mahs HOH-vehn*
Your wife / daughter is beautiful.	**Su / Tu esposa / hija es guapísima.** *soo / too ehs-POH-sah / EE-hah ehs wah-PEE-see-moh*
Your husband / son is handsome.	**Su / Tu esposo / hijo es guapo.** *soo / too ehs-POH-soh / EE-hoh ehs WAH-poh*
What a beautiful baby!	**¡Que bebé tan mono!** *keh beh-BEH tahn MOH-noh*
Are you here on business?	**¿Está aquí por negocios?** *ehs-TAH ah-KEE pohr neh-GOH-thyohs*

I am vacationing.	**Estoy de vacaciones.**
	ehs-TOY deh vah-kah-THYOH-nehs
I'm attending a conference.	**Estoy asistiendo a una conferencia.**
	ehs-TOY ah-sees-TYEHN-doh ah OO-nah kohn-feh-REHN-thyah
How long are you staying?	**¿Por cuánto tiempo se va a quedar?**
	pohr KWAHN-toh TYEHM-poh seh vah ah keh-DAHR
What are you studying?	**¿Qué estudia?**
	keh ehs-TOO-dyah
I'm a student.	**Soy estudiante.**
	soy ehs-too-DYAHN-teh
Where are you from?	**¿De dónde es / eres?**
	deh DOHN-deh ehs / EH-rehs

PERSONAL DESCRIPTIONS

African-American	**negro -a**
	NEH-groh -grah
Asian	**Asiático -a**
	ah-see-AH-tee-koh -kah
biracial	**birracial**
	bee-rrah-THYAHL
black	**negro -a**
	NEH-groh -grah
blond(e)	**rubio -a**
	ROO-byoh -byah
blue eyes	**los ojos azules**
	lohs OH-hohs ah-SOO-lehs
brown eyes	**los ojos marrones**
	lohs OH-hohs mah-RROH-nehs
brunette	**de cabello oscuro**
	deh kah-BEHL-yoh oh-SKOO-roh

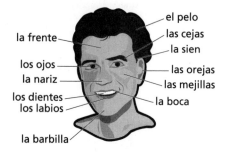

el pelo
la frente
las cejas
la sien
los ojos
las orejas
la nariz
las mejillas
los dientes
los labios
la boca
la barbilla

curly / kinky hair	**pelo rizado**
	PEH-loh REE-thah-doh
eyebrows	**las cejas**
	lahs THEH-hahs
eyelashes	**las pestañas**
	lahs pehs-TAH-nyahs
face	**la cara**
	lah KAH-rah
fat	**gordo -a**
	GOHR-doh -dah
freckles	**las pecas**
	lahs PEH-kahs
green eyes	**los ojos verdes**
	lohs OH-hohs VEHR-dehs
hazel eyes	**los ojos de color avellana**
	OH-hohs deh koh-LOHR ah-vehl-
	LYAH-nah
long hair	**pelo largo**
	PEH-loh LAHR-goh

mocha-skinned	**moreno -a** *moh-REH-noh -nah*
moles	**los lunares** *lohs looh-NAH-rehs*
pale	**pálido -a** *PAH-lee-doh*
redhead	**pelirrojo -a** *peh-lee-RRO-hoh -hah*
short	**bajo -a** *BAH-hoh -hah*
short hair	**pelo corto** *PEH-loh KOHR-toh*
straight hair	**pelo lacio** *PEH-loh LAH-thyoh*
tall	**alto -a** *AHL-toh -tah*
tanned	**bronceado -a** *brohn-theh-AH-doh -dah*
thin	**delgado -a** *dehl-GAH-doh -dah*
white	**blanco -a** *BLAHN-koh -kah*

DISPOSITIONS AND MOODS

angry	**enfadado -a** *ehn-fah-DAH-doh -dah*
anxious	**ansioso -a** *ahn-SYOH-soh -sah*
confused	**confundido -a** *kohn-foon-DEE-doh -dah*
depressed	**deprimido -a** *deh-pree-MEE-doh -dah*
enthusiastic	**entusiasmado -a** *ehn-too-syahs-MAH-doh -dah*

Listen Up: Nationalities

Soy alemán -a. *soy ah-leh-MAHN -nah*	I'm German.
Soy argentino -a. *soy ahr-hehn-TEE-noh -nah*	I'm Argentinean.
Soy boliviano -a. *soy boh-lee-VYAH-noh -nah*	I'm Bolivian.
Soy brasileño -a. *soy brah-see-LEH-nyoh -nyah*	I'm Brazilian.
Soy chino -a. *soy CHEE-noh -nah*	I'm Chinese.
Soy colombiano -a. *soy koh-lohm-BYAH-noh -nah*	I'm Colombian.
Soy costarricense. *soy kohs-tah-rree-THEHN-seh*	I'm Costa Rican.
Soy ecuatoriano -a. *soy eh-kwah-toh-RYAH-noh -nah*	I'm Ecuadorian.
Soy español -a. *soy ehs-pah-NYOHL -lah*	I'm Spanish.
Soy francés. *soy frahn-THEHS*	I'm French.
Soy guatemalteco -a. *soy wah-teh-mahl-TEH-koh -kah*	I'm Guatemalan.
Soy hindú. *soy een-DOO*	I'm Hindu.
Soy hondureño -a. *soy ohn-doo-REH-nyoh -nyah*	I'm Honduran
Soy italiano -a. *soy ee-tah-LYAH-noh -nah*	I'm Italian.
Soy japonés / japonesa. *soy hah-poh-NEHS -NEH-sah*	I'm Japanese.
Soy mexicano -a. *soy meh-hee-KAH-noh -nah*	I'm Mexican.
Soy nicaragüense. *soy nee-kah-rah-WEHN-seh*	I'm Nicaraguan.

Soy panameño -a. *soy pah-nah-MEH-nyoh -nyah*	I'm Panamanian.
Soy paraguayo -a. *soy pah-rah-WAH-yoh -yah*	I'm Paraguayan.
Soy peruano -a. *soy peh-roo-AH-noh -nah*	I'm Peruvian.
Soy puertorriqueño -a. *soy pwehr-toh-rree-KEH-nyoh -nyah*	I'm Puerto Rican.
Soy ruso -a. *soy ROO-soh -sah*	I'm Russian.
Soy salvadoreño -a. *soy sahl-vah-doh-REH-nyoh -nyah*	I'm Salvadorian.
Soy uruguayo -a. *soy oo-roo-WAH-yoh -yah*	I'm Uruguayan.
Soy venezolano -a. *soy veh-neh-thoh-LAH-noh -nah*	I'm Venezuelan.

For more nationalities, see p230 and English / Spanish dictionary.

happy	**feliz / alegre** *feh-LEETH / ah-LEH-greh*
sad	**triste** *TREES-teh*
stressed	**estresado -a** *ehs-treh-SAH-doh -dah*
tired	**cansado -a** *kahn-SAH-doh -dah*

PROFESSIONS

What do you do for a living?	**¿En qué trabaja usted? / ¿En qué trabajas?** *ehn keh trah-BAH-hah oo-STEHD / ehn keh trah-BAH-has*
Here is my business card.	**Aquí tiene mi tarjeta de presentación.** *ah-KEE TYEH-neh mee tahr-HEH-tah deh preh-sehn-tah-THYOHN*
I am ____	**Soy ____** *soy*
an accountant.	**contable.** *kohn-TAH-bleh*
an artist.	**artista.** *ahr-TEES-tah*
a craftsperson.	**artesano -a.** *ahr-teh-SAH-noh -nah*
a designer.	**diseñador -a.** *dee-seh-nyah-DOHR -DOH-rah*
a doctor.	**doctor.** *dohk-TOHR*
an editor.	**editor -a.** *eh-dee-TOHR -TOH-rah*
an educator.	**docente / pedagogo** *doh-THEHN-teh / peh-dah-GOH-goh*
an engineer.	**ingeniero -a.** *een-heh-NYEH-roh -rah*
a government employee.	**funcionario.** *foon-thyoh-NAH-ryoh*
a homemaker.	**ama de casa.** *AH-mah deh KAH-sah*
a lawyer.	**abogado -a.** *ah-boh-GAH-doh -dah*

a military professional.	**militar.**
	mee-lee-TAHR
a musician.	**músico -a.**
	MOO-see-koh -kah
a nurse.	**enfermero -a**
	ehn-fehr-MEH-roh -rah
a salesperson.	**vendedor -a.**
	vehn-deh-DOHR -DOH-rah
a writer.	**escritor -a.**
	ehs-kree-TOHR -TOH-rah

DOING BUSINESS

I'd like an appointment.	**Quiero pedir una cita.**
	KYEH-roh peh-DEER OO-nah SEE-tah
I'm here to see _____.	**Estoy aquí para ver a _____.**
	ehs-TOY ah-KEE pa-rah vehr ah
May I photocopy this?	**¿Puedo fotocopiar esto?**
	PWEH-doh foh-toh-koh-PYAHR EHS-toh
May I use a computer here?	**¿Puedo utilizar el ordenador?**
	PWEH-doh oo-tee-lee-THAHR ehl ohr-dehn-ah-DOHR
What's the password?	**¿Cuál es la contraseña?**
	kwahl ehs lah kohn-trah-SEH-nyah
May I access the Internet?	**¿Puedo acceder a Internet?**
	PWEH-doh ahk-theh-DEHR ah een-tehr-NEHT
May I send a fax?	**¿Puedo enviar un fax?**
	PWEH-doh ehn-vee-AHR oon fahks
May I use the phone?	**¿Puedo usar el teléfono?**
	PWEH-doh oo-SAHR ehl teh-LEH-foh-noh

PARTING WAYS

Keep in touch.

No pierdas el contacto.
noh PYEHR-dahs ehl kohn-TAHK-toh

Please write or email.

Por favor escríbame o envíeme un e-mail.
pohr fah-VOHR ehs-KREE-bah-meh oh ehn-VEE-eh-meh oon EE-mehl

Here's my phone number. Call me.

Aquí tiene mi número de teléfono. Llámeme.
ah-KEE TYEH-neh mee NOO-meh-roh deh teh-LEH-foh-noh. YAH-meh-meh

May I have your phone number / e-mail please?

¿Me puede dar su número de teléfono / dirección de e-mail, por favor?
meh PWEH-deh dahr soo NOO-meh-roh deh teh-LEH-foh-noh / dee-rehk-THYOHN deh EE-mehl pohr fah-VOHR

May I have your card?

¿Me puede dar su tarjeta?
meh PWEH-deh dahr soo tahr-HEH-tah

Give me your address and I'll write you.

Déme su dirección y le escribiré.
DEH-meh soo dee-rehk-THYOHN ee leh ehs-kree-bee-REH

TOPICS OF CONVERSATION

As in the United States, the weather and current affairs are common conversation topics.

THE WEATHER

It's so ____	**Hace tanto ____** *AH-theh TAHN-toh*
Is it always so ____ ?	**¿Hace siempre tanto -a ____ ?** *AH-theh SYEHM-preh TAHN-toh -tah*
sunny.	**sol.** *sohl*
rainy.	**lluvia.** *YOOV-yah*
humid.	**humedad.** *oo-mee-DAHD*
warm.	**calor.** *kah-LOHR*
cool.	**frío.** *FREE-oh*
windy.	**viento.** *VYEHN-toh*
Do you know the weather forecast for tomorrow?	**¿Usted sabe el pronóstico del tiempo para mañana?** *oo-STEHD SAH-beh ehl proh-NOHS-tee-koh dehl TYEHM-poh PAH-rah mah-NYAH-nah*

THE ISSUES

What do you think about ____	**¿Qué opina usted de ____** *keh oh-PEE-nah oos-TEHD deh*
democracy?	**la democracia?** *lah deh-moh-KRAH-thyah*
socialism?	**el socialismo?** *ehl soh-thyah-LEES-moh*
Democrats?	**los demócratas?** *lohs deh-MOH-krah-tahs*

Republicans?	**los republicanos?**
	lohs reh-poo-blee-KAH-nohs
the environment?	**el medio ambiente?**
	ehl MEH-dyoh ahm-BYEHN-teh
women's rights?	**los derechos de la mujer?**
	lohs deh-REH-chohs deh lah
	moo-HEHR
gay rights?	**los derechos de los homo-sexuales?**
	lohs deh-reh-chos deh lohs oh-moh-sehk-SWAH-lehs
the economy?	**la economía?**
	lah eh-koh-noh-MEE-ah
What political party do you belong to?	**¿A qué partido político pertenece usted?**
	ah keh pahr-TEE-doh poh-LEE-tee-koh pehr-teh-NEH-theh oos-TEHD
What did you think of the American election?	**¿Qué opina de las elecciones americanas?**
	keh oh-PEE-nah deh lahs eh-lehk-THYOH-nehs ah-meh-ree-KAH-nahs
What do you think of the war in ____?	**¿Qué opina de la guerra en ____?**
	keh oh-PEE-nah deh lah GEH-rrah ehn

RELIGION

Do you go to church / temple / mosque?	**¿Va usted a la iglesia / al templo / a la mezquita?**
	vah oos-TEHD ah lah ee-GLEH-syah / ahl TEHM-ploh / ah lah mehth-KEE-tah
Are you religious?	**¿Es usted religioso?**
	ehs ooh-STEHD reh-lee-HYOH-soh

I'm ____ / I was raised ____	**Soy ____ / Fui criado ____** *soy / FOO-ee kree-AH-doh*
agnostic.	**agnóstico.** *ahg-NOHS-tee-koh*
atheist.	**ateo -a.** *ah-TEH-oh -ah*
Buddhist.	**budista.** *boo-DEES-tah*
Catholic.	**católico.** *kah-TOH-lee-koh*
Greek Orthodox.	**ortodoxo griego.** *orh-toh-DOHK-soh GRYEH-goh*
Hindu.	**hindú.** *een-DOO*
Jewish.	**judío.** *hoo-DEE-oh*
Muslim.	**musulmán.** *moo-sool-MAHN*
Protestant.	**protestante.** *proh-tehs-TAHN-teh*
I'm spiritual but I don't attend services.	**Soy espiritual pero no asisto a oficios religiosos.** *soy ehs-pee-ree-TWAHL peh-roh noh ah-SEES-toh ah oh-FEE-thyohs rreh-lee-HYOH-sohs*
I don't believe in that.	**Yo no creo en eso.** *yoh noh KREH-oh ehn EH-soh*
That's against my beliefs.	**Eso va en contra de mis creencias.** *EH-soh vah ehn KOHN-trah deh mees kreh-EHN-thyahs*
I'd rather not talk about it.	**Preferiría no hablar de ello.** *preh-feh-ree-REE-ah noh ah-BLAHR deh EH-yoh*

GETTING TO KNOW SOMEONE

Following are some conversation starters.

MUSICAL TASTES

What kind of music do you like?	**¿Qué tipo de música le gusta?** *keh TEE-poh deh MOO-see-kah leh GOOS-tah*
I like _____	**Me gusta _____** *meh GOOS-tah*
classical.	**la música clásica.** *lah MOO-see-kah KLAH-see-kah*
country and western.	**la música country.** *lah MOO-see-kah KOHN-tree*
disco.	**la música disco.** *lah MOO-see-kah DEES-koh*
hip hop.	**el hip hop.** *ehl eep ohp*
jazz.	**el jazz.** *ehl jahs*
New Age.	**ehl New Age.** *ehl (as in English)*
opera.	**la ópera.** *lah OH-peh-rah*
pop.	**la música pop.** *lah MOO-see-kah pohp*
reggae.	**el reggae.** *ehl REH-geh*
rock 'n' roll.	**el rock and roll.** *ehl rroh-kahnd-ROHL*
show-tunes / musicals.	**los musicales.** *lohs moo-see-KAH-lehs*
techno.	**el techno.** *ehl TEHK-noh*

HOBBIES

What do you like to do in your spare time?	**¿Qué le gusta hacer en su tiempo libre?**
	keh leh GOO-stah ah-THEHR ehn soo TYEHM-poh LEE-breh
I like ____	**Me gusta ____**
	meh GOOS-tah
camping.	**ir de acampada.**
	eer deh ah-kahm-PAH-dah
cooking.	**cocinar.**
	koh-thee-NAHR
dancing.	**bailar.**
	bah-ee-LAHR
drawing.	**dibujar.**
	dee-boo-HAHR
eating out.	**comer fuera.**
	koh-MEHR FWEH-rah
going to the movies.	**ir al cine.**
	eer ahl THEE-neh
hanging out.	**pasar el rato.**
	pah-SAHR ehl RAH-toh
hiking.	**salir de excursión.**
	sah-LEER deh ehks-koor-SYOHN
painting.	**pintar.**
	peen-TAHR
piano.	**el piano.**
	ehl PYAH-noh
playing guitar.	**tocar la guitarra.**
	toh-KAHR lah gee-TAH-rrah

For other instruments, see the English / Spanish dictionary.

reading.	**leer.**
	leh-EHR
sewing.	**coser.**
	koh-SEHR
shopping.	**ir de compras.**
	eer deh kohm-PRAHS

sports.	**los deportes.**
	lohs deh-POHR-tehs
traveling.	**viajar.**
	vyah-HAR
watching TV.	**ver televisión.**
	vehr teh-leh-vee-SYOHN
Do you like to dance?	**¿Le gusta bailar?**
	leh GOOS-tah bah-ee-LAHR
Would you like to go out?	**¿Le gustaría salir?**
	leh goos-tah-REE-ah sah-LEER
May I buy you dinner sometime?	**¿Le puedo invitar a cenar algún día?**
	leh PWEH-doh een-vee-TAHR ah THEH-nahr ahl-GOON DEE-oh
What kind of food do you like?	**¿Qué tipo de comida le gusta?**
	keh TEE-poh deh koh-MEE-dah leh GOOS-tah

For a full list of food types, see Dining in Chapter 4.

Would you like to go _____	**¿Le gustaría ir _____**
	leh goos-tah-REE-ah eer
to a movie?	**al cine?**
	ahl THEE-neh
to a concert?	**a un concierto?**
	ah oon kohn-THYEHR-toh
to the zoo?	**al zoo?**
	ahl thoh
to the beach?	**a la playa?**
	ah lah PLAH-yah
to a museum?	**a un museo?**
	ah oon moo-SEH-oh
for a walk in the park?	**a dar un paseo por el parque?**
	ah dahr oon pah-SEH-oh pohr ehl PAHR-keh
dancing?	**a bailar?**
	ah bah-ee-LAHR

Would you like to get ____	**¿Le gustaría ir ____**
	leh goos-tah-REE-ah eer
lunch?	**a almorzar?**
	ah ahl-mohr-THAHR
coffee?	**a tomar un café?**
	ah toh-MAHR oon kah-FEH
dinner?	**a cenar?**
	ah theh-NAHR
What kind of books do you like to read?	**¿Qué tipo de libros le gusta leer?**
	keh TEE-poh deh LEE-brohs leh GOOS-tah leh-EHR
I like ____	**Me gusta / gustan ____**
	meh GOOS-tah / GOOS-tahn
auto-biographies.	**las autobiografías.**
	lahs ow-toh-bee-oh-grah-FEE-ahs
biographies.	**las biografías.**
	lahs bee-oh-grah-FEE-ahs
history.	**los libros de historia.**
	lohs LEE-brohs deh ee-STOH-ryah
mysteries.	**los libros de misterio.**
	lohs LEE-brohs deh mee-STEH-ryoh
novels.	**las novelas.**
	lahs noh-VEH-lahs
plays.	**las obras dramáticas.**
	lahs OH-brahs drah-MAH-tee-kahs
romance.	**los romances.**
	lohs roh-MAHN-thehs
Westerns.	**los libros sobre el oeste americano.**
	lohs LEE-brohs SOH-breh ehl WEH-steh ah-meh-ree-KAH-noh

For dating terms, see Nightlife in Chaper 10.

POPULAR TOPICS OF CONVERSATION

Sports is a sure-fire winner. Spain's two top-selling newspapers, **As** and **Marca,** both exclusively cover soccer, boasting circulations way ahead of the regular dailies **El País** and **El Mundo;** there are copies of them on practically every cafe table.

Bullfights are okay to discuss, provided you discuss them as a fan and not a critic. Have a look at Hemingway's *Death in the Afternoon:* Though written in the 1930s, it remains the most authoritative account in English today. If, on the other hand, you regard bullfighting as a cruel blood sport, you might venture expressing your views in Cataluña and the Basque country, where the *corrida* is far from revered.

More risky topics are **religion, war, Gibraltar** (the controversial British enclave at the foot of Andalucía), and the politics of the late dictator **General Franco.** These subjects were taboo, but today it's sometimes permissible to broach them, provided that you're sufficiently familiar with Spanish viewpoints and prejudices.

SPANIARDS BY REGION

Spaniards are proud, confident, volatile, demonstrative, passionate, and unpredictable. So go the clichés. They can also be diffident, reflective, considerate, slow-speaking and so relaxed and laid-back, they're almost horizontal. All this of course varies from person to person, town to town, and province to province. And though nothing is black and white, we can make certain generalizations.

Madrileños can tend to be *macho, chulo* (pushy), and prone to talking quickly, crisply, and loudly. They can either be distant or, when they get to know you, very generous. Many locals in **Andalucía** think work is over-rated, relish a laugh or a party *(juerga)*, and talk with a lazily truncated accent. In **Castile** and the **Northern Provinces** bordering the Atlantic, from the **Basque Country** to **Galicia,** residents tend to be thoughtful, taciturn, and hard-working. Most visitors find the Spanish spoken here much clearer and easier to understand. In **Cataluña** people are noted for being close, dour, stubborn, regionalistic (particularly when it comes to speaking their own guttural-sounding language), and business obsessed.

"In Madrid they give you things. In Barcelona everything is based on trade and profit," is one resident American writer's observation. (He cited, as an example, the free tapas that accompany a drink in many Madrid bars—a rarity in Barcelona.) However, anyone who has gotten to know a Catalan knows he too can be extremely generous.

Spaniards attach the utmost importance to the **family unit.** Older people are still held in respect (though perhaps not quite as much as they were), while children continue to be worshipped and spoiled outrageously. Even the poorest family will make sure their children are dressed as elegantly as possible, especially at fiesta times.

Personal relationships sometimes have a priority over **business relationships,** and people are not unduly concerned with keeping strict time where schedules are concerned. Deadlines are an objective to be met if possible, but it's not the end of the world if they aren't. Great importance is attached to appearance. Smart stylish clothes are appreciated, and suits are worn in most business offices—though jeans and casual gear are making inroads in some.

It's a touchy-feely society. And it's becoming more **equal.** Men sometimes hug each other as well as women. Though the macho ethic still holds strong, it's not unknown now for men to occasionally do the cooking and help with the housework, especially among middle-class workers in bigger cities. **Women** occupy an increasingly important place in society and business since Franco's death. They have been given more impetus since the election of Zapatero's socialist party and his appointment of several women to key cabinet posts. You'll also see them in increasingly important positions in all types of daily work.

The general attitude of Spanish people to visiting **Americans** is—at least outwardly—as warm and welcoming as it is to other nationalities. This applies to general day-to-day social contact. Should you, however, find yourself at a dinner table or in a bar with Spaniards ready to discuss international matters, you may get a somewhat different reaction. While courtesy prevents many informed and opinionated Spaniards from expressing critical views with their trans-Atlantic hosts, after a glass or two of wine, some might strongly express their disapproval of the Iraqi "War" (90% of Spaniards opposed this venture and demonstrated accordingly). Spain's most popular newspaper *El País* regularly criticizes the Bush administration, and many of its readers support these views. So be prepared.

The average family-obsessed Spaniard, more interested in acquiring the latest accouterments and comforts than in politics, alternatively tends to regard the U.S. with a blend of envy and awe. This attitude is reflected in the Americanized style of certain TV programs, the number of U.S.-style food and cafe chains (Burger King, McDonald's, Starbucks), and the appearance of multi-purpose shopping malls in the new satellite towns that are burgeoning around the big cities. Since the '50s many aspects of urban architecture have been inspired by American models, a trend begun by Franco in the 1950s perhaps partly in homage to the much-needed U.S. aid his country began to receive then. Stretches of Madrid's Gran Vía and new AZCA business zones have a vaguely Manhattan-ish look, and the country's Mediterranean coast is studded with Florida-style condominiums.

Provinces such as Cataluña and the Basque country still tend to look on Europe as their spiritual home, with little envy directed across the Atlantic. It's in these regions that any criticism of the U.S., as mentioned earlier, is likely to be strongest.

In today's Spain there's an increasing interest in learning **foreign languages,** headed by **English,** which has long replaced French as a priority. Since 2000, much more English is being taught in schools and language academies.

FUN FACTS

In general, Spaniards identify themselves as being from a particular **region** (Galicia, Aragón, and so on) rather than from the country as a whole. It's therefore useful, when you're talking with locals, to know a little something about the part of the country they hail from.

People stay up late all over Spain, and even on weekdays it's not unusual to go to bed around 1am. Many bars and restaurants stay open into the early hours. **Entertaining** is frequently done in restaurants rather than at home.

The average day starts early, with **breakfast,** eaten out, as early as 5:30 or 6am. You'll get a chance here to see locals drinking huge *coñacs* or *copas de anís* to kick-start the day— "breakfasts" that could lay the inexperienced on his or her ear. Accompanying them are rich, cholesterol-high *churros* or *porras*. And of course practically everyone smokes! So if you like healthy, wholesome food, smoke-free air, and weak coffee, stick to the hotel buffet. If you want to see and taste the real Spain, eat breakfast out. (A rule of thumb: The more basic the bar, the friendlier the clientele.)

CHAPTER SIX

MONEY & COMMUNICATIONS

This chapter covers money, the mail, phone, Internet service, and other tools you need to connect with the outside world.

MONEY

Do you accept ____

¿Aceptan ____
ah-THEHP-tahn

Visa / MasterCard / Discover / American Express / Diners' Club? credit cards?

Visa / MasterCard / Discover / American Express / Diners' Club?
Pronounced as in english
tarjetas de crédito?
tahr-HEH-tahs deh KREH-dee-toh

bills?

billetes?
bee-YEH-tehs

coins?

monedas?
moh-NEH-dahs

checks?

cheques?
CHEH-kehs

travelers checks?

cheques de viaje?
CHEH-kehs deh VYAH-heh

money transfer?

giro de dinero?
HEE-roh deh dee NEH-roh

May I wire transfer funds here?

¿Me pueden girar dinero aquí?
meh PWEH-den hee-RAHR dee-NEH-roh ah-KEE

Would you please tell me where to find ____

Por favor, ¿puede decirme dónde puedo encontrar ____
pohr fah-VOHR PWEH-deh deh-THEER-meh DOHN-deh PWEH-doh ehn-kohn-TRAHR

a bank?

un banco?
oon BAHN-koh

a credit bureau?	**una agencia de crédito?** *OO-nah ah-HEHN-thyah deh KREH-dee-toh*
an ATM?	**un cajero automático?** *oon kah-HEH-roh ow-toh-MAH-tee-koh*
a currency exchange?	**una oficina de cambio de moneda?** *OO-nah ah-fee-THEE-nah deh KAHM-byoh deh moh-NEH-dah*
A receipt, please.	**Un recibo, por favor.** *oon reh-THEE-boh pohr fah-VOHR*
Would you tell me ____	**Me puede decir ____** *meh PWEH-deh deh-THEER*
today's interest rate?	**la tasa de interés de hoy?** *lah TAH-sah deh een-teh-REHS deh oy*
the exchange rate for dollars to ____?	**la tasa de cambio de dólares a ____?** *lah TAH-sah deh KAHM-byoh deh DOH-lah-rehs ah*
Is there a service charge?	**¿Cobran recargo?** *KOH-brahn reh-KAHR-goh*
May I have a cash advance on my credit card?	**¿Puedo sacar dinero en efectivo de mi tarjeta de crédito?** *PWEH-doh sah-KAHR dee-NEH-roh ehn eh-fehk-TEE-voh deh mee tahr-HEH-tah deh KREH-dee-toh*
Will you accept a credit card?	**¿Aceptarían una tarjeta de crédito?** *ah-thehp-tah-REE-ahn OO-nah tahr-HEH-tah deh KREH-dee-toh*

Listen Up: Bank Lingo

Por favor, firme aquí. *pohr fah-VOHR FEER-meh ah-KEE*	Please sign here.
Aquí está su recibo. *ah-KEE ehs-TAH soo reh-THEE-boh*	Here is your receipt.
Por favor, ¿puedo ver su pasaporte? *pohr fah-VOHR PWEH-doh vehr soo pah-sah-POHR-teh*	May I see your ID, please?
Aceptamos cheques de viaje. *ah-sehp-TAH-mohs CHEH-kehs deh VYAH-heh*	We accept travelers checks.
Solo en efectivo. *SOH-loh ehn eh-fehk-TEE-voh*	Cash only.

May I have smaller bills, please.	**Me puede dar billetes más pequeños, por favor.** *meh PWEH-deh dahr bee-YEH-tehs mahs peh-KEH-nyohs pohr fah-VOHR*
Can you make change?	**¿Puede darme cambio?** *PWEH-deh DAHR-meh KAHM-byoh*
I only have bills.	**Sólo tengo billetes.** *SOH-loh TEHNG-goh bee-YEH-tehs*
Some coins, please.	**Déme también algunas monedas, por favor.** *DEH-meh tahm-BYEHN ahl-GOO-nahs moh-NEH-dahs pohr fah-VOHR*

ATM Machine

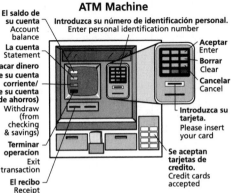

El saldo de su cuenta
Account balance

Introduzca su número de identificación personal.
Enter personal identification number

La cuenta
Statement

Aceptar
Enter

Borrar
Clear

Cancelar
Cancel

Sacar dinero (De su cuenta corriente/ De su cuenta de ahorros)
Withdraw (from checking & savings)

Introduzca su tarjeta.
Please insert your card

Terminar operacion
Exit transaction

El recibo
Receipt

Se aceptan tarjetas de crédito.
Credit cards accepted

COMMUNICATIONS

PHONE SERVICE

Where can I buy or rent a cell phone?

¿Dónde puedo comprar o alquilar un teléfono móvil?
DOHN-deh PWEH-doh kohm-PRAHR oh ahl-kee-LAHR oon teh-LEH-foh-noh MOH-veel

What rate plans do you have?

¿Qué planes de tarifas tienen?
keh PLAH-nehs deh tah-REE-fahs TYEH-nehn

Is this good throughout the country?

¿El móvil funciona en todo el país?
ehl MOH-veel foon-THYON-nah ehn TOH-doh ehl pah-EES

May I have a prepaid phone?

¿Me puede dar un teléfono pre-pagado?
meh PWEH-deh dahr oon teh-LEH-foh-noh preh-pah-GAH-doh

Where can I buy a phone card?	**¿Dónde puedo comprar una tarjeta de teléfono?** *DOHN-deh PWEH-doh kohm-PRAHR OO-nah tahr-HEH-tah deh teh-LEH-fon-noh*
May I add more minutes to my phone card?	**¿Puedo añadirle más minutos a la tarjeta de teléfono?** *PWEH-doh ah-nyah-DEER-leh mahs mee-NOO-tohs ah lah tahr-HEH-tah deh teh-LEH-fon-noh*

MAKING A CALL

May I dial direct?	**¿Puedo marcar directamente?** *PWEH-doh MAHR-kahr dee-rehk-tah-MEHN-teh*
Operator please.	**Operadora, por favor.** *oh-peh-rah-DOH-rah pohr fah-VOHR*
I'd like to make an international call.	**Quiero hacer una llamada internacional.** *KYEH-roh ah-THEHR OO-nah yah-MAH-dah een-tehr-nah-thyoh-NAHL*

Fuera de Servicio

Before you stick your coins or bills in a vending machine, watch out for the little sign that says *Fuera de Servicio* (Out of Service).

Listen Up: Telephone Lingo

¿Diga? / ¿Dígame? /
¿Sí?
*DEE-gah / DEE-gah-
meh / see*

Hello?

¿A qué número?
ah keh NOO-meh-roh

What number?

Lo siento, la línea está
ocupada.
*loh SYEHN-toh lah LEE-
neh-ah ehs-TAH oh-koo-
PAH-dah*

I'm sorry, the line is busy.

Por favor, cuelgue y
marque el número
de nuevo.
*pohr fah-VOHR KWEHL-
geh ee MAHR-keh ehl NOO-
meh-roh deh NWEH-voh*

Please, hang up and redial.

Lo siento. No contestan.
*loh SYEHN-toh noh
kohn-TEH-stahn*

I'm sorry, nobody is answering.

Su tarjeta tiene diez
minutos.
*soo tahr-HEH-tah TYEH-
neh dyeth mee-NOO-tohs*

Your card has ten minutes left.

COMMUNICATIONS

I'd like to make a collect call.	**Quiero hacer una llamada a cobro revertido.** *KYEH-roh ah-THEHR OO-nah yah-MAH-dah ah KOH-broh reh-vehr-TEE-doh*
I'd like to use a calling card.	**Quiero utilizar una tarjeta de teléfono.** *KYEH-roh oo-tee-lee-THAR OO-nah tahr-HEH-tah deh teh-LEH-foh-noh*
Bill my credit card.	**Cárguelo a mi tarjeta de crédito.** *kar-GWEH-loh ah mee tahr-HEH-tah deh KREH-dee-toh*
May I bill the charges to my room?	**¿Puedo cargarlos a mi habitación?** *PWEH-doh kahr-GAHR-lohs ah mee ah-bee-tah-THYOHN*
Information, please.	**Información, por favor.** *een-fohr-mah-THYOHN pohr fah-VOHR*
I'd like the number for ____.	**Necesito el número para ____.** *neh-the-THEE-toh ehl NOO-meh-roh PAH-rah*
I just got disconnected.	**Se me ha cortado la llamada.** *seh meh ah kohr-TAH-doh lah lay-MAH-dah*
The line is busy.	**La línea está ocupada.** *lah LEE-neh-ah ehs-TAH oh-koo-PAH-dah*

INTERNET ACCESS

Where is an Internet café?	**¿Dónde hay un café con acceso a Internet?**
	DOHN-deh aye oon kah-FEH kohn ahk-THEH-soh ah een-tehr-NET
Is there a wireless hub nearby?	**¿Hay un nodo de conexión inalámbrica cerca de aquí?**
	aye oon NOH-doh deh koh-nehk-SYOHN ee-nah-LAHM-bree-kah THEHR-kah deh ah-KEE
How much do you charge per minute / hour?	**¿Cuánto cobra por minuto / hora?**
	KWAHN-toh KOH-brah pohr mee-NOO-toh / OH-rah
Can I print here?	**¿Puedo imprimir aquí?**
	PWEH-doh eem-pree-MEER ah-KEE
Can I burn a CD?	**¿Puedo grabar un CD?**
	PWEH-doh grah-BAHR oon seh-DEH
Would you please help me change the language preference to English?	**¿Me puede ayudar a cambiar la opción de idioma al inglés?**
	meh PWEH-deh ah-yoo-DAHR ah kahm-BYAHR lah ohp-THYOHN deh ee-DYOH-mah ahl eeng-GLEHS

May I scan something?	**¿Puedo escanear algo?** *PWEH-doh ehs-kah-neh-AHR AHL-goh*
Can I upload photos?	**¿Puedo cargar mis fotos?** *PWEH-doh kahr-GAHR mees FOH-tohs*
Do you have a USB port so I can download music?	**¿Tiene un puerto USB para poder descargar música?** *TYEH-neh oon PWEHR-toh oo-EH-seh-BEH PAH-rah poh-DEHR dehs-kahr-GAHR MOO-see-kah*
Do you have a machine compatible with iTunes?	**¿Tiene una máquina compatible con iTunes?** *TYEH-nehn OO-nah MAH-kee-nah kohm-pah-TEE-bleh kohn ay-TOONS*
Do you have a Mac?	**¿Tienen un ordenador Macintosh?** *TYEH-nehn oon ohr-deh-nah-DOHR mah-keen-TOHSH*
Do you have a PC?	**¿Tienen ordenadores?** *TYEH-nehn ohr-deh-nah-DOH-rehs*
Do you have a newer version of this software?	**¿Tiene la última versión de este software?** *TYEH-neh lah OOL-tee-mah vehr-SYOHN deh EHS-teh SOHFT-wehr*
Do you have broadband?	**¿Tiene conexión de Internet de alta velocidad?** *TYEH-neh koh-nehk-SYOHN deh een-tehr-NEHT deh AHL-tah veh-loh-thee-DAHD*
How fast is your connection speed here?	**¿Qué velocidad de conexión tienen aquí?** *keh veh-loh-thee-DAHD deh koh-nehk-SYOHN TYEH-nehn ah-KEE*

GETTING MAIL

Where is the post office?	**¿Dónde está la oficina de correos?** *DOHN-deh ehs-TAH lah ah-fee-THEE-nah deh koh-RREH-ohs*
May I send an international package?	**¿Puedo enviar un paquete internacional?** *PWEH-doh ehn-vee-AHR oon pah-KEH-teh een-tehr-nah-thyoh-NAHL*
Do I need a customs form?	**¿Necesito un formulario de aduanas?** *neh-theh-SEE-toh oon fohr-moo-LAHR-yoh deh ah-DWAH-nahs*
May I insure the package?	**¿Puedo asegurar el paquete?** *PWEH-doh ah-seh-goo-RAHR ehl pah-KEH-teh*
Please, mark it fragile.	**Por favor, márquelo frágil.** *pohr fah-VOHR MAHR-keh-loh FRAH-heel*
Please, handle with care.	**Por favor, trátelo con cuidado.** *pohr fah-VOHR TRAH-teh-loh kohn koo-ee-DAH-doh*
Do you have twine?	**¿Tiene cuerda?** *TYEH-neh KWEHR-dah*
Where is a DHL office?	**¿Dónde hay una oficina de DHL?** *DOHN-deh aye OO-nah oh-fee-THEE-nah deh deh AH-cheh EH-leh*
Do you sell stamps?	**¿Vende sellos?** *VEHN-deh SEH-yohs*
Do you sell postcards?	**¿Vende postales?** *VEHN-deh pohs-TAH-lehs*
May I send that as a first class letter?	**¿Puedo enviarla por correo ordinario?** *PWEH-doh ehn-vee-AHR-lah pohr koh-RREH-oh ohr-dee-NAH-ryoh*

COMMUNICATIONS

Listen Up: Postal Lingo

¡Próximo! *PROHK-see-moh*	Next!
Por favor, póngalo aquí. *pohr fah-VOHR POHNG-gah-loh ah-KEE*	Please, set it here.
¿Qué modalidad? *keh moh-dah-lee-DAHD*	Which class?
¿Qué tipo de servicio quiere? *keh TEE-poh deh sehr-VEE-thyoh KYEH-reh*	What kind of service would you like?
¿En qué puedo servirle? *ehn keh PWEH-doh sehr-VEER-leh*	How can I help you?
ventanilla de entregas *vehn-tah-NEE-yah deh ehn-TREH-gahs*	dropoff window
ventanilla de recogidos *vehn-tah-NEE-yah deh reh-koh-HEE-dohs*	pickup window

How much to send that express / air mail?	**¿Cuánto cuesta enviar esto por correo urgente / correo aéreo?** *KWAHN-toh KWEHS-tah ehn-VEE-ahr EHS-toh pohr koh-RREH-oh oor-HEHN-teh / koh-RREH-oh ah-EH-reh-oh*
Do you offer overnight delivery?	**¿Tienen entrega de un día para otro?** *TYEH-nehn ehn-TREH-gah deh oon DEE-ah PAH-rah OH-troh*

How long will it take to reach the United States?

¿Cuánto tardará en llegar a los Estados Unidos?
KWAHN-toh tahr-dah-RAH ehn yeh-GAHR ah lohs ehs-TAH-dohs oo-NEE-dohs

I'd like to buy an envelope.

Quiero comprar un sobre.
KYEH-roh kohm-PRAHR oon SOH-breh

May I send it airmail?

¿Puedo enviarlo por correo aéreo?
PWEH-doh ehn-VYAHR-loh pohr koh-RREH-oh ah-EH-reh-oh

I'd like to send it certified / registered mail.

Quiero enviarlo por correo certificado.
KYEH-roh ehn-VYAHR-loh pohr koh-RREH-oh thehr-tee-fee-KAH-doh

MONEY MATTERS

Since 2002, the **euro**—official abbreviation "EUR"—has replaced the *peseta* as Spain's official currency. For more details on the euro, check **www.europa.eu.int/euro.** For today's exchange rates, try **www.oanda.com** or **www.nyforeignexchange.com.**

It makes sense to buy some euros before you leave home, to avoid lines at airport ATMs when you arrive, often early in the morning. You can exchange money through many U.S. banks, or **American Express** (✆ **800/673-3782;** www.americanexpress.com). When you change money, ask for some small bills or loose change. Petty cash will come in handy for tipping or public transportation. Consider keeping the change separate from your larger bills, so that it's readily accessible, and you'll be less of a target for theft.

These days, traveler's checks are less necessary because most cities have 24-hour ATMs that let you withdraw small amounts of cash as needed. You can get checks at any American Express office or by calling ✆ **800/221-7282. Visa** offers traveler's checks at Citibank locations nationwide (✆ **800/732-1322**). **MasterCard** (✆ **800/223-9920;** www.mastercard-credit-cards.com) also sells traveler's checks.

The easiest way to get money abroad is through an ATM. PLUS, Cirrus, and other ATM networks operate in virtually every town in Spain. It's a good idea to call and find out your daily withdrawal limit before you leave home. If you need cash fast over the weekend, when all banks and American Express offices are closed, you can go to an ATM or have money wired to you from **Western Union** (✆ **800/325-6000;** www.westernunion.com).

Major credit cards are accepted throughout Spain. Keep in mind that if you use a credit card in an ATM, you'll need to know your PIN (personal identification number). You'll also be charged a conversion fee, on which interest will accrue from the day of your withdrawal, even if you pay your monthly bill on time. It's always wise to call your credit card company to let them know where and when you're traveling; otherwise, they may question charges far from home, and refuse to honor your bill.

WHAT TO DO IF YOUR WALLET IS LOST OR STOLEN

If your wallet is lost or stolen, inform all your credit card companies immediately. (You'll be best-prepared for this situation if you've recorded your credit cards' emergency numbers and stored them someplace other than your wallet.) File a report at the nearest police precinct, as well, because your creditors or insurer may require a police report number or record of the loss. Identity theft or fraud are potential complications of losing your wallet—especially if you've lost your driver's license as well. It's wise to notify the major credit-reporting bureaus immediately to place a fraud alert on your records. The three major U.S. credit-reporting agencies are **Equifax** (© 800-766-0008; www.equifax.com), **Experian** (© 888/397-3742; www.experian.com), and **TransUnion** (© 800/680-7289; www.transunion.com). If you need emergency cash over the weekend, when all banks and American Express offices are closed, you can have money wired to you via **Western Union** (© 800/325-6000; www.westernunion.com).

STAYING IN TOUCH

Cellphones You can use your own **mobile phone** in Spain with the help of a "roaming" system, which you activate before you set off from home—contact your local phone company for details. You can purchase an international cellphone from home before departing. **Cellular Abroad** offers packages for many popular destinations (www.cellularabroad.com/index.html). Alternatively, on arrival you can rent one from a company called **Spain Cell Phone** on a short- or long-term

basis. Their number is ✆ **687-558-529** and their website is
www.puertademadrid.com/rentacellphone. Outgoing call
rates are inexpensive and incoming calls are free. Contracts
vary with Spanish mobiles; you can pay monthly or use
rechargeable cards which you pay for in advance.

Embassy   If you lose your passport, fall seriously ill, get into
legal trouble, or have some other serious problem, advise the
United States Embassy in Madrid, ✆ **91-587-22-00.** You can
also contact the U.S. Consulate in Barcelona at ✆ **93-280-22-
27,** open Monday to Friday, 9am to 1pm.

Emergencies   A centralized phone number for fire, police,
or ambulance is ✆ **112.**

Information Offices in the U.S.   The **Tourist Office of
Spain** provides sightseeing information, events calendars,
train and ferry schedules, and more. The main office is in New
York, 666 Fifth Ave., 35th Floor, New York, NY 10103
(✆ **212/265-8822**). Other offices are located at: 8383 Wilshire
Blvd., Suite 956, Beverly Hills, CA 90211 (✆ **323/658-7188);**
845 N. Michigan Ave., Suite 915E, Chicago, IL 60611
(✆ **312/642-1992);** and 1395 Brickell Ave., Suite 1130, Miami,
FL 33131 (✆ **305/358-1992**).

Postage Rates   Mailing a basic letter (small envelope or postcard) to the U.S. will cost 0.78€ for regular service. Leave your
letters with your hotel concierge, mail them in a post office, or
drop them in yellow post boxes called *buzones.* Buy stamps
in an *oficina de correos* (post office) or—if you don't like
standing in lines—in an *estanco* (a government-licensed tobac-
conist easily recognized by its brown and yellow logo). For further information, check the Spanish Post office website:
www.correos.es.

Telephone Use   Phoning from your **hotel room** can cost 40% more than the normal rate. Economical alternatives are **locutorios** (call centers with fax services) or street **phone booths** (known as *cabinas*), which have dialing instructions in English. Make local calls by inserting a 0.25€ coin for 3 minutes. Many only take **phone cards,** which you can buy from *estancos*. For national inquiries dial ✆ **11818.** For international inquiries dial ✆ **11825.** Operators on both lines usually speak sufficient English to get you through to the right city and number. To make international calls, dial 00 and then the country code (U.S. and Canada 1, U.K. 44, Ireland 353, Australia 61, New Zealand 64).

Numbers beginning with **900** in Spain are **toll-free.** Calling a 1-800 number in the States from Spain costs the same as an overseas call. If you have an **American calling card** that you would like to use to call home, you will have to figure out the company's access number in Spain. Check with the company before traveling. The AT&T access code for Spain is **900/99-0011;** for Sprint it is **900/99-0013.**

Time   Spain is 6 hours ahead of Eastern Standard Time in the United States. Daylight saving time is in effect from the last Sunday in March to the last Sunday in September.

CHAPTER SEVEN

CINEMA

Is there a movie theater nearby?	**¿Hay algún cine por aquí cerca?** *aye ahl-GOON THEE-neh pohr ah-KEE THEHR-kah*
What's playing tonight?	**¿Qué películas hay en cartelera?** *keh peh-LEE-koo-lahs ay ehn cahr-teh-LEHR-ah*
Is that in English or Spanish?	**¿Está en inglés o español?** *eh-STAH ehn eeng-GLEHS oh ehs-pah-NYOHL*
Are there English subtitles?	**¿Tiene subtítulos en inglés?** *TYEH-neh soob-TEE-too-lohs ehn eeng-GLEHS*
Is the theater air conditioned?	**¿El teatro tiene aire acondicionado?** *ehl teh-AH-troh TYEH-neh AYE-reh ah-kohn-dee-thyoh-NAH-doh*
How much is a ticket?	**¿Cuánto cuesta la entrada?** *KWAHN-toh KWEH-stah lah ehn-TRAH-dah*
Do you have a _____ discount?	**¿Ofrecen un descuento para _____** *oh-FREH-sehn oon dehs-KWEHN-toh PAH-rah*
senior	**mayores de 65 años?** *mah-YOH-rehs deh seh-SEHN-tah ee THEEN-koh AHN-yohs*
student	**estudiantes?** *ehs-too-DYAHN-tehs*
children's	**niños?** *NEE-nyohs*

What time is the movie showing?	**¿A qué hora muestran la película?**
	ah keh OH-rah MWEHS-trahn lah peh-LEE-koo-lah
How long is the movie?	**¿Cuánto dura la película?**
	KWAHN-toh DOO-rah lah peh-LEE-koo-lah
May I buy tickets in advance?	**¿Se pueden comprar entradas por anticipado?**
	seh PWEH-dehn kohm-PRAHR ehn-TRAH-dahs pohr ahn-tee-thee-PAH-thoh
Is it sold out?	**¿Están agotadas las localidades?**
	eh-STAHN ah-goh-TAH-dah lahs loh-kah-lee-DAH-thes
When does it begin?	**¿A qué hora empieza?**
	ah keh OH-rah ehm-PYEH-thah

PERFORMANCES

Do you have ballroom dancing?	**¿Tienen bailes de salón?**
	TYEH-nehn bah-EE-lehs deh sah-LOHN
Are there any plays showing right now?	**¿Hay ahora alguna obra en cartelera?**
	aye ah-OH-rah ahl-GOO-nah OH-brah ehn cahr-teh-LEH-rah
Is there a dinner theater?	**¿Hay teatro de cena?**
	aye teh-AH-troh deh THEH-nah
Where can I buy tickets?	**¿Dónde puedo comprar las entradas?**
	DOHN-deh PWEH-doh kohm-PRAHR lahs ehn-TRAH-thas
Are there student discounts?	**¿Ofrecen descuentos para estudiantes?**
	oh-FREH-sehn dehs-KWEHN-tohs PAH-rah ehs-too-DYAHN-tehs

CULTURE

Listen Up: Box Office Lingo

¿Qué le gustaría ver? *keh leh goos-tah-REE-ah vehr*	What would you like to see?
¿Cuántos? *KWAHN-tohs*	How many?
¿Para dos adultos? *PAH-rah dohs ah-DOOL-tohs*	For two adults?
¿Con mantequilla? ¿Sal? *kohn mahn-teh-KEE-yah sahl*	With butter? Salt?
¿Algo más? *AHL-goh mahs*	Would you like anything else?

I need ____ seats.	**Quiero ____ entradas.** *KYEH-roh ____ ehn-TRAH-thas*

For a full list of numbers, see p7.

An aisle seat.	**Una butaca de pasillo.** *OO-nah boo-TAH-kah deh pah-SEE-yoh*
Orchestra seat, please.	**Una butaca de patio, por favor.** *OO-nah boo-TAH-kah deh PAH-tyoh pohr fah-VOHR*
What time does the play start?	**¿A qué hora comienza la obra?** *ah keh OH-rah koh-MYEHN-thah lah OH-brah*
Is there an intermission?	**¿Hay un descanso?** *aye oon dehs-KAHN-soh*
Do you have an opera house?	**¿Tienen un teatro de la ópera?** *TYEH-nehn oon teh-AH-troh deh lah OH-peh-rah*

Is there a local symphony?	**¿Hay una sinfonía local?** *aye OO-nah seen-foh-NEE-ah loh-KAHL*
May I purchase tickets over the phone?	**¿Puedo comprar entradas por teléfono?** *PWEH-doh kohm-PRAHR ehn-TRAH-thas pohr teh-LEH-foh-noh*
What time is the box office open?	**¿A qué hora abre la taquilla?** *ah keh OH-rah AH-breh lah tah-KEE-yah*
I need space for a wheelchair, please.	**Necesito espacio para una silla de ruedas, por favor.** *neh-theh-SEE-toh ehs-PAH-thyoh PAH-rah OO-nah SEE-yah deh RWEH-dahs pohr fah-VOHR*
Do you have private boxes available?	**¿Tiene palcos privados disponibles?** *TYEH-neh PAHL-kohs pree-VAH-dohs dees-poh-NEE-blehs*
Is there a church that gives concerts?	**¿Hay alguna iglesia que ofrezca conciertos?** *aye ahl-GOO-nah ee-GLEH-syah keh oh-FRETHS-kah kohn-THYEHR-tohs*
A program, please.	**Un programa, por favor.** *oon proh-GRAH-mah pohr fah-VOHR*
Please show us to our seats.	**Por favor llévenos a nuestros asientos.** *pohr fah-VOHR YEH-veh-nohs ah NWEHS-trohs ah-SYEHN-tohs*

CULTURE

MUSEUMS, GALLERIES & SIGHTS

Do you have a museum guide? **¿Tiene un guía del museo?**
TYEH-neh oon GEE-ah dehl moo-SEH-oh

Do you have guided tours? **¿Ofrecen visitas guiadas?**
oh-FREH-sehn vee-SEE-tahs gee-AH-dahs

What are the museum hours? **¿Qué horario tiene el museo?**
keh oh-RAH-ryoh TYEH-ne ehl moo-SEH-oh

Do I need an appointment? **¿Necesito inscribirme?**
neh-theh-SEE-toh een-skree-BEER-meh

What is the admission fee? **¿Cuánto cuesta la entrada?**
KWAHN-toh KWEH-stah lah ehn-TRAH-dah

Do you have _____ **¿Ofrecen _____**
oh-FREH-thehn

  student discounts? **descuentos para estudiantes?**
dehs-KWEHN-tohs PAH-rah ehs-too-DYAHN-tehs

  senior discounts? **descuentos para mayores de 65 años?**
dehs-KWEHN-tohs PAH-rah mah-YOH-rehs deh seh-SEHN-teh ee THEEN-koh AHN-yohs

Do you have services for the hearing impaired? **¿Tienen servicios para personas con discapacidad auditiva?**
TYEH-nehn sehr-VEE-thyohs PAH-rah pehr-SOH-nahs kohn dees-kah-pah-thee-DAHD ow-dee-TEE-vohs

Do you have audio tours in English? **¿Tienen audioguías en inglés?**
TYEH-nehn ow-dyoh-GEE-ahs ehn eeng-GLEHS

FAVORITE MOMENTS

Sitting in *Sol* or *Sombra* at a Bullfight Love it or hate it, this unique microcosm of death, catharsis, and rebirth can be one of the most evocative and memorable events you'll experience in Spain. Tickets are for seats in the *sombra,* or shade (essential in high summer), or in the *sol,* or sun.

Running with The Bulls in Pamplona Wine flows during this exhilarating, dangerous event—when reckless souls run with herds of furious bulls down the medieval streets of Navarra's most famous town.

Being Riveted by Flamenco Staccato foot stomping, castanet rattling, hand clapping, and sultry guitar sounds accompany this heart-rending expression of conflict and pain, an Andalusian specialty said to have originated in Asia.

Beholding the Prado's Masterpieces Over 4,000 priceless paintings, many acquired by Spanish kings, fill Madrid's world-famous museum. Look out for Goya's once scandalous *Naked Maja* and *Las Meninas* (The Maids of Honor) by Velázquez.

Feasting on Tapas in the Tascas *Tapas*—those bite-size tidbits served in *tascas,* washed down with sherry, *vino,* or beer—are a quintessentially Spanish treat. They can be as simple as *chorizo* (spicy sausage) or exotic as *gambas* (deep-fried shrimp).

Sipping Sherry in Its Home Town, Jerez de la Frontera Sherry (Jerez) is Spain's most famous drink, dating back to Roman times. Jerez de la Frontera's hundred *bodegas* (cellars) yield vintages for every taste, from dry pale *finos* to rich dark *olorosos.*

SIGHTSEEING

Wandering the Winding Alleys of Barcelona's Gothic Quarter   The labyrinthine **Barri Gótic,** with its central **Ciutat Vella** (old city), are medieval bastions of art and architecture that inspired artists from Picasso to native-born Joan Miró.

Going Gaga over Gaudí   Barcelona is studded with the UNESCO-listed *moderniste* works of reclusive celibate architect Antoní Gaudí y Cornet. A highlight is his still unfinished **Sagrada Familia** cathedral.

Following the Ancient Pilgrim Route to Santiago de Compostela   The scenic medieval route taken by European pilgrims to the shrine of St. James (Santiago) in Galicia is avidly followed (on foot) by many visitors today.

Riding the Ferry from Ibiza to Formentera   The Balearic port of Ibiza links Spain atmospherically with Greece. The 30-minute sea trip to its tiny neighbor Formentera, across turquoise waters and past rocky islets, is a classic Homeresque voyage in miniature.

CALENDAR OF EVENTS

The dates given below are only approximate. Sometimes the exact days may not be announced until several weeks before the actual festival. For details, check with the **National Tourist Office of Spain** (www.okspain.org).

January

Granada Reconquest Festival   The whole city celebrates the Christian's victory over the Moors in 1492, and the highest tower is opened just this day to the public. *January 2.*

Three Kings Day (Día de los Reyes)   Lavish parades are staged throughout the main arteries of cities all over the country in anticipation of the Feast of the Epiphany. *January 6.*

St. Anthony's Day (Día de San Antonio)   At La Puebla, on the island of **Majorca,** bonfires, dancing, and revellers dressed as devils and other religious events honor St. Anthony. *January 17.*

February

Madrid Carnaval The carnival kicks off with a big parade along the Paseo de la Castellana, culminating in a masked ball at the Círculo de Bellas Artes on the following night. *Fancy-dress competitions last until February 28.*

March

Fallas de Valencia This centuries-old fiesta today centers around the burning of huge satirical papier-mâché images of current political and show biz celebrities. Bullfights, firework displays, and parades precede the conflagration. *March 12-19.*

Semana Santa (Holy Week) in Seville Usually the last week of March, **Seville's Holy Week festivities** are the most elaborate in Spain. From **Palm Sunday until Easter Sunday,** processions with hooded penitents move to the wail of the *saeta,* a love song to the Virgin or Christ. *Pasos* (heavy floats) bear images of the Virgin or Christ. Make hotel reservations way in advance.

April

Feria de Sevilla (Seville Fair) Spain's most colorful week of revelry, with parades of elegant riders accompanied by beautiful women in traditional Andalusian garb, all-night flamenco dancing, entertainment booths, and dancing in the streets. Book early, have a full wallet, and check with the Seville Tourist Office for exact dates. *Second week after Easter.*

May

Moors and Christians (Moros y Cristianos) At Alcoy, near Alicante, this centuries-old battle is re-enacted between Moorish and Christian soldiers in lavish period costumes. *May 2-5.*

Fiesta de San Isidro Madrileños run wild with a 2-week celebration honoring their city's patron saint. Food fairs, Castilian folkloric events, street parades, parties, music, dances, bullfights, and other festivities mark the occasion. Book early. *Mid-May.*

SIGHTSEEING

June

Hogueras de San Juan   Alicante's answer to Valencia's *Fallas*. Satirical effigies are burned on bonfires to celebrate the summer solstice, followed by parades and fireworks. *June 20-24.*

Verbena de Sant Joan   Barcelona dances until dawn, with bonfires and fireworks at Montjuich. *June 23-24.*

July

Fiesta de San Fermín, Pamplona   Vividly described in Ernest Hemingway's first novel, *The Sun Also Rises,* the running of bulls through the medieval streets of Pamplona is the most raucously popular celebration in Spain. It includes copious wine tasting, fireworks and, of course, bullfights. *July 6-14.*

August

Fiestas of La Paloma   Madrid's torrid mid-summer celebration of the Virgen de la Paloma. Children's games, floats, music, flamenco, and zarzuelas, along with street fairs. *August 1-15.*

Málaga Fair (Feria de Málaga)   Ten days of colorful Andalusian fun with wine, castanets, flamenco, and parades of carriages drawn by Arab horses. *Weekend before August 19.*

Battle of the Tomatoes (La Tomatina)   Truckloads of tomatoes provide ammunition for a mock gory battle that paints the town of **Buñol, Valencia** red. *First Wednesday in August.*

September

San Sebastián International Film Festival   Spain's top movie fest takes place in the modern auditorium of its most beautiful coastal town. *Second week in September.*

December

Día de los Santos Inocentes   On this countrywide holiday, the Spanish play many practical jokes and in general do *loco* things to one another—it's the Spanish equivalent of April Fools' Day. *December 28.*

CHAPTER EIGHT

SHOPPING

This chapter covers the phrases you'll need to shop in a variety of settings, from the mall to the town square artisan market. We also threw in the terminology you'll need to visit the barber or hairdresser.

For coverage of food and grocery shopping, see p110.

GENERAL SHOPPING TERMS

Please tell me _____	**¿Me puede decir _____** *meh PWEH-deh deh-THEER*
how to get to a mall?	**cómo llego a un centro comercial?** *KOH-moh YEH-goh ah oon THEHN-troh koh-mehr-THYAHL*
the best place for shopping?	**el mejor lugar para ir de compras?** *ehl meh-HOHR loo-GAHR pah-rah EER deh KOHM-prahs*
how to get downtown?	**cómo llego al centro?** *KOH-moh YEH-goh ahl THEHN-troh*
Where can I find a _____	**¿Dónde puedo encontrar una _____** *DOHN-deh PWEH-doh ehn-kohn-TRAHR OO-nah*
shoe store?	**tienda de zapatos?** *TYEHN-dah deh thah-PAH-tohs*
men's / women's / children's clothing store?	**tienda de ropa para hombres / mujeres / niños?** *TYEHN-dah deh RROH-pah PAH-rah HOM-brehs / moo-HEH-rehs / NEE-nyohs*

designer fashion shop?	**tienda de moda de diseño?**
	TYEHN-dah deh MOH-dah deh
	dee-SEH-nyoh
vintage clothing store?	**tienda de ropa antigua?**
	TYEHN-dah deh RROH-pah ahn-
	TEE-wah
jewelry store?	**joyería?**
	hoh-yeh-REE-yah
bookstore?	**librería?**
	ee-breh-REE-ah
toy store?	**juguetería?**
	hoo-geh-teh-REE-ah
stationery store?	**papelería?**
	peh-pehl-eh-REE-ah
antique shop?	**tienda de antigüedades?**
	TYEHN-dah deh ahn-tee-gweh-
	DAH-dehs
cigar shop?	**tienda de cigarros?**
	TYEHN-dah deh see-GAH-rrohs
souvenir shop?	**tienda de recuerdos?**
	TYEHN-dah deh reh-KWEHR-
	dohs
Where can I find a flea market?	**¿Dónde puedo encontrar un mercadillo?**
	DOHN-deh PWEH-doh ehn-kohn-
	TRAHR oon mehr-kah-DEE-yoh

Flea Markets

In Madrid, the most famous flea market is the one held on Sundays at "El Rastro." Many cities do not have flea markets at all, so it's best to ask.

CLOTHES SHOPPING

I'd like to buy ____	**Quiero comprar ____** *KYEH-roh kohm-PRAHR*
men's shirts.	**camisas para hombres.** *kah-MEE-sahs PAH-rah OHM-brehs*
women's shoes.	**zapatos para mujeres.** *thah-PAH-tohs PAH-rah moo-HEH-rehs*
children's clothes.	**ropa para niños.** *RROH-pah PAH-rah NEE-nyohs*
toys.	**juguetes.** *hoo-GEH-tehs*

For a full list of numbers, see p7.

I'm looking for a size ____	**Busco una talla ____** *BOOS-koh OO-nah TAH-yah*
small.	**pequeña.** *peh-KEH-nyah*
medium.	**mediana.** *meh-DYAH-nah*
large.	**grande.** *GRAHN-deh*
extra-large.	**extra grande.** *EHS-trah GRAHN-deh*

los pendientes
el collar

la camisa
la corbata
la chaqueta

el vestido
el reloj

el cinturón

los pantalones

los zapatos

I'm looking for ____	**Busco ____**
	BOOS-koh
a silk blouse.	**una blusa de seda.**
	OO-nah BLOO-sah deh SEH-dah
cotton pants.	**pantalones de algodón.**
	pahn-tah-LOH-nehs deh ahl-goh-DOHN
a hat.	**un sombrero.**
	oon sohm-BREH-roh
sunglasses.	**gafas de sol.**
	GAH-fahs deh sohl
underwear.	**ropa interior.**
	RROH-pah een-teh-RYOHR
cashmere.	**cachemira.**
	kah-che-MEER-ah
socks.	**calcetines.**
	kahl-seh-TEE-nehs
sweaters.	**jerséis.**
	hehr-SEH-ees

las gafas

la camiseta

los vaqueros

las zapatillas
de deporte

a coat.	**un abrigo.**
	oon ah-BREE-goh
a swimsuit.	**un bañador.**
	oon bahn-yah=DOHR
May I try it on?	**¿Me lo puedo probar?**
	meh loh PWEH-doh proh-BAHR
Do you have fitting rooms?	**¿Tiene probadores?**
	TYEH-neh proh-bah-DOH-rehs
This is _____	**Esto me queda _____**
	EHS-toh meh KEH-dah
too tight.	**muy apretado.**
	MOO-ee ah-preh-TAH-doh
too loose.	**muy suelto.**
	MOO-ee SWEHL-toh
too long.	**muy largo.**
	MOO-ee LAHR-goh
too short.	**muy corto.**
	MOO-ee KOHR-toh
This fits great!	**¡Esto me queda fenomenal!**
	EHS-toh meh KEH-dah feh-noh-meh-NAHL

Thanks, I'll take it.	**Gracias, me lo llevo.**
	GRAH-thyahs meh loh YEH-voh
Do you have that in _____	**¿Lo tiene en _____**
	loh TYEH-neh ehn
a smaller / larger size?	**una talla más pequeña / grande?**
	OO-nah TAH-yah mahs peh-KEH-nyah / GRAHN-deh
a different color?	**un color diferente?**
	oon koh-LOHR dee-feh-REHN-teh
How much is it?	**¿Cuánto cuesta?**
	KWAHN-toh KWEHS-tah

ARTISAN MARKET SHOPPING

Is there a craft / artisan market?	**¿Hay algún mercado de artesanías?**
	aye ahl-GOON mehr-KAH-doh deh ahr-teh-SAH-nee-ahs
That's beautiful. May I look at it?	**¡Eso es precioso! ¿Puedo verlo?**
	EH-soh ehs preh-SYOH-soh PWEH-doh VEHR-loh
Is that open every day of the week?	**¿Alore todos los días de la semana?**
	ah-LOH-reh TOH-dohs lohs DEE-ahs deh lah seh-MAH-nah
How much does that cost?	**¿Cuánto cuesta eso?**
	KWAHN-toh KWEHS-tah EH-soh
That's too expensive.	**Es muy caro.**
	ehs MOO-ee KAH-roh
How much for two?	**¿Cuánto por los / las dos?**
	KWAHN-doh pohr lohs / lahs dohs

Listen Up: Market Lingo

Se ruega no tocar los artículos. *seh RWEH-gah noh toh-KAHR lohs ahr-TEE-kuh-los*	Please don't handle the goods.
Aquí tengo su cambio. *ah-KEE TEHNG-goh soo KAHM-byoh*	Here is your change.
Dos por cuarenta, señor. *dohs pohr kwah-REHN-tah sehn-YOHR*	Two for forty, sir.

Do I get a discount if I buy two or more?	**¿Me da un descuento si compro dos o más?** *meh dah oon dehs-KWEHN-toh see KOHM-proh dohs oh mahs*
Do I get a discount if I pay in cash?	**¿Me da un descuento si pago en efectivo?** *meh dah oon desh-KWEHN-toh see PAH-goh ehn eh-FEHK-tee-voh*
No thanks, maybe I'll come back.	**No gracias, quizás vuelva más tarde.** *noh GRAH-thyahs kee-SAHS VWEHL-vah mahs TAHR-deh*
Would you take $____?	**¿Aceptaría €____?** *ah-THEHP-tah-REE-ah ____ eh-oo-rohs*

For a full list of numbers, see p7.

That's a deal!	**¡Trato hecho!**
	TRAH-toh EH-choh
Do you have a less expensive one?	**¿Tiene uno -a menos caro -a?**
	TYEH-neh oon / OO-nah MEH-nohs KAH-roh / KAH-rah
Is there tax?	**¿Hay impuestos?**
	aye eem-PWEHS-tohs
May I have the VAT forms? (Europe only)	**¿Me puede dar los formularios para el IVA?**
	meh PWEH-deh dahr lohs fohr-moo-LAHR-yohs PAH-rah ehl ee-veh-AH

BOOKSTORE / NEWSSTAND SHOPPING

Is there a ____ nearby?	**¿Hay ____ por aquí cerca?**
	aye ____ pohr ah-KEE THEHR-kah
a bookstore	**una librería**
	OO-nah lee-breh-REE-ah
a newsstand	**un quiosco**
	oon kee-OHS-koh
Do you have ____ in English?	**¿Tiene ____ en inglés?**
	TYEH-neh ____ ehn eeng-GLEHS
books	**libros**
	LEE-brohs
newspapers	**periódicos**
	pehr-YOH-dee-kohs
magazines	**revistas**
	reh-VEES-tahs
books about local history	**libros acerca de la historia local**
	LEE-brohs ah-THEHR-kah deh lah ees-TOHR-yah loh-KAHL

SHOPPING FOR ELECTRONICS

Before buying a DVD to take home, ask whether it will play on a DVD player in your home country.

Can I play this in the United States?	**¿Puedo tocar esto en Estados Unidos?**
	PWEH-doh toh-KAHR EHS-toh ehn ehs-TAH-dohs oo-NEE-dohs?
Will this game work on my game console in the United States?	**¿Funcionará este juego en mi consola de juegos en los Estados Unidos?**
	foon-thyoh-nah-RAH EHS-teh HWEH-goh ehn mee kohn-SOH-lah deh HWEH-gohs ehn lohs ehs-TAH-dohs oo-NEE-dohs
Do you have this in a U.S. market format?	**¿Tiene esto en un formato para el mercado de los Estados Unidos?**
	TYEH-neh EHS-toh ehn oon fohr-MAH-toh PAH-rah ehl mehr-KAH-doh deh lohs ehs-TAH-dohs oo-NEE-dohs
Can you convert this to a U.S. market format?	**¿Puede convertir esto a un formato para el mercado de los Estados Unidos?**
	PWEH-deh kohn-vehr-TEER EHS-toh ah oon fohr-MAH-toh PAH-rah ehl mehr-KAH-doh deh lohs ehs-TAH-dohs oo-NEE-dohs
Will this work with a 110 VAC adapter?	**¿Esto funcionará con un adaptador de 110 VAC?**
	EHS-toh foon-thyoh-nah-RAH kohn oon ah-dahp-tah-DOHR deh SYEHN-toh ee dyehs VOHL-tyohs deh koh-RRYEHN-teh ahl-TEHR-nah

Do you have an adapter plug for 110 to 220?	**¿Tiene un adaptador de 110 / 220 voltios?** *TYEH-neh oon ah-dahp-tah-DOHR deh THYEHN-toh ee dyehs / doh-THYEHN-tohs ee VEH-een-teh VOHL-tyohs*
Do you sell electronics adapters here?	**¿Vende adaptadores para aparatos electrónicos?** *VEHN-deh ah-dahp-tah-DOH-rehs PAH-rah ah-pah-RAH-tohs eh-lehk-TROH-nee-kohs*
Is it safe to use my laptop with this adapter?	**¿Es seguro utilizar mi ordenador portátil con este adaptador?** *ehs seh-GOO-roh oo-tee-lee-THAHR mee ohr-deh-nah-DOHR pohr-TAH-teel kohn EHS-teh ah-dahp-tah-DOHR*
If it doesn't work, may I return it?	**Si no funciona, ¿puedo devolverlo?** *see noh foon-THYOH-nah PWEH-doh deh-vohl-VEHR-loh*
May I try it here in the store?	**¿Puedo probarlo aquí en la tienda?** *PWEH-doh proh-BAHR-loh ah-KEE ehn lah TYEHN-dah*

AT THE BARBER / HAIRDRESSER

Do you have a style guide?	**¿Tiene una guía de estilo?** *TYEH-neh OO-nah GEE-ah deh eh-STEE-loh*
A trim, please.	**Un recorte, por favor.** *oon rreh-KOHR-teh pohr fah-VOHR*
I'd like it bleached.	**Me gustaría teñirme el pelo rubio.** *meh goos-tah-REE-ah tehn-YEER-meh ehl PEH-loh deh ROO-byoh*

Would you change the color _____	**¿Me puede _____ el color?** *meh PWEH-deh _____ ehl koh-LOHR*
darker?	**oscurecer** *oh-skuh-reh-THEHR*
lighter?	**aclarar** *ah-klah-RAHR*

Would you just touch it up a little?	**¿Lo puede retocar un poco?** *loh PWEH-deh reh-toh-KAHR oon POH-koh*
I'd like it curled.	**Me gustaría rizado.** *meh goos-tah-REE-ah ree-THAH-doh*
Do I need an appointment?	**¿Es necesario pedir cita?** *ehs neh-theh-SAH-ryoh peh-DEER THEE-tah*
Wash, dry, and set.	**Lavar, secar y peinar.** *lah-VAHR seh-KAHR ee peh-ee-NAHR*
Do you do permanents?	**¿Hacen permanentes?** *AH-thehn pehr-mah-NEHN-tehs*
May I make an appointment?	**¿Puedo pedir cita?** *PWEH-doh peh-DEER THEE-tah*
Please use low heat.	**Por favor use poco calor.** *pohr fah-VOHR OO-seh POH-koh kah-LOHR*
Please don't blow dry it.	**Por favor no me lo seque con secador.** *pohr fah-VOHR noh meh loh SEH-keh kohn seh-kah-DOHR*
Please dry it curly / straight.	**Por favor séquelo rizado / lacio.** *pohr fah-VOHR SEH-keh-loh ree-THAH-doh / LAH-thyoh*
Would you fix my braids?	**¿Me puede arreglar las trenzas?** *meh PWEH-deh ah-rreh-GLAHR lahs TREHN-thahs*

Would you fix my highlights?	**¿Me puede retocar los reflejos / las mechas?** *meh PWEH-deh reh-toh-KAHR lohs reh-FLEH-hohs / lahs meh-CHAHS*
Do you wax?	**¿Hacen depilación con cera?** *AH-sehn deh-pee-lah-THYOHN kohn THEH-rah*
Please wax my ____	**Me quiero depilar ____, por favor.** *meh KYEH-roh deh-pee-LAHR pohr fah-VOHR*
legs.	**las piernas.** *lahs PYEHR-nahs*
bikini line.	**las ingles.** *lahs een-GLEHS*
eyebrows.	**las cejas.** *lahs THEH-hahs*
upper lip.	**el labio superior.** *ehl LAH-byoh soo-pehr-YOHR*
Would you trim my beard, please?	**¿Me podría recortar la barba, por favor?** *meh poh-DREE-ah reh-kohr-TAHR lah BAHR-bah pohr fah-VOHR*
A shave, please.	**Un afeitado, por favor.** *oon ah-feh-ee-TAH-doh pohr fah-VOHR*
Use a fresh blade please.	**Por favor, utilice una cuchilla nueva.** *pohr fah-VOHR oo-tee-LEE-theh OO-nah kuh-CHEE-yah NWEH-vah*
Sure, cut it all off.	**Vale, córtemelo todo.** *VAH-leh KOHR-teh-meh-loh TOH-doh*

UNDERSTANDING VAT

When you buy something in Spain, you pay an internal tax, known as VAT in most of Europe, but as IVA in Spain. The rate ranges from 7% for foodstuffs to 16% of the total worth of your merchandise. Some luxury items such as fur coats, gold items, and silverware can be taxed as high as 33%.

At shops with "tax free for tourists" signs you can get a refund, provided your total purchases exceed a certain sum (around 90€). Complete three copies of a form that the store will give you, detailing the nature of your purchase and its value. Citizens of non-EU countries show the purchase and the form to the Spanish Customs Office when they leave the country. Be sure not to pack these items in your checked baggage. You then present the validated form to the airport branch of the Banco Exterior de España, which will refund the tax, minus a commission. For more info, check out **www.globalrefund.com.**

BEST BUYS & WHERE TO FIND THEM

Spain is renowned for its craftspeople, many of whom still work in the time-honored and labor-intensive traditions of their grandparents. It's hard to go wrong if you stick to beautiful handcrafted Spanish objects—hand-painted tiles, ceramics, and porcelain; hand-woven rugs; handmade sweaters; and intricate embroideries. And, of course, jewelry—especially gold set with Majorca pearls, which represents good value and unquestioned luxury.

Some of the world's finest **leather goods** are made in Spain. Excellent **shoes** are available—some highly fashionable. But be advised that prices for shoes and quality clothing are generally higher in Spain than in the U.S.

In **Madrid,** the best street for middle-range shoe shops is **Augusto Figueroa** in the district of Chueca. Over in Calle Serrano, Spain's most stylish shopping street, you'll find one of the most well-known names in the world of footwear, **Farrutx,** which originates on the Balearic island of **Majorca** and has branches in all major Spanish mainland cities. Its *zapaterías* (shoe shops) produce elegant quality leather goods that also include belts and handbags. (If you're visiting **Majorca,** take a trip out to the inland town of **Inca**—it's filled with shops selling a wide variety of leather goods at highly competitive prices.)

Another notable name is **Loewe,** whose main **Madrid** branch has been the most elegant leather store in Spain since 1846. Its gold medal-winning designers have always kept abreast of changing tastes and styles, but the inventory still retains a timeless chic. The store sells luggage, handbags, and jackets for men and women (in leather or suede).

The equally well-stocked **Barcelona** branch is part of the stylish *moderniste* Casa Morera, in Passeig de Gracia's famed *Mansana de la Discordia*. Also in Barcelona, the **Hermengildo Muxart** leather and footwear shop in Carrer Rosselló produces boots, shoes, and sandals, designed by the owner, that are works of art.

Ceramics   The little-known but evocatively named town of **Talavera de la Reina** produces hand-painted ceramic tiles, plates, and pottery that are sold in major cities all over the country. The more famous **Lladró** porcelain figurines from **Valencia,** with their predominant pale grays and blues, are widely sold both in towns and tourist resorts. Lladró's mecca in **Madrid** is Lasarte in the Gran Vía. Other ceramics to look for are those from Manises, Puente del Arzobispo, Alcora, Granada, and Seville. One of the best shops to find them is the **Antigua Casa Talavera** in **Madrid.** Sangria pitchers, dinnerware, tea sets, plates, and vases are all handmade. There's also a series of tiles depicting famous paintings in the Prado.

Pearls & Steel   Also highly popular and available everywhere are **Majorica Pearls** (artificial) and **Toledo steel** products such as **ornamental swords.** The former come from the country town of **Manacor** at the eastern end of the island of **Mallorca;**

the latter, are produced in the historic city of **Toledo,** just under an hour from Madrid. The steel is not from Toledo but actually transported from the northern areas around Bilbao, and achieves its unique quality after being tempered in the mineral-rich waters of the Tagus River, which curves round the city.

Carpets & Rugs   There's always a good choice of *alfombras* (carpets) in all main Spanish towns. If you're in **Madrid,** look no further than **Ispahan,** located in a 19th-century building in stylish Serrano Street. Behind its bronze handmade doors you'll find three whole floors devoted to carpets from around the world.

Hand-Woven Embroidery   The **Balearic Islands** (especially Majorca) specialize in this delicately attractive product. In Palma de Mallorca's **Can Bonet,** located in Plaça Federico Chopin, shoppers avidly seek out bridal chests and elegant dinner settings. The highly popular **Madrid** branch in Calle Nuñez de Balboa has a similar display.

Flea Markets   These abound in Spain. The most famous is **Madrid's Rastro** (Sunday mornings only), which extends south from the Plaza Cascorro and offers a wide range of bargain clothes, as well as general junk and antiques of varying quality. It's worth seeing for the atmosphere alone, but it usually gets very crowded and you should beware of pickpockets. **Barcelona's** pricier **Antiques Market** takes place every Thursday in front of the cathedral in the city's Barri Gótic. Be ready to haggle.

DEPARTMENT STORES

El Corte Inglés (The English Cut), Spain's largest department-store chain, sells hundreds of souvenirs and Spanish handicrafts. It also sells glamorous fashion articles, such as Pierre Balmain designs, for about a third less than equivalent items in most European capitals. Stores are widespread throughout the country.

SHOPPING

FNAC, the comprehensive French store, has offices in various cities. Its largest branch, in Madrid, provides a wealth of media fare from a multilingual book section with everything from current bestsellers to travel and history, to a huge stock of CDs.

GALLERIES

If you want to buy original art, **Madrid**'s galleries are the best, renowned throughout Europe for their ability to discover and encourage new talent. For the most eclectic choice, head for **Calle Claudio Coello,** in the top-drawer Salamanca district. Key galleries lining this street are **Galeria Kreisler,** owned by Ohio-born Edward Kreisler and specializing in figurative and contemporary paintings, **sculptures,** and graphics; **Guillermo de Osma,** which features 20th-century **avant-garde** art from Kandinsky to Klee; and **Oliva Arauna,** whose main focus is sculpture, with a strong interest in **photography** and **video.**

In **Barcelona,** check out the Barri Gótic's **Antoni de Barnola,** which sells mainly Spanish **contemporary** artists' work, and the elegant 19th-century **Sala Parés,** an institution on the Barcelona art scene, which specializes in **figurative** and **historical** paintings. **Calle Consell de Cent** in the Eixample district offers a stylish selection of galleries: **Carlos Taché** at number 290 often displays works by top local artists such as Tapiés (so don't expect low-priced bargains here), and the **Fundación La Caixa** at the *moderniste* **Palau Macaya** in Passeig de San Joan 108 combines **modern** Catalan paintings with **photograph** exhibitions.

Andalusian capital **Seville** has a number of rewarding galleries. One of the most prominent is **Rafael Ortiz** at Calle Marmoles 12, which specializes in fine arts, and sculpture (www.galeriarafaelortiz.com). Out in the Balearic Islands, **Palma de Mallorca**'s leading gallery is **Sala Pelaires,** in a 17th-century palace at Calle Pelaires 5.

CHAPTER NINE
SPORTS & FITNESS

STAYING FIT

Is there a gym nearby?	**¿Hay un gimnasio cerca de aquí?** *aye oon heem-NAH-syoh THEHR-kah deh ah-KEE*
Do you have free weights?	**¿Tienen sala de pesas?** *TYEH-nehn SAH-lah deh PEH-sahs*
I'd like to go for a swim.	**Me gustaría nadar.** *meh goos-tah-REE-ah nah-DAHR*
Do I have to be a member?	**¿Tengo que ser socio del gimnasio?** *TEHNG-goh keh sehr SOH-syoh dehl heem-NAH-syoh*
May I come here for one day?	**¿Puedo venir por un día, nada más?** *PWEH-doh veh-NEER pohr oon DEE-ah NAH-dah mahs*
How much does a membership cost?	**¿Cuánto cuesta abonarse al gimnasio?** *KWAHN-toh KWEHS-tah ah-boh-NAHR-seh ahl heem-NAH-syoh*

I need to get a locker please.	**Necesito un casillero, por favor.** *neh-theh-SEE-toh oon kah-see-YEH-roh pohr fah-VOHR*
Do you have a lock?	**¿Tiene un candado?** *TYEH-neh oon kahn-DAH-doh*
Do you have treadmills?	**¿Hay cintas de correr?** *ay THEEN-tahs deh koh-RREHR*
Do you have stationary bikes?	**¿Hay bicicletas estáticas?** *ay bee-thee-KLEH-tahs ehs-TAH-tee-kahs*
Do you have handball / squash courts?	**¿Hay canchas de balonmano / squash?** *ay KAHN-chahs deh bah-lohn-MAH-noh / skwahsh?*
Are they indoor courts?	**¿Son canchas interiores?** *sohn KAHN-chahs een-teh-RYOH-rehs*
I'd like to play tennis.	**Me gustaría jugar al tenis.** *meh goos-tah-REE-ah hoo-GAHR ahl TEH-nees*
Would you like to play?	**¿Le gustaría jugar?** *leh goos-tah-REE-ah hoo-GAHR*
I'd like to rent a racquet.	**Quiero alquilar una raqueta.** *KYEH-roh ahl-kee-LAHR OO-nah rrah-KEH-tah*
I need to buy some ____	**Necesito comprar ____** *neh-theh-SEE-toh kohm-PRAHR*
new balls.	**pelotas nuevas.** *peh-LOH-tahs NWEH-vahs*
safety glasses.	**gafas de protección.** *GAH-fahs deh proh-tehk-THYOHN*
May I rent a court for tomorrow?	**¿Puedo alquilar una cancha para mañana?** *PWEH-doh ahl-kee-LAHR OO-nah KAHN-chah PAH-rah mah-NYAH-nah*

May I have clean towels?	**¿Me puede dar toallas limpias?** *meh PWEH-deh dahr toh-AH-yahs LEEM-pyahs*
Where are the showers / locker-rooms?	**¿Dónde están las duchas / los vestuarios?** *DOHN-deh ehs-TAHN lahs DOO-chas / lohs vehs-TWAHR-yohs*
Do you have a workout room for women only?	**¿Tienen una sala para mujeres solamente?** *TYEH-nehn OON-ah SAH-lah PAH-rah moo-HEH-rehs soh-lah-MEHN-teh*
Do you have aerobics classes?	**¿Tienen clases de aerobic?** *TYEH-nehn KLAH-sehs deh ah-eh-roh-BEEK*
Do you have a women's pool?	**¿Tienen piscina para mujeres?** *TYEH-nehn pee-THEE-nah PAH-rah moo-HEH-rehs*
Let's go for a jog.	**Vamos a hacer footing.** *VAH-mohs ah ah-THEHR FOO-teeng*
That was a great workout.	**Ha estado fenomenal el entrenamiento.** *ah eh-STAH-doh feh-noh-meh-NAHL ehl ehn-trehn-ah-MYEHN-toh*

CATCHING A GAME

Where is the stadium?	**¿Dónde está el estadio?** *DOHN-deh ehs-TAH ehl ehs-TAH-dyoh*

Do you have a bullfight?	**¿Tienen corridas de toros?** *TYEH-nehn koh-RREE-dahs deh TOH-rohs*
Who is your favorite toreador / matador?	**¿Quién es su torero favorito?** *kyehn ehs soo toh-REH-roh fah-voh-REE-toh*
Who is the best goalie?	**¿Quién es el mejor portero?** *kyehn ehs ehl meh-HOHR pohr-TEH-roh*
Are there any women's teams?	**¿Hay equipos de mujeres?** *aye eh-KEE-pohs deh moo-HEH-rehs*
Do you have any amateur / professional teams?	**¿Hay equipos de amateur / profesionales?** *ay eh-KEE-pohs deh ah-mah-TYOOR / proh-feh-syoh-NAHL-ehs*
Is there a game I could play in?	**¿Puedo jugar en algún partido?** *PWEH-doh hoo-GAHR en ahl-GOON pahr-TEE-doh*
Which is the best team?	**¿Cuál es el mejor equipo?** *kwahl ehs ehl meh-HOHR eh-KEE-poh*
Will the game be on television?	**¿Van a echar el partido por la tele?** *vahn ah eh-CHAHR ehl pahr-TEE-doh pohr lah TEH-leh*
Where can I buy tickets?	**¿Dónde puedo comprar entradas?** *DOHN-deh PWEH-doh kohm-PRAHR ehn-TRAH-dahs*
The best seats, please.	**Los mejores asientos, por favor.** *lohs meh-HOH-rehs ah-SYEHN-tohs pohr fah-VOHR*
The cheapest seats, please.	**Los asientos más baratos, por favor.** *lohs ah-SYEHN-tohs mahs bah-RAH-tohs pohr fah-VOHR*

How close to the court are these seats?	**¿A qué distancia del campo de fútbol / cancha de baloncesto / tenis están estos asientos?** *ah keh dee-STAHN-thyah dehl KAHM-poh de FOOT-bahl / KAHN-chah de bah-lohn-SEHS-tah / TEH-nees ehs-TAHN EHS-tohs ah-SYEHN-tohs*
May I have box seats?	**¿Me puede dar butacas en un palco?** *meh PWEH-deh dahr boo-TAH-kahs ehn oon PAHL-koh*
Wow! What a game!	**¡Caray! ¡Qué partido!** *kah-RAH-ee keh pahr-TEE-doh*
Go! Go! Go!	**¡Venga, venga, venga!** *VEHN-gah, VEHN-gah, VEHN-gah*
Oh No!	**¡Noooo!** *noh*
Give it to them!	**¡Dale!** *DAH-leh*
Go for it!	**¡Ve por él!** *veh pohr ehl*
Score!	**¡Gol!** *gohl*
What's the score?	**¿Cómo van?** *KOH-moh vahn*
Who's winning?	**¿Quién va ganando?** *kyehn vah gah-NAHN-doh*

HIKING

Where can I find a guide to hiking trails?	**¿Dónde puedo encontrar una guía de senderos?** *DOHN-deh PWEH-doh ehn-kohn-TRAHR OO-nah GEE-ah deh sehn-DEH-rohs*

Do we need to hire a guide?	**¿Necesitamos contratar a un guía?** *neh-theh-see-TAH-mohs kohn-trah-TAHR ah oon GEE-ah*
Where can I rent equipment?	**¿Dónde puedo alquilar equipo?** *DOHN-deh PWEH-doh ahl-kee-LAHR eh-KEE-poh*
We need more ropes and carabiners.	**Necesitamos más cuerda y mosquetones.** *neh-theh-see-TAH-mohs mahs KWEHR-dah ee mohs-keh-TOHN-ehs*
Where can we go mountain climbing?	**¿Dónde podemos ir a hacer alpinismo?** *DOHN-deh poh-DEH-mohs eer ah ah-THEHR ahl-pee-NEES-moh*
Are the routes _____	**¿Están _____ los senderos?** *ehs-TAHN _____ lohs sehn-DEH-rohs*
well marked?	**bien marcados** *byehn mahr-KAH-dohs*
in good condition?	**en buenas condiciones** *ehn BWEH-nahs kohn-deeth-YOH-nehs*
What is the altitude there?	**¿A qué altura está?** *ah keh ahl-TOO-rah eh-STAH*

How long will it take?	**¿Cuánto tiempo tardará?**
	KWAHN-toh TYEHM-poh tahr-da-RAH
Is it very difficult?	**¿Es muy difícil?**
	ehs MOO-ee dee-FEE-theel
I'd like a challenging climb but I don't want to take oxygen.	**Me gustaría un ascenso desafiante, pero no quiero tener que llevar oxígeno.**
	meh goos-tah-REE-ah oon ah-THEHN-soh deh-sah-fee-AHN-teh peh-roh noh KYEH-roh teh-NEHR keh yeh-VAHR ohk-SEE-heh-noh
I want to hire someone to carry my excess gear.	**Quiero contratar a alguien que cargue mi exceso de equipo.**
	KYEH-roh kohn-trah-TAHR ah AHLG-yehn keh KAHR-geh mee ehk-THEH-soh deh eh-KEE-poh
We don't have time for a long route.	**No tenemos tiempo para hacer una ruta larga.**
	noh teh-NEH-mohs TYEHM-poh PAH-rah ah-THEHR OO-nah RROO-tah LAHR-gah
I don't think it's safe to proceed.	**No creo que sea prudente continuar.**
	noh KREH-oh keh SEH-ah proo-DEHN-teh kohn-tee-NWAHR
Do we have a backup plan?	**¿Tenemos una alternativa de regreso?**
	teh-NEH-mohs OO-nah ahl-tehr-nah-TEE-vah deh reh-GREH-soh
If we're not back by tomorrow, send a search party.	**Si no hemos regresado mañana, envía un equipo de rescate.**
	see noh EH-mohs rreh-greh-SAH-doh mah-NYAH-nah ehn-VEE-ah oon eh-KEE-poh deh rrehs-KAH-teh

Are the campsites marked?	**¿Los campamentos están marcados?**
	lohs kahm-pah-MEHN-tohs ehs-TAHN mahr-KAH-dohs
Can we camp off the trail?	**¿Podemos acampar lejos del sendero?**
	poh-DEH-mohs ah-kahm-PAHR LEH-hohs dehl sehn-DEH-roh
Is it okay to build fires here?	**¿Está permitido hacer fogatas aquí?**
	ehs-TAH pehr-mee-TEE-doh ah-THEHR foh-GAH-tahs ah-KEE
Do we need permits?	**¿Necesitamos permisos?**
	neh-theh-see-TAH-mohs pehr-MEE-sohs

For more camping terms, see p87.

BOATING OR FISHING

When do we sail?	**¿Cuándo partimos / salimos?**
	KWAHN-doh pahr-TEE-mohs / sah-LEE-mohs
Where are the life preservers?	**¿Dónde están los salvavidas?**
	DOHN-deh ehs-TAHN lohs sahl-vah-VEE-dahs
Can I purchase bait?	**¿Puedo comprar cebo?**
	PWEH-doh kohm-PRAHR THEH-boh
Can I rent a pole?	**¿Puedo alquilar una caña de pescar?**
	PWEH-doh ahl-kee-LAHR OO-nah KAH-nyah deh pehs-KAHR

How long is the voyage?	**¿Cuanto dura el viaje?**
	KWAHN-toh DOO-rah ehl VYAH-heh
Are we going up river or down?	**¿Vamos río arriba o río abajo?**
	VAH-mohs REE-oh ah-RREE-bah
	oh REE-oh ah-BAH-hoh
How far are we going?	**¿Cuanta distancia vamos a recorrer?**
	KWAHN-tah dee-STAHN-seeah
	VAH-mohs ah reh-KOH-rrehr
How fast are we going?	**¿A qué velocidad viajamos?**
	ah keh veh-loh-thee-DAHD vyoh-
	HAH-mohs
How deep is the water here?	**¿Cuál es la profundidad del aqua?**
	kwahl ehs lah proh-foon-dee-
	DAHD dehl AH-wah
I got one!	**¡Pesqué uno!**
	pehs-KEH OO-noh
I can't swim.	**No sé nadar.**
	noh seh nah-DAHR
Can we go ashore?	**¿Podemos bajarnos en la orilla?**
	poh-DEH-mohs bah-HAHR-nohs
	ehn lah oh-REE-yah

For more boating terms, see p66.

DIVING

I'd like to go snorkeling.	**Me gustaría hacer buceo con tubo.**
	meh goo-stah-REE-ah ah-THEHR
	boo-THEH-oh kohn TOO-boh
I'd like to go scuba diving.	**Me gustaría hacer buceo con escafandra.**
	meh goo-stah-REE-ah ah-THEHR
	boo-THEH-oh kohn ehs-kah-FAHN-
	drah
I have a NAUI / PADI certification.	**Tengo certificación NAUI / PADI.**
	TEHNG-goh thehr-tee-fee-kah-
	THYOHN EH-neh ah oo ee / peh ah
	deh ee

I need to rent gear.	**Necesito alquilar equipo.** *neh-theh-SEE-toh ahl-kee-LAHR* *eh-KEE-poh*
We'd like to see some shipwrecks if we can.	**Nos gustaría ver algunos naufragios si podemos.** *nohs goo-stah-REE-ah vehr ahl-GOO-nohs now-FRAH-hyohs see poh-DEH-mohs*
Are there any good reef dives?	**¿Hay buenos lugares para buceo en arrecifes?** *aye BWEH-nohs loo-GAH-rehs PAH-rah boo-THEH-oh ehn ah-rreh-THEE-fehs*
I'd like to see a lot of sea-life.	**Quiero ver mucha fauna marina.** *KYEH-roh vehr MOO-chah FAH-oo-nah mah-REE-nah*
Are the currents strong?	**¿Las corrientes son fuertes?** *lahs koh-RRYEHN-tehs sohn FWEHR-tehs*
How clear is the water?	**¿Qué grado de claridad tiene el agua?** *keh GRAH-doh deh klah-ree-DAHD TYEH-neh ehl AH-wah*
I want / don't want to go with a group	**Quiero / No quiero ir con un grupo.** *KYEH-roh / NOH kyeh-roh eer kohn oon GROO-poh*
Can we charter our own boat?	**¿Podemos fletar nuestra propia barca?** *poh-DEH-mohs fleh-TAHR NWEHS-trah PROH-pyah BAHR-kah*

SURFING

I'd like to go surfing.	**Me gustaría hacer surf.** *meh goo-stah-REE-ah ah-THEHR SOORF*
Are there any good beaches?	**¿Hay buenas playas?** *aye BWEH-nahs PLAH-yahs*
Can I rent a board?	**¿Puedo alquilar una tabla?** *PWEH-doh ahl-kee-LAHR OO-nah TAH-blah*
How are the currents?	**¿Cómo son las corrientes?** *KOH-moh sohn lahs koh-RRYEHN-tehs*
How high are the waves?	**¿Qué altura tienen las olas?** *keh ahl-TOO-rah TYEH-nehn lahs OH-lahs*
Is it usually crowded?	**¿Está generalmente abarrotada de gente?** *eh-STAH heh-neh-rahl-MEHN-teh ah-bah-rah-TAH-dah deh HEHN-teh*
Are there facilities on that beach?	**¿Hay instalaciones en esa playa?** *aye een-stah-lah-THYOH-nehs ehn EH-sah PLAH-yah*
Is there wind surfing there also?	**¿Hay también windsurfing?** *aye tahm-BYEHN weend-SOOR-feeng*

GOLFING

I'd like to reserve a tee-time, please.	**Quiero reservar hora de salida, por favor.**
	KYEH-roh rreh-sehr-VAHR OH-rah deh sah-LEE-dah pohr fah-VOHR
Do we need to be members to play?	**¿Tenemos que ser miembros para jugar?**
	teh-NEH-mohs keh sehr MYEHM-brohs PAH-rah hoo-GAHR
How many holes is your course?	**¿Cuántos hoyos tiene el campo?**
	KWAHN-tohs OH-yohs TYEH-neh ehl KAHM-poh
What is par for the course?	**¿Cuál es el par del campo?**
	kwahl ehs ehl pahr dehl KAHM-poh
I need to rent clubs.	**Necesito alquilar los palos.**
	neh-theh-SEE-toh ahl-kee-LAHR lohs PAH-lohs
I need to purchase a sleeve of balls.	**Necesito alquilar una funda de bolas.**
	neh-theh-SEE-toh ahl-kee-LAHR OO-nah FOON-dah deh BOH-lahs
I need a glove.	**Necesito un guante.**
	neh-theh-SEE-toh oon GWAHN-teh
I need a new hat.	**Necesito un sombrero nuevo.**
	neh-theh-SEE-toh oon sohm-BREH-roh NWEH-voh

Do you require soft spikes?	**¿Es necesario que lleve zapatos con clavos?**
	ehs neh-thee-SAH-ryoh keh YEH-veh thah-PAH-tohs kohn KLAH-vohs
Do you have carts?	**¿Tienen carritos?**
	TYEH-nehn kah-RREE-tohs
I'd like to hire a caddy.	**Quiero contratar a un caddie.**
	KYEH-roh kohn-trah-TAHR ah oon KAH-dee
Do you have a driving range?	**¿Tienen un campo de práctica?**
	TYEH-nehn oon KAHM-poh deh PRAHK-tee-kah
How much are the greens fees?	**¿Cuánto es la cuota para jugar?**
	KWAHN-toh ehs lah KWOH-tah PAH-rah hoo-GAHR
Can I book a lesson with the pro?	**¿Puedo reservar una lección con el profesional?**
	PWEH-doh rreh-sehr-VAHR OO-nah lehk-THYOHN kohn ehl proh-feh-syoh-NAHL
I need to have a club repaired.	**Necesito reparar un palo de golf.**
	neh-seh-SEE-toh rreh-pah-RAHR oon PAH-loh deh gohlf
Is the course dry?	**¿Está seco el campo?**
	ehs-TAH SEH-koh ehl KAHM-poh
Are there any wildlife hazards?	**¿Hay peligros de vida silvestre?**
	aye peh-LEEG-rohs deh VEE-dah seel-VEHS-treh
How many meters is the course?	**¿De cuántos metros es el campo?**
	deh KWAHN-tohs MEH-trohs ehs ehl KAHM-poh
Is it very hilly?	**¿Está lleno de colinas pequeñas?**
	ehs-TAH YEH-noh deh koh-LEE-nahs peh-KEH-nyahs

SPECTATOR SPORTS

Bullfighting

The bullfight is an inimitably Spanish experience—and inevitably controversial. Some people view it as nothing more than a cruel blood sport; others as a highly skilled art form that requires courage, showmanship, and gallantry.

The *corrida* (bullfight) season lasts from early spring until around mid-October. Fights are held in a *plaza de toros* (bullring). Tickets fall into three classifications, and prices are based on whether you're in the *sol* (sun), the cheapest seats; *sombra* (shade), the most expensive tickets; or the mid-range *sol y sombra* seats, in a mixture of sun and shade.

The initial parade—a highly colorful spectacle with all the bullfighters clad in their *trajes de luces,* or luminous suits—is followed by three stages: The first is the **tercio de capa (cape),** during which the matador studies and tests the bull with various passes. The second portion, the **tercio de varas (sticks),** begins with the lance-carrying *picadores* on horseback, who weaken the bull by jabbing him in the shoulder area. The *picadores* are followed by the agile *banderilleros,* who try to puncture the bull with pairs of colored darts.

The final **tercio de muleta** is all about the lone fighter and the bull. Instead of a cape, the matador uses a small red cloth known as a *muleta,* which requires a bull to lower its head. (The *picadores* and *banderilleros* have worked to achieve this.) Using the *muleta* as a lure, the matador wraps the bull around himself in various passes. The most dangerous is the *natural,* in which the matador holds the *muleta* in his left hand, the sword in his right. After a number of passes, the matador kills the bull.

The highest official at the ring may then award the matador an ear, or perhaps both ears, or ears and tail. Spectators cheer a superlative performance by waving white handkerchiefs, imploring the judge to award a prize. The bullfighter may be carried away as a hero, or, if he has displeased the crowd, he may be jeered and have seat cushions thrown at him. At a major fight, usually six bulls are killed by three matadors in one afternoon.

There are bullrings in practically every town and village in Spain. Madrid's **Las Ventas** bullring is the largest of all and features top matadors. Seville's **Maestranza** is Spain's second largest. Get tickets from the bullring itself or in travel agencies or store chains like the Corte Inglés. It is highly recommended that you buy tickets for your bullfight online, especially if your Spanish- speaking skill and vocabulary is still growing. Contact **Tauro Entrada** at **www.tauroentrada.com.**

Soccer

If you're in **Madrid,** head for the **Santiago Bernabeu** stadium (capacity 75,000), whose team **Real Madrid** is the most successful in Spain. Get tickets for matches from Estadio Santiago Bernabeu, Paseo de la Castellana 144. Even bigger is **Barcelona's Nou Camp** stadium (capacity 115,000) where the local team **Barça,** Madrid's great rivals, play regularly.

You can also purchase tickets online. Check out **www.madrid-football-tickets.com** for tickets to games in Madrid and **www.euro-football.co.uk** for tickets in Barcelona. Tickets will be securely delivered to your hotel or place of residence in Spain without a hassle.

ACTIVE SPORTS

Golf

The largest concentration is along Spain's Mediterranean coast, especially on the **Costa del Sol.** Two of Spain's top golf courses are the following: **Sotogrande,** Paseo del Parque s/n, San Roque, Cádiz (② **956-78-50-14;** fax 956-79-50-29), designed by the famed Robert Trent Jones, and **La Manga,** Los Belones, Cartagena (② **968-175-000,** ext. 1360; fax 968-175-058;

www.golf.lamangaclub.com). The latter, located right beside
the Mediterranean resort of La Manga, was rated Europe's leading golf resort in 2001.

Horseback Riding

You can rent a horse and gallop off into the sunset in many parts
of the country, from sophisticated city sports complexes like
those in Madrid and Barcelona, to Mediterranean mainland and
island resort areas. The website **www.riding-adventures.com**
gives details of inclusive riding holidays in two of Spain's favorite
areas: the Gredos Mountains in Castile and the Alpujarras
Mountains in Andalucía's Granada province. Further information is available on **www.spain-horse-riding.com.**

Skiing

The largest and best-run ski resorts and facilities can be found in
three main areas: **Solynieve,** high in the southerly **Sierra
Nevada;** the Pyrenean resort of **La Molina** (www.lamolina.com);
and the mighty mountains of the **Picos de Europa** in the north
offer many opportunities for great skiing. Check out
www.spain.info/TourSpain/Deportes/Esqui/?Language=en for a
comprehensive listing of all Spanish ski resorts.

Walking

If you're in Madrid, the nearby **Guadarrama** and **Gredos** mountains are excellent walking areas. In Cataluña, the **Pyrenees** are
a great favorite. In Andalucía, the **Alpujarra** range below the
Sierra Nevada is increasingly popular. In Northern Spain the
magnificent **Picos de Europa,** which extend from Asturias into
Cantabria, are a walker's heaven. There are plenty of companies
that organize walking and hiking tours of Spain's beautiful countryside. However, you might like to put together your own walking tours. Check out **www.walkingworld.com.**

Windsurfing
The best place for this exhilarating sport is the unspoiled white beaches of the **Costa de la Luz,** on Spain's southwest Atlantic coast. The top windsurf town is southernmost **Tarifa.**

BEST OUTFITTERS
Diving
Scuba-diving, meanwhile, is provided by **www.divingin spain.com,** based at Mijas-Costa in Southern Spain.

Fishing
Freshwater anglers should take a look at **www.ebrolake fishing.co.uk,** which arranges fishing trips in one of Spain's largest rivers, the Ebro near Zaragoza in Aragón province. (Needless to say, this area was a favorite with Hemingway.)

Hiking
For sports outfitters, try **www.idealspain.com** ("Sport in Spain" section). Valencia-based **walking** holidays are arranged by **Walks in Spain** (www.walksinspain.com). **New Experience Holidays** (www.newex.co.uk) provides routes and guides for off-beat **hikes** in the wild mountains of Teruel and Galicia.

Rock Climbing
If **rock climbing** is your thing you'll find details on www.talisman-activities.co.uk, which covers cliff-scaling in the Pyrenees, Picos de Europa, and Andalucían mountains.

Sailing
If you want to hire **sailboats** in the clear-watered Balearic Islands—probably the best area in Spain for this activity—check with the Dutch-run **Mona Lisa Charters Company** (www.monalisacharter.com). For details of Costa del Sol **yachting** vacations, check www.idealspain.com/dawnapproach.htm.

CHAPTER TEN

For coverage of movies and cultural events, see Chapter Seven,
"Culture."

CLUB HOPPING

Where can I find ____	**¿Dónde puedo encontrar ____** *DOHN-deh PWEH-doh ehn-kohn-TRAHR*
a good nightclub?	**una buena discoteca?** *OO-nah BWEH-nah dees-koh-TEH-kah*
a club with a live band?	**un bar con música en vivo?** *oon bahr kohn moo-see-kah ehn VEE-voh*
a reggae club?	**un local de reggae?** *oon loh-KAHL deh RREH-geh*
a hip hop club?	**un local o una discoteca de hip hop?** *oon loh-KAHL oh OO-nah dees-koh-TEH-kah deh HEEP-hohp*
a techno club?	**un discoteca de música techno?** *oon dees-koh-TEH-kah deh MOO-see-kah TEHK-noh*
a jazz club?	**un club de jazz?** *oon kloob deh jahs*
a country-western club?	**un club de música country?** *oon kloob deh MOO-see-kah KOHN-tree*
a singles bar?	**un bar para solteros?** *oon bahr PAH-rah sohl-TEH-rohs*
a club with Latin music?	**un local con música latina?** *oon loh-KAHL kohn MOO-see-kah lah-TEE-nah*

a gay / lesbian club?	**una discoteca de gays / lesbianas?**
	OO-nah dees-koh-TEH-kah deh gehs / lehs-bee-AH-nahs
a club where I can dance?	**una discoteca dónde pueda bailar?**
	OO-nah dees-koh-TEH-kah DOHN-deh PWEH-dah bah-ee-LAHR
the most popular club in town?	**el bar / la discoteca más marchoso -a?**
	ehl bahr / lah dees-koh-TEH-kah mahs marh-CHOH-soh -sah
a piano bar?	**un bar con piano?**
	oon barh kohn PYAH-noh
the most upscale club?	**el local / la discoteca más exclusivo -a?**
	ehl loh-KAHL / lah dees-koh-TEH-kah mahs ehks-kloo-SEE-voh -vah
What's the cover charge?	**¿Cuánto cuesta la entrada?**
	KWAHN-toh KWEH-stah lah ehn-TRAH-thah
Do they have a dress code?	**¿Tienen un código de vestimenta?**
	TYEH-nehn oon KOH-dee-goh deh vehs-tee-MEHN-tah
Is it expensive?	**¿Es caro?**
	ehs KAH-roh
What's the best time to go?	**¿Cuál es la mejor hora para ir?**
	kwahl ehs lah meh-HOHR OH-ra PAH-rah eer
What kind of music do they play there?	**¿Qué tipo de música tocan?**
	keh TEE-poh deh MOO-see-kah TOH-kahn

Is it smoking?	**¿Permiten fumar?**
	pehr-MEE-tehn foo-MAHR
Is it nonsmoking?	**¿Se prohíbe fumar?**
	seh proh-EE-beh foo-MAHR
I'm looking for _____	**Estoy buscando _____**
	ehs-TOY boos-KAHN-doh
a good cigar shop.	**una buena tienda de cigarros.**
	OO-nah BWEH-nah TYEHN-dah deh thee-GAH-rrohs
a pack of cigarettes.	**un paquete de cigarrillos.**
	oon pah-KEH-teh deh thee-gah-REE-yohs
I'd like _____, please.	**Déme _____, por favor.**
	kee-SYEH-rah _____ pohr fah-VOHR
a bottle of beer	**una botella de cerveza**
	OO-nah boh-TEH-yah deh thehr-VEH-thah
a beer on tap	**una cerveza de barril**
	OO-nah thehr-VEH-thah deh bah-RREEL

Do You Mind If I Smoke?

¿Tienes un cigarrillo?	Do you have a cigarette?
TYEH-nehs oon thee-gah-RREE-yoh	
¿Tienes fuego?	Do you have a light?
TYEH-nehs FWEH-goh	
¿Te puedo ofrecer fuego? /	May I offer you a light?
¿Te doy fuego?	
teh PWEH-doh ohfreh-thehr	
FWEH-goh / teh doy FWEH-goh	
Prohibido fumar.	Smoking not permitted.
proh-ee-BEE-doh foo-MAHR	

| a shot of tequila / vodka | **un chupito de tequila / vodka** |
| | *oon choo-PEE-toh deh teh-KEE-lah / VOHD-kah* |

For a full list of drinks, see p100.

Make it a double, please!	**¡Que sea doble, por favor!**
	keh SAY-ah DOH-bleh pohr fah-VOHR
With ice, please.	**Con hielo, por favor.**
	kohn YEH-loh pohr fah-VOHR
And one for the lady / the gentleman!	**¡Y uno para la dama / el caballero!**
	ee OO-noh PAH-rah lah DAH-mah / ehl kah-bah-YEH-roh
How much for a bottle / glass of beer?	**¿Cuánto cuesta una botella / un copa de cerveza?**
	KWAHN-toh KWEHS-tah pohr OO-nah boh-TEH-yah / oon KOH-pah deh thehr-VEH-thah
I'd like to buy a drink for that girl / guy over there.	**Quiero comprarle una copa a esa chica / ese chico de allí.**
	KYEH-roh kohm-PRAHR-leh OO-nah KOH-pah ah EH-sah CHEE-kah / EH-soh CHEE-koh deh ah-YEEH
A pack of cigarettes, please.	**Un paquete de cigarrillos, por favor.**
	oon pah-KEH-teh deh thee-gah-RREE-yohs pohr fah-VOHR
Do you have a lighter or matches?	**¿Tienes mechero o cerrilas?**
	TYEH-nehs meh-CHEH-roh oh theh-REE-yahs
Do you smoke?	**¿Fumas?**
	FOO-mahs
Would you like a cigarette?	**¿Quieres un cigarrillo?**
	KYEH-rehs oon thee-gah-RREE-yoh

May I run a tab?	**¿Puedo crear una cuenta?** *PWEH-doh kreh-AHR OO-nah* *KWEHN-tah*
What's the cover?	**¿Cuánto cuesta la entrada?** *KWAHN-toh KWEHS-tah lah* *ehn-TRAH-thah*

ACROSS A CROWDED ROOM

Excuse me; may I buy you a drink?	**Perdona, ¿te puedo invitar a una copa?** *pehr-DOH-nah teh PWEH-doh* *een-vee-TAHR ah OO-nah KOH-* *pah*
You look amazing.	**Se ve maravilloso -a.** *seh veh mah-rah-vee-YOH-soh -* *sah*
You look like the most interesting person in the room.	**Se te ve la persona más interesante.** *seh teh veh lah pehr-SOH-nah* *mahs een-teh-reh-SAHN-teh*
Would you like to dance?	**¿Quieres bailar?** *KYEH-rehs bah-ee-LAHR*

The Grammar of Intimacy

When you are drinking or dancing with another person of your age, especially when both of you are young, the informal mode of address, **tú**, is more common.

Do you like fast or slow music? | ¿Prefieres la música lenta o la rápida?
preh-FYEH-rehs la moo-thee-kah LEHN-tah oh RAH-pee-dah

Give me your hand. | **Dame la mano.**
DAH-meh lah MAH-noh

What would you like to drink? | ¿Qué quieres beber?
keh KYEH-rehs beh-BEHR

You're a great dancer. | **Bailas fenomenal.**
BAY-lahs feh-noh-mee-NAHL

I don't know that dance style. | **No conozco esa manera de bailar.**
noh koh-NOH-thkoh EH-sah mah-NEH-rah deh bay-LAHR

Do you like this song? | ¿Te gusta esta canción?
teh GOOS-tah EHS-tah kahn-THYOHN

You have nice eyes! | ¡Tienes unos ojos preciosos!
TYEH-nehs OO-nohs OH-hohs preh-THYOH-sohs

For a full list of features, see p132.

May I have your phone number? | ¿Me puedes dar tu número de teléfono?
meh PWEH-dehs dahr too NOO-meh-roh deh teh-LEH-foh-noh

GETTING CLOSER

You're very attractive. | **Te encuentro muy atractivo -a.**
teh ehn-KWEHN-troh MOO-ee ah-trahk-TEE-voh -vah

I like being with you. | **Me gusta estar contigo.**
meh GOOS-tah ehs-TAHR kohn-TEE-goh

I like you.	**Me gustas.** *meh GOOS-tahs*
I want to hold you.	**Quiero abrazarte.** *KYEH-roh ah-brah-THAHR-teh*
Kiss me.	**Bésame.** *BEH-sah-meh*
May I give you _____	**¿Te puedo dar _____** *teh PWEH-doh dahr*
a hug?	**un abrazo?** *oon ah-BRAH-thoh*
a kiss?	**un beso?** *oon BEH-soh*
Would you like _____	**¿Te gustaría _____** *teh goos-tah-REE-ah*
a back rub?	**un masaje de espalda?** *oon mah-SAH-heh deh* *ehs-PAHL-dah*
a massage?	**un masaje?** *oon mah-SAH-heh*

SEX

Would you like to come inside?	**¿Quieres entrar?** *KYEH-rehs ehn-TRAHR*
May I come inside?	**¿Puedo entrar?** *PWEH-doh ehn-TRAHR*
Let me help you out of that.	**Déjame que te ayude a quitarte eso.** *DEH-hah-meh keh teh ah-YOO-deh ah kee-TAHR-teh EH-soh*
Would you help me out of this?	**¿Me puedes ayudar a quitarme esto?** *meh PWEH-dehs ah-yoo-DAHR ah kee-TAHR-meh EHS-toh*
You smell so good.	**Hueles tan bien.** *WEH-lehs tahn byehn*

You're beautiful / handsome.	**Eres preciosa / guapísimo.** *EH-rehs preh-THYOH-sah / wah-PEE-see-moh*
May I?	**¿Me dejas?** *me DEH-hahs*
OK?	**¿Está bien?** *ehs-TAH byehn*
Like this?	**¿Así?** *ah-SEE*
How?	**¿Cómo?** *KOH-moh*

HOLD ON A SECOND

Please don't do that.	**Por favor no hagas eso.** *pohr fah-VOHR noh AH-gahs EH-soh*
Stop, please.	**Para, por favor.** *PAH-rah pohr fah-VOHR*
Do you want me to stop?	**¿Quieres que pare?** *KYEH-rehs keh PAH-reh*
Let's just be friends.	**Seamos sólo amigos.** *seh-AH-mohs SOH-loh ah-MEE-gohs*
Do you have a condom?	**¿Tienes un condón?** *TYEH-nehs oon kohn-DOHN*
Are you on birth control?	**¿Utilizas métodos anticonceptivos?** *oo-tee-LEE-thahs MEH-toh-dohs ahn-tee-kohn-thehp-TEE-vohs*
I have a condom.	**Tengo un condón.** *TEHNG-goh oon kohn-DOHN*
Do you have anything you should tell me first?	**¿Tienes que decirme algo primero?** *TYEH-nehs keh deh-THEER-meh AHL-goh pree-MEH-roh*

Don't Mix the Message

Te deseo. *teh deh-SEH-oh*	I desire you. This is pretty much a physical expression.
Te quiero. *teh KYEH-roh*	While this literally means "I want you," in Spanish, it means "I love you" in the romantic and erotic sense but it is also used by parents, when they tell their children that they love them.
Te amo. *teh AH-moh*	This is used very seriously, only in romantic love. You'd better not be saying this without a ring in your pocket.

BACK TO IT

That's it.	**Así.** *ah-SEE*
That's not it.	**Así no.** *ah-SEE noh*
Here.	**Aquí.** *ah-KEE*
There.	**Ahí.** *ah-EE*
More.	**Más.** *mahs*
Harder	**Más duro.** *mahs DOO-roh*
Faster	**Más rápido.** *mahs RRAH-pee-doh*
Deeper	**Más profundo.** *mahs proh-FOON-doh*
Slower.	**Más lento.** *mahs LEHN-toh*
Easier.	**Más suave.** *mahs SWAH-veh*

COOLDOWN

You're great.	**Eres tremendo -a.**
	EH-rehs treh-MEHN-doh -dah
That was great.	**Eso estuvo fabuloso.**
	EH-soh ehs-TOO-voh fah-boo-LOH-soh
Would you like ____	**¿Quieres ____**
	KYEH-rehs
a drink?	**un trago?**
	oon TRAH-goh
a snack?	**algo de comer?**
	AHL-goh deh koh-MEHR
a shower?	**ducharte?**
	doo-CHAHR-teh
May I stay here?	**¿Me puedo quedar aquí?**
	meh PWEH-doh keh-DAHR ah-KEE
Would you like to stay here?	**¿Te gustaría quedarte aquí?**
	teh goos-tah-REE-ah keh-DAHR-teh ah-KEE
I'm sorry. I have to go.	**Lo siento. Me tengo que ir.**
	loh SYEHN-toh meh TEHN-goh keh eer
Where are you going?	**¿Adónde vas?**
	ah-DOHN-deh vahs
I have to work early.	**Tengo que trabajar temprano.**
	TEHN-goh keh trah-bah-HAHR tehm-PRAH-noh
I'm flying home in the morning.	**Mañana regreso en un vuelo a casa.**
	mah-NYAH-nah rreh-GREH-soh ehn oon VWEH-loh ah KAH-sah
I have an early flight.	**Tengo un vuelo temprano.**
	TEHNG-goh oon VWEH-loh tehm-PRAH-noh

I think this was a mistake.	**Creo que esto ha sido un error.** *KREH-oh keh EHS-toh ah SEE-doh oon eh-RROHR*
Will you make me breakfast too?	**¿Puedes hacerme a mí también el desayuno?** *PWEH-dehs ah-THEHR-meh ah mee tahm-BYEHN ehl deh-sah-YOH-noh*
Stay. I'll make you breakfast.	**Quédate. Te preparo el desayuno.** *KEH-dah-teh preh-PAH-roh ehl deh-sah-YOO-noh*

IN THE CASINO

How much is this table?	**¿Cuánto cuesta esta mesa?** *KWAHN-toh KWEHS-tah EHS-tah MEH-sah*
Deal me in.	**Repártame las cartas.** *reh-PAHR-tah-meh lahs KAHR-tahs*
Put it on red!	**¡Ponlo en rojo!** *POHN-loh ehn ROH-hoh*
Put it on black!	**¡Ponlo en negro!** *POHN-loh ehn NEH-groh*
Let it ride!	**¡Déjalo ir!** *DEH-hah-loh eer*
21!	**¡21!** *veh-een-TYOO-noh*
Snake-eyes!	**¡Dos unos!** *dohs OO-nohs*
Seven.	**Siete.** *SYEH-teh*

For a full list of numbers, see p7.

Damn, eleven.	**Once, maldita sea.** *OHN-seh mahl-DEE-tah SEH-ah*
I'll pass.	**Paso / Me reservo.** *PAH-soh / meh reh-SEHR-voh*
Hit me!	**¡Dame!** *DAH-meh*
Split.	**Rompa.** *RROHM-pah*
Are the drinks complimentary?	**¿Son gratis las copas?** *sohn GRAH-tees lahs KOH-pahs*
May I bill it to my room?	**¿Me lo puede añadir a la factura de mi habitación?** *meh lo PWEH-deh ahn-YAH-deer ah lah fahk-TOO-rah deh mee ah-bee-tah-THYOHN*
I'd like to cash out.	**Quiero llevarme el dinero.** *KYEH-roh yeh-VAHR-meh ehl dee-NEH-roh*
I'll hold.	**Me quedo.** *meh KEH-doh*
I'll see your bet / I call.	**Igualo la apuesta.** *ee-GWAH-loh lah ah-PWEHS-tah*
Full house!	**¡Full!** *fool*
Royal flush.	**Escalera real.** *ehs-kah-LEH-rah reh-AHL*
Straight.	**Escalera.** *ehs-kah-LEH-rah*

NIGHTLIFE

SPANISH MUSIC & DANCE

The word that probably comes to mind when someone mentions Spanish music is **flamenco.** Its *cante jondo,* a melancholy lament sung by Andalusian gypsies, has its origins in North Africa (the legendary Al-Andalus, whose 8th century invaders gave the province its name). Accompanied by the guitar and danced by exotically clad dancers, flamenco is riveting—an almost painfully moving experience for aficionados. **Seville** and **Madrid** are where it's seen at its best today, in a variety of *tablaos* and nightspots. A passionate *cantaor,* whose untimely death at 42 transformed him into a cult, was **El Camarón.** One of today's leading female singers is **La Macanita.**

When searching for flamenco in Seville, you might start out with reservations at **Tablao Los Gallos,** Plaza de Santa Cruz 11 (© **95-421-69-81**), or its competitor **El Arenal,** Calle Rodó 7 (© **95-421-64-92**). Two great finds for flamenco in Madrid include **Café de Chinitas,** Torija 7 (© **91-547-15-02**), and **Las Tapas,** Plaza de España 9 (© **91-542-05-20**). In Barcelona, be sure to try out **Los Tarantos,** Placa Reial 17 (© **93-318-30-67**), the oldest flamenco club in Barcelona. Remember that most clubs have a cover charge and more often than not do not serve dinner with your show.

TOP SUMMER MUSIC FESTIVALS

Veranos en la Villa   Program of folkloric dancing, pop and classical music, zarzuelas, and flamenco held at various venues in **Madrid.** The Tourist Office will provide details closer to the event (www.munimadrid.es). *June/July.*

International Music and Dance Festival, Granada International artists perform at the Alhambra and other venues. This is a major event on the European cultural calendar. Book well ahead (© **95-822-18-44;** www.granadafestival.org). *Last week in June through the first week in July.*

Jazz Festivals   San Sebastián (© 94 344 00-34; www.jazzaldia.com) and **Vitoria-Gasteiz** in Alava (www.jazzvitoria.com) are the two biggest jazz events in northern Spain. *July.* **Santander Music and Dance Festival**   One of the most important musical events in Spain. Held in Palacio de Festivales (© 94-221-05-08; www.festivalsantander.com). *August.*

RECOMMENDED MOVIES, MUSIC CDS & BOOKS

One notable Spanish **director** of the 1950s was **J. A. Bardem,** with his neorealistic/satirical works such as *Death of a Cyclist* (1955). **Luis Buñuel** dominated the scene up to the '70s—even when filming in Mexico or France—with his striking *Los Olvidados, Viridiana,* and *The Discreet Charm of the Bourgeoisie.* Stark '60s statements were *Furtivos* and *Pascual Duarte,* while the *Spirit of the Beehive* and *El Sol del Membrillo* by the reflective and unprolific **Victor Erice** have assumed the rank of cult classics. With his simple, dance-driven stories, **Carlos Saura** produced some of the most impressive movies of the '80s, including his unique modern version of *Carmen.*

More recent movies by young award-winning directors have sensitively covered social problems such as unemployment *(Lunes al Sol)* and domestic abuse *(Te Doy Mis Ojos).* Chilean born **Alejandro Almenabar**'s stylishly surreal horror flicks, *Open Your Eyes* and *The Others,* set new levels of imaginative filming (the first was remade as *Tangerine Sky* with Tom Cruise and the latter—filmed in Spain but shot in English—with Nicole Kidman). More lurid, though stylish, are the works of **Alex de la Iglesia,** whose *La Comunidad* is a minor classic of black humor.

The best-known, best-loved Spanish director today is the flamboyant **Pedro Almódovar,** whose stylish and anarchically kitsch post-*movida* movies included the hilarious *Women on the Verge of a Nervous Breakdown.* He won an Oscar for best foreign language film with *All About My Mother* in 2000; and two of his earlier actors, Antonio Banderas and Penelope Cruz, have now become international stars.

For a cross section of all that **Spanish music** has to offer, look for recordings by the following: **El Camarón** *(cante jondo);* **Ketama** "rock-flamenco"; **Joan Manuel Serrat** (folk *cantautor* or singer-composer in both Castilian and Catalan); **Joaquin Sabina** (earthy *baladist;* look for his "Dímelo en la Calle"); **Alicia de Larrocha** (classical piano pieces); **Andrés Segovia** (classical guitar); and **Nicanor Zabaleta** (harp).

Among the top post–Civil War **novelists** are **Carmen Laforet**, whose *Nada* (1944) describes a young girl's life in a muted and austere Barcelona; stream-of-consciousness stylist **Rafael Sánchez Ferlosio,** whose 1955 prize-winner *El Jarama* (or "The One Day of the Week") deals—entirely in dialogue form—with a Sunday picnic among middle-class Madrileños that ends in tragedy; and the Joyce-influenced **Juan Goytisolo,** whose semi-biographical *Señas de Identidad* (1966) recounts its hero's attempts to reconcile life in his homeland with life as an exile in Paris. One of today's most popular and readable writers is adventure storyteller **Arturo Pérez-Reverte,** whose books have been translated into various languages. His *Capitán Alatriste* is currently being made into a new Spanish film with Viggo Mortensen in the title role.

Key novelists who deal intriguingly with more contemporary situations are **Javier Marias, Eduardo Mendoza,** and **Juan Marsé.** The most impressive female writer is probably **Almudena Grandes,** whose *Los Aires Difíciles* deals with troubled characters who have escaped the Spanish capital to find a new life near Cádiz on the south coast.

CLASSICAL COMPOSERS

Spain's top three classical composers are **Isaac Albeñiz, Manuel de Falla,** and **Enrique Granados.**

Albeñiz (1860–1909), a Mozart-style prodigy who was playing piano in concerts at the age of 4 and stowed away on a ship to South America at 10, is renowned for his evocative *Iberia* suite comprising 12 virtuoso pieces. **De Falla** (1876–1946) is best remembered for the *Sombrero de Tres Picos* ("Three Cornered Hat") ballet-opera and his poetic piano piece *Noches en Los Jardines de España* ("Nights in the Gardens of Spain"). **Granados** (1867–1916) is famous for his evocative *Danzas Españolas* and *Goyescas*. His death was tragic and unexpected: He drowned in the English Channel during World War I when a German submarine torpedoed the ship he was sailing in, upon returning from a concert in London.

Other Spanish "nationalist" composers who also produced enduring works are **Joaquín Turina** (1882–1949), who wrote *Oración del Torero* and *Danzas Fantasticas,* and **Joaquín Rodrigo** (1901–1999), known for the world-famous *Concierto de Aranjuez.* **Federic Mompou** (1893–1987), more impressionist in style, produced fragile haunting works influenced by Chopin and Satie.

GETTING TICKETS

Your hotel receptionist or concierge will usually be able to book your tickets; make your request at the same time you reserve your room. Tickets are also now widely sold through savings banks. If you're in **Madrid,** the most comprehensive ticket agency is **Localidades Galicia,** Plaza del Carmen 1 (© **91-531-27-32**). Other agencies include **Casa de Catalunya** (© **91-538-33-00**) and **Corte Inglés** (© **91-432-93-00;** www.elcorteingles.es), both of which have satellite offices throughout Madrid.

In **Barcelona,** you can buy tickets from the desk inside the **Boulevard Rosa** shopping center (Passeig de Gracia 53; Mon–Sat 10am–8:30pm). For pop concert reservations try the **Taquilles Gran/Vía Aribau** booth near the University (Mon–Sat 10am–1pm and 4:30–7:30pm).

CHAPTER ELEVEN

HEALTH & SAFETY

This chapter covers the terms you'll need to maintain your health and safety—including the most useful phrases for the pharmacy, the doctor's office, and the police station.

AT THE PHARMACY

Please fill this prescription.	**Por favor, dispense esta receta.** *pohr fah-VOHR dee-SPEHN-seh EHS-tah rreh-THEH-tah*
Do you have something for ____	**¿Tiene algo para ____** *TYEH-neh AHL-goh PAH-rah*
a cold?	**un catarro?** *oon kah-TAH-rroh*
a cough?	**la tos?** *lah TOHS*
I need something ____	**Necesito algo para ____** *neh-theh-SEE-toh AHL-goh PAH-rah*
to help me sleep.	**ayudarme a dormir.** *ah-yoo-DAHR-meh ah dohr-MEER*
to help me relax.	**relajarme.** *rreh-lah-HAHR-meh*
I want to buy ____	**Quiero comprar ____** *KYEH-roh kohm-PRAHR*
condoms.	**condones.** *kohn-DOH-nehs*
an antihistamine.	**un antihistamínico.** *oon ahn-tee-ees-tah-MEE-nee-koh*
antibiotic cream.	**una crema antibiótica.** *OO-nah KREH-mah ahn-tee-BYOH-tee-koh*

aspirin.	**aspirina.**
	ahs-pee-REE-nah
non-aspirin pain reliever.	**un analgésico sin aspirina.**
	oon ah-nahl-HEH-see-koh
	seen ahs-pee-REE-nah
medicine with codeine.	**medicina con codeína.**
	meh-dee-SEE-nah kohn koh-
	deh-EE-nah
insect repellant.	**repelente contra insectos.**
	rreh-peh-LEHN-teh KOHN-
	trah een-SEHK-tohs
I need something for ___	**Necesito algo para ___.**
	neh-theh-SEE-toh AHL-goh
	PAH-rah
corns.	**los callos.**
	lohs KAH-yohs
congestion.	**la congestión nasal.**
	lah kohn-hehs-TYOHN nay-
	SAHL
warts.	**las verrugas.**
	lahs veh-RROO-gahs
constipation.	**el estreñimiento.**
	ehl ehs-treh-nyee-MYEHN-toh
diarrhea.	**la diarrea.**
	lah dyah-RREH-ah
indigestion.	**la indigestión.**
	lah een-dee-hehs-TYOHN
nausea.	**la náusea.**
	lah NOW-seh-ah
motion sickness / seasickness.	**el mareo.**
	ehl mah-REH-oh
acne.	**el acné.**
	ehl ahk-NEH

AT THE DOCTOR'S OFFICE

I would like to see ____	**Necesito ver a ____.**
	neh-theh-SEE-toh vehr ah
a doctor.	**un doctor.**
	oon dohk-TOHR
a chiropractor.	**un quiropráctico.**
	oon kee-roh-PRAHK-tee-koh
a gynecologist.	**un ginecólogo.**
	oon hee-neh-KOH-loh-goh
an eye / ears / nose / throat specialist.	**un otorrinolaringólogo.**
	oon oh-toh-rree-noh-lah-reen-GOH-loh-goh
a dentist.	**un dentista.**
	oon dehn-TEES-tah
an optometrist.	**un oculista.**
	oon oh-kuh-LEES-tah
Do I need an appointment?	**¿Necesito cita?**
	neh-theh-SEE-toh THEE-tah
I have an emergency.	**Necesito atención médica urgente.**
	neh-theh-SEE-toh ah-then-THYOHN MEH-dee-kah oor-HEHN-teh
I need an emergency prescription refill.	**Necesito con urgencia que me dispensen de nuevo esta receta.**
	neh-theh-SEE-toh kohn oor-HEHN-thyah keh meh dee-SPEHN-sehn deh noo-EH-voh EH-stah reh-THEH-tah
Please call a doctor.	**Por favor llame a un médico.**
	pohr fah-VOHR YAH-meh ah oon MEH-dee-koh
I need an ambulance.	**Necesito una ambulancia.**
	neh-theh-SEE-toh OO-nah ahm-boo-LAHN-syah

SYMPTOMS

For a full list of body parts, see p228.

My ____ hurts.	**Me duele el / la / los / las ____.**
	meh DWEH-leh ehl / lah / lohs / lahs
My ____ is stiff.	**Siento entumecimiento en el / la ____.**
	see-EHN-toh ehn-too-meh-thee-MYEHN-toh ehn ehl / lah
I think I'm having a heart attack.	**Creo que estoy teniendo un ataque al corazón.**
	KREH-oh keh ehs-TOY teh-NYEHN-doh oon ah-TAH-keh ahl koh-rah-THOHN
I can't move.	**No me puedo mover.**
	noh meh PWEH-doh moh-VEHR
I fell.	**Me caí.**
	meh kah-EE
I can't get up.	**No me puedo levantar.**
	noh meh PWEH-doh leh-vahn-TAHR
I fainted.	**Me desmayé.**
	meh dehs-mah-YEH
I have a cut on my ____.	**Tengo un corte en el / la / los / las ____.**
	TEHN-goh oon KOHR-teh ehn ehl / lah / lohs / lahs
I have a headache.	**Tengo dolor de cabeza.**
	TEHN-goh doh-LOHR deh kah-BEH-thah
My vision is blurry	**Tengo visión borrosa.**
	TEHN-goh vee-SYOHN boh-RROH-sah
I feel dizzy.	**Me siento mareado -a.**
	meh SYEHN-toh mah-reh-AH-doh -dah

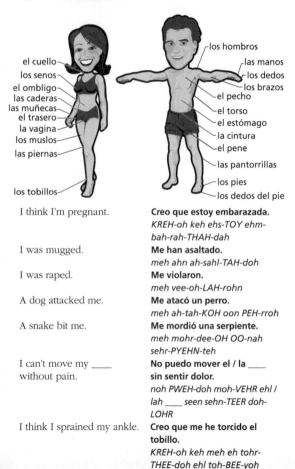

el cuello
los senos
el ombligo
las caderas
las muñecas
el trasero
la vagina
los muslos
las piernas
los tobillos

los hombros
las manos
los dedos
los brazos
el pecho
el torso
el estómago
la cintura
el pene
las pantorrillas
los pies
los dedos del pie

I think I'm pregnant.	**Creo que estoy embarazada.** *KREH-oh keh ehs-TOY ehm-bah-rah-THAH-dah*
I was mugged.	**Me han asaltado.** *meh ahn ah-sahl-TAH-doh*
I was raped.	**Me violaron.** *meh vee-oh-LAH-rohn*
A dog attacked me.	**Me atacó un perro.** *meh ah-tah-KOH oon PEH-rroh*
A snake bit me.	**Me mordió una serpiente.** *meh mohr-dee-OH OO-nah sehr-PYEHN-teh*
I can't move my ____ without pain.	**No puedo mover el / la ____ sin sentir dolor.** *noh PWEH-doh moh-VEHR ehl / lah ____ seen sehn-TEER doh-LOHR*
I think I sprained my ankle.	**Creo que me he torcido el tobillo.** *KREH-oh keh meh eh tohr-THEE-doh ehl toh-BEE-yoh*

MEDICATIONS

I need morning-after pills.	**Necesito píldoras del día siguiente / poscoitales.** *neh-theh-SEE-toh PEEL-doh-rahs dehl DEE-ah see-GYEHN-teh / pohs-kohee-TAH-lehs*
I need birth control pills.	**Necesito píldoras anticonceptivas.** *neh-theh-SEE-toh PEEL-doh-rahs ahn-tee-kohn-thehp-TEE-vahs*
I lost my eyeglasses and need new ones.	**He perdido mis gafas y necesito unas nuevas.** *eh pehr-DEE-do mees GAH-fahs ee neh-theh-SEE-toh OO-nahs NWEH-vahs*
I need new contact lenses.	**Necesito lentillas nuevas.** *neh-theh-SEE-toh lehn-TEE-yahs NWEH-vahs*
I need erectile dysfunction pills.	**Necesito píldoras para la disfunción eréctil.** *neh-theh-SEE-toh PEEL-doh-rahs PAH-rah lah dees-foon-THYOHN eh-REHK-teel*
It's cold in here!	**¡Hace frío aquí!** *AH-theh FREE-oh ah-KEE*
I am allergic to ____	**Soy alérgico a ____** *soy ah-LEHR-hee-koh ah*
penicillin.	**la penicilina.** *lah peh-nee-thee-LEE-nah*
antibiotics.	**los antibióticos.** *lohs ahn-tee-BYOH-tee-kohs*
sulfa drugs.	**las sulfamidas.** *lahs sool-fah-MEE-dahs*
steroids.	**los esteroides.** *lohs ehs-teh-ROH-EE-dehs*
I have asthma.	**Tengo asma.** *TEHNG-goh AHS-mah*

HEALTH & SAFETY

DENTAL PROBLEMS

I have a toothache.	**Tengo dolor de muelas.**
	TEHNG-goh doh-LOHR deh MWEH-lahs
I chipped a tooth.	**Se me partió un diente.**
	seh meh pahr-tee-OH oon DYEHN-teh
My bridge came loose.	**Se me ha desrendido un puente.**
	seh meh hah dehs-prehn-DEE-doh oon PWEHN-teh
I lost a crown.	**Perdí una corona.**
	pehr-DEE OO-nah koh-ROH-nah
I lost a denture plate.	**Se me ha perdido la dentadura postiza.**
	seh meh hah pehr-DEE-doh lah dehn-tah-DOO-rah pohs-TEE-thah

AT THE POLICE STATION

I'm sorry, did I do something wrong	**Lo siento, ¿hice algo mal?**
	loh SYEHN-toh EE-theh AHL-goh mahl
I am _____	**Soy _____**
	soy
American.	**estadounidense.**
	eh-STAH-doh-oo-nee-dehn-seh
British.	**británico.**
	bree-TAH-nee-koh
Canadian.	**canadiense.**
	kah-nah-DYEHN-seh
Irish.	**irlandés.**
	eer-lahn-DEHS
Australian.	**australiano.**
	ows-trah-LYAH-noh
New Zealandese.	**neozelandés.**
	neh-oh-theh-lahn-DEHS

Listen Up: Police Lingo

Su carné de conducir, matrículación y seguro, por favor. *soo KAHR-neh deh kohn-doo-THEER mah-tree-koo-lah-THYON ee seh-GOO-roh pohr fah-VOHR*	Your license, registration, and insurance, please.
La multa es de ___ euros y me la puede pagar directamente a mí. *lah MOOL-tah ehs deh ___ EHOO-rohs ee meh lah PWEH-deh pah-GAHR dee-REHK-tah-mehn-teh ah MEE*	The fine is $10. You can pay me directly.
Su pasaporte, por favor. *soo pah-sah-POHR-teh pohr fah-VOHR*	Your passport, please.
¿A dónde va? *ah DOHN-deh vah*	Where are you going?
¿Por qué tiene tanta prisa? *pohr keh TYEH-neh TAHN-tah PREE-sah*	Why are you in such a hurry?

The car is a rental.	**El coche es alquilado.** *ehl KOH-cheh ehs ahl-kee-LAH-doh*
Do I pay the fine to you?	**¿Le pago la multa a usted?** *leh PAH-goh lah MOOL-tah ah oos-TEHD*
Do I have to go to court?	**¿Tengo que ir al juzgado?** *TEHN-goh keh eer ahl hooth-GAH-doh*

When?	**¿Cuándo?**
	KWAHN-doh
I'm sorry, I speak little Spanish.	**Lo siento, hablo muy poco español.**
	loh SYEHN-toh AH-bloh mwee POH-koh ehs-pah-NYOHL
I need an interpreter.	**Necesito un intérprete.**
	neh-theh-SEE-toh oon een-TEHR-preh-teh
I'm sorry, I don't understand the ticket.	**Lo siento, no entiendo la multa.**
	loh SYEHN-toh noh ehn-TYEHN-doh lah MOOL-tah
May I call my embassy?	**¿Puedo llamar a mi embajada?**
	PWEH-doh yah-MAHR ah mee ehm-bah-HA-dah
I was robbed.	**He sido víctima de un robo.**
	eh SEE-doh VEEK-tee-mah deh oon ROH-boh
I was mugged.	**Me han asaltado.**
	meh ahn ah-sahl-TAH-doh
I was raped	**Me violaron.**
	meh vee-oh-LAH-rohn
Do I need to make a report?	**¿Tengo que poner una denuncia en comisaría?**
	TEHNG-goh keh poh-NEHR OO-nah deh-NOON-thyah en koh-mee-sah-REE-ah
Somebody broke into my room.	**Alguien entró en mi habitación.**
	AHLG-yehn ehn-TROH ehn mee ah-bee-tah-THYOHN
Someone stole my purse / wallet.	**Alguien me robó el bolso / la cartera.**
	AHLG-yehn meh rroh-BOH ehl BOHL-soh / lah kahr-TEH-rah

STAYING HEALTHY

Spain should not pose any major health hazards. The rich cuisine—garlic, olive oil, and wine—may give some travelers mild diarrhea, so take along some appropriate medicine, and moderate your eating habits, if necessary. Even though the water is generally safe, cautious travelers will want to stick to bottled water. Fish and shellfish from the polluted Mediterranean should only be eaten cooked (even though today sea purification methods have improved considerably).

Medications Pack prescription medications in your carry-on luggage. Carry written prescriptions in generic, rather than brand-name, form. Also bring along copies of your prescriptions in case you lose your pills or run out.

Pharmacies are open during normal shopping hours (usually 9:30am–2pm and 5:30–8pm.) and each posts a list of pharmacies that are open late or 24 hours a day. For details check the local newspaper or dial ✆ **010.**

For holistic medicine enthusiasts there's a wide choice of *herbolarios* (herbal clinics) providing natural health products. Two top *herbolarios* in Madrid and Barcelona include: **Salud Madrid,** Calle José Ortega y Gasset 77 (✆ **91-309-53-90**), and **Herbolari Ferran,** Placa Reial 18 (✆ **93-304-20-05**).

Sickness Away from Home Spanish medical facilities are among the best in the world. If a medical emergency arises, your hotel staff can usually put you in touch with a reliable doctor.

For an English-speaking **doctor** or **dentist,** contact the U.S. Embassy in Madrid or the U.S. Consulate in Barcelona. Also consult **Unidad Médica Anglo-Americana,** an English speaking medical center in the heart of Madrid, Conde de Arandá 1 Madrid (✆ **91-435-18-23** with a 24-hour answering service;

www.unidadmedica.com; Mon–Fri 9am–8pm and Sat
10am–1pm). It is also possible to join the **International
Association for Medical Assistance to Travelers (IAMAT)**
(✆ **716/754-4883** or 416/652/0137), which provides free
information on healthy travel and listings of English-speaking
doctors around the world.

DRIVING SAFETY

Driving through dramatic landscapes can be a joy, but in
congested major cities it can be a potentially dangerous night-
mare. It always feels like rush hour, though theoretically peak
travel time is from 8 to 10am, 1 to 2pm, and 4 to 6pm, Monday
through Saturday. Parking is next to impossible except in
expensive garages. Save your car rentals, therefore, for excur-
sions. If you drive from one big city to another, ask at your hotel
for the nearest garage or parking space, and leave your car
there until you're ready to leave.

Speed limits are 50km per hour in towns, 90kmph on
most highways, and 120kmph on major highways. Be careful:
Spanish drivers tend to be very impatient, and the number of
accidents is high, especially on weekends, during *puentes,* and
in August (avoid roads during these periods if you can). To rent
a car you need a passport and valid license, plus a valid credit
card or prepaid voucher. Though it's not essential, an international license is available from offices of the American
Automobile Association (AAA).

Because of increasing crime in major cities and in coastal
tourist areas, leave valuables in your hotel safe when you go
out. Hold on to your passport, however, as the police often
stop foreigners for identification checks. Keep valuables in
front pockets and carry only enough cash for the day's needs.
Keep a separate record of your passport number, traveler's
check numbers, and credit card numbers.

Purse snatching is common. Criminals often work in pairs, grabbing purses from pedestrians, cyclists, and even from cars. In one popular scam, criminals smear the back of the victim's clothing with mustard, ice cream, or the like. An accomplice then pretends to help clean up the mess, all the while picking the victim's pockets. If your car is standing still, a thief may open the door or break a window, so keep the doors locked while driving, and store valuables in the trunk.

TRAVEL INSURANCE

Check your existing insurance policies before you buy travel insurance to cover trip cancellation, lost luggage, medical expenses, or rental car accidents; you're likely to have partial or complete coverage.

Popular companies include: **Access America** (✆ **800/284-8300;** www.accessamerica.com); **Travel Assistance International** (✆ **800/821-2828;** www.travelassistance.com); **Travel Guard International** (✆ **800/826-4919;** www.travelguard.com); **Travel Insured International** (✆ **800/243-3174;** www.travelinsured.com); and **Travelex Insurance Services** (✆ **888/457-4602;** www.travelex-insurance.com).

Trip Cancellation Insurance   These come in three forms: first, when a prepaid tour gets cancelled, and there's no refund; second, when you or a family member gets sick or dies, and you can't travel (this may not cover a pre-existing condition); and third, when bad weather makes travel impossible. Some insurers cover events such as jury duty, local natural disasters, even job loss. A few provide for cancellations due to terrorist activities. Check the fine print before signing on, and only buy trip cancellation insurance from a reputable travel insurance agency.

Medical Insurance   Most health insurance policies cover you if you get sick away from home—but check, particularly if you're insured by an HMO. Most out-of-country hospitals make you pay your bills up front and send you a refund after you've returned home and filed the necessary paperwork. Members of **Blue Cross/Blue Shield** can now use their cards at select hospitals in most major cities worldwide. Call © **800/810-BLUE** or log on to www.bluecares.com for a list of hospitals. Some credit cards (American Express and certain gold and platinum Visas and MasterCards, for example) offer automatic flight insurance against death or dismemberment. Consult your card company for details. **MEDEX International** (© **888/MEDEX-00** or 410/453-6300; www.medexassist.com) specializes in a wide range of travel insurance for individuals. You might also check out **Travel Assistance International** (© **800/821-2828;** www.travelassistance.com). Also consider buying travel insurance for emergency medical evacuation. Otherwise, if you have to buy a one-way, same-day ticket home and forfeit your non-refundable round-trip ticket, you could lose a chunk of money.

Lost Luggage Insurance   Take any valuables or irreplaceable items with you in your carry-on luggage. If you file a lost luggage claim, be prepared to answer detailed questions about the baggage contents, and file a claim immediately, as most airlines enforce a 21-day deadline. Make a list estimating the value of items insured before you leave home to make sure you're properly compensated if luggage is lost. Once you've filed a complaint, follow up, as there are no laws governing the length of time it takes for a carrier to reimburse you. If you arrive at a destination without your bags, ask the airline to forward them to your hotel or next destination. If your bag is delayed or lost, the airline may reimburse you for reasonable expenses, such as a toothbrush or a set of clothes, but they're not legally obliged to.

CHAPTER TWELVE

CULTURE GUIDE

ART HISTORY BASICS

Spain's art ranges from Romanesque frescoes to Velázquez's royal portraits to Picasso's *Guernica*. Its architecture runs from Moorish palaces to Gothic cathedrals, Gaudí's Art Nouveau creations, and Frank Gehry's metallic flower in the Basque region, the Bilbao Guggenheim Museum. This brief overview should help you make sense of it all. Many examples of the styles and artists below can be found at the Madrid's glorious and extensive **Museo del Prado** (http://museoprado.mcu.es).

Romanesque (10th–13th c.)

From the 8th century, most of Spain was under **Moorish** rule. The Muslims took the Koranic injunction against graven images so seriously that they produced no art in the Western traditional sense. Instead, you will find remarkably intricate **geometric designs** and swooping, exaggerated letters of **Kufic inscriptions** played out in woodcarving, painted tiles, and plasterwork on Moorish palaces. These decorations are of the highest aesthetic order (see "Architecture 101" later in this chapter).

Starting with the late-10th-century Reconquest, **Christian** Spaniards began producing art in the eastern and northern provinces. **Painting** and **mosaics** in Catalonia show the Byzantine influence of northern Italy. **Sculptures** along the northerly pilgrimage route to Santiago de Compostela are related to French models, though they are often more symbolic (and primitive looking) than realistic. **Significant examples include:**

- A Mozarab (a Christian living under Moorish rule), the monk Beatus de Liébana illuminated the 10th-century **Códex del Beatus** or "Commentary on the Apocalypse" manuscript in an influential hybrid style, which includes many Arabic devices. Its pages are now dispersed internationally; the best remaining chunk is in **Gerona's (Girona's) Catedral.**

- Most of **Catalonia**'s great **Romanesque** paintings were detached from their village churches in the early 20th century and are now housed in Barcelona's **Museu Nacional d'Art de Catalunya** on Montjuich hill at the western end of the city.

- Over in north-westerly **Galicia,** you'll find the most imposing example of Romanesque sculpture in the 12th-century Pórtico de la Gloria in **Santiago de Compostela's Cathedral.**

Gothic (13th–16th c.)

The influence of Catalonia and France continued to dominate in the **Gothic** era—though, in painting especially, a dollop of Italian style and a dash of Flemish attention to detail were added, often set against a solid gold-leaf background. In the art of this period, colors became more varied and vivid, compositions more complex, lines more fluid and with a sense of motion, and features more expressive. **Significant artists and examples include:**

- **Jaime Huguet** (1415–1492) The primary artist in the Catalán School, Huguet mixed Flemish and Italian influences with true local Catalán Romanesque conventions. He left works in his native **Barcelona's Palau Reial** and **Museu Nacional d'Art de Catalunya.**

- **Bartolomé Bermejo** (active 1474–1498) Though Andalusian by birth, Bermejo was the lead painter in the Italianate Valencian School, and the first Spanish painter to use oils. Some of his best early paintings are in Madrid's Museo del Prado; one of his last is *La Pietat* (1498) in the **Catedral de Barcelona.**

- **Fernando Gallego** (1466–1507) The leader of the Gothic Castilian School worked in a strong Flemish style melded to Spanish traditions, most evident in his masterpiece triptych in **Salamanca's Catedral Viejo.**

Renaissance (16th c.)

Renaissance means "rebirth," and in this case refers to classical ideals originating in ancient Greece and Rome. Artists strove for greater naturalism, using recently developed techniques such as linear perspective to achieve new heights of realism. The style started in Italy, and slowly displaced Spain's Gothic tendencies. When the Renaissance finally got rolling in Spain, the style had already mutated into the baroque.

Renaissance art flowered in Castile, where its greatest artists strove for court appointments at Toledo (though sculpture really flowered in Valladolid). **Significant artists include:**

- **Pedro Berruguete** (1450–1504)   The court painter to Ferdinand and Isabella worked for a time in Italy's Urbino, where he picked up an Italian softness, ethereality, and chiaroscuro, enhancing his Flemish-influenced obsession with details and Spanish-style gold backgrounds. His works are in the **Catedral de Avila** and **Jaén's Museo Provincial.**

- **Alonso Berruguete** (1488–1561)   Pedro's talented son was not only court painter to Charles V, but also the greatest native sculptor in Spain, having traveled to Italy to study painting under Filippino Lippi and sculpture under Michelangelo. The latter studies lent him a powerful natural style intent on expressing the psychology of his figures in such masterworks as the *San Sebastián* (1526–1532) in **Valladolid's Museo Nacional de Escultura** and a *reredos* (a floor piece with Biblical scenes in relief, 1539–1543) in the **Catedral de Toledo.**

- **Juan de Juni** (1507–1577)   A Frenchman who also took up Michelangelo's sensibilities, sculptor Juni developed a Catalán Renaissance style that predicted the baroque in its expressiveness and drama. His greatest works are in

Valladolid, including the *Entombments* (1544) in the **Museo Nacional de Escultura** and an altarpiece (1551) in the **Cathedral,** and a *Deposition* (1571) in the **Cabildo Catedral de Segovia.**

- **El Greco** (1540–1614)   Spain's most significant Renaissance artist was actually from Crete. Domenikos Thetocopoulos (his real name) traveled first to Italy, where he picked up Tintoretto's color palette in Venice and the twisting figures of late Renaissance mannerism in Rome. Then he headed to Toledo (then Spain's capital) to seek his fortune with a combination of weirdly lit scenes, broodingly dark colors, crowded compositions, eerily elongated figures, and a mystical touch. He never became court painter, though plenty of religious commissions and lesser nobility portraits came his way. **Toledo's churches** and **Casa y Museo de El Greco** retain many of his works, as does Madrid's Museo del Prado; other works are scattered across Spain in collections at Sitges, Bilbao, Valencia, Seville, Cuenca, El Escorial, and **Madrid's Thyssen-Bornemisza** and **Fine Arts museums.**

Baroque (17th–18th c.)

The **baroque** was Spain's greatest artistic era, producing several painters who rank among Europe's greatest. A more theatrical and decorative take on the Renaissance, the baroque had a rich exuberance that dovetailed nicely with Spain's Counter-Reformation fervor. The style mixes a kind of superrealism based on the use of peasant models and the chiaroscuro (dramatically playing areas of harsh lighting off dark shadows) of Caravaggio, with compositional complexity and explosions of dynamic fury, movement, color, and figures.

Many baroque commissions were officially sanctioned religious subjects or noble and royal portraits, but middle-class merchants, flush with wealth from the American colonies, were also ravenous for smaller genre scenes. **Significant artists** include:

- **José de Ribera** (1591–1652) The greatest master of chiaroscuro and *tenebrism* after Caravaggio, Ribera cranked out numerous, pale, wrinkle-faced, flaccid-armed *St. Jeromes*. He worked mostly in Italy, but largely at the Spanish court in Naples, then under Spanish rule, so many of his earthly realistic works found their way back home, including *Archimedes* (1630) in Madrid's Museo del Prado.

- **Diego Velázquez** (1599–1660) Spain's greatest painter, a prodigy who became Philip IV's court painter at 24, Velázquez studied in Italy where he polished his unflinchingly naturalistic technique. Though his position meant the bulk of his work was portraiture (and he did this better than anyone), he was a master of all painting genres. The collection in Madrid's Museo del Prado spans his career, from the early *Adoration of the Magi* (1619) to the *Surrender of Breda* (1634) to his masterpiece *Las Meninas* (1656).

- **Francisco de Zurbarán** (1598–1664) Seville's master of chiaroscuro, Zurbarán had a unique style that used the orangey glow of candles to light his clay figures, rather than the out-of-frame white light of Ribera and Caravaggio. **Seville's Museo Provincial** has several of his works. The *Defense of Cadiz* (1634) in Madrid's Museo del Prado shows how he was adapting and lightening his dark style to adapt to prevailing tastes.

- **Bartolomé Esteban Murillo** (1617–1682) Zubarán's Seville competitor, Murillo created work with a distinctly brighter, more saccharine and sentimental quality. His approach was well-suited to Counter-Reformation devotional images, which were used as models throughout Spain and Europe for the next few centuries. He eventually developed an *estilo vaporoso* (vaporous style) of loose brushwork, rich colors, and soft contours that loosely parallels the French rococo. His native Seville's **Museo Provincial** preserves several devout paintings. The best of his patented (and oft-copied) *Immaculate Conceptions* are in Madrid's Museo del Prado.

Bourbon Rococo & Neoclassical (18th–19th c.)

Spain's turbulent late 18th and early 19th centuries are best seen in the progression of work by the unique master Goya. His works started in the prevailing **rococo** style (a chaotic, frothy version of the baroque) but soon went off on its own track. This century also saw the rise of Spanish **neoclassicism,** often seen as dry, academic, and rather uninteresting. Significant artists include:

- **Francisco de Goya** (1746–1828)   Goya started as a painter of frothy, pastel-colored rococo works often of silly, joyful scenes (*Parasol,* 1777). He then became a courtly portraitist in the position of principal painter to Charles IV (*Family of Charles IV,* 1800), but his republican tendencies and encroaching deafness left him angry and prone to paint and engrave satirical attacks on the social system (*Los Caprichos,* 1796–1798). He turned increasingly to more harshly, realistically painted works with the French Invasion (*Clothed Maja* and *Naked Maja,* 1800–1803; the *Third of May,* 1808; *Execution,* 1814), but after the Restoration he was turned away by the new court. He retreated to his house, a deaf embittered old man, where he painted the deeply disturbing mythological/psychological *Black Paintings* (1821–1822). He spent his final 4 years in Bordeaux, apparently happier, and returned to the brighter color and simpler, happier themes of his youth. All of these works, along with 108 more, are in Madrid's Museo del Prado.

- **Madrid's Palacio Real**   The Bourbons imported many artists, including **Anton Mengs** (1728–1779) from Bohemia and **Tiepolo** (1696–1770) from Italy, to decorate their palace in the high baroque/emergent rococo style.

20th Century

Spain became an artistic hotbed again at the turn of the 20th century—even if Barcelona's own Picasso moved to Paris. Though cubism and surrealism were born in France, Spanish artists were key to both movements. **Cubists,** including Spaniards Picasso and Gris, accepted that the canvas was flat but painted objects from all points of view at once, rather than using optical tricks like perspective to fool viewers into seeing three dimensions; the effect is a fractured, imploded look. **Surrealists** such as Dalí and Miró tried to express the inner working of their minds in paint, plumbing their ids for imagery. Significant artists include:

- **Joan Miró** (1893–1983) Greatest of the surrealists in Spain, Miró created largely appealing work with a whimsical and childlike quality (save the dark works he did during the Spanish Civil War). The Catalán tended toward bright colors, especially blue, and was an accomplished sculptor as well (the assemblages often look like three-dimensional versions of his paintings). **Barcelona's Fundació Joan Miró** is the best place to get an overview of his work.

- **Pablo Picasso** (1881–1973) The most important artist of the last century, Picasso dipped his brush into several of the significant early-20th-century movements, helping to establish cubism and redefine surrealism in the process. Though he lived in France after 1904, Spain has always hungrily acquired his works to serve as stars of modern art museums from **Bilbao's Guggenheim Museum** to **Madrid's Centro de Arte Reina Sofía,** which houses his masterpiece *Guernica* (1937)—a bleak, confusing polemic against the horrors of war. Many of his early works are housed in **Barcelona's**

Museu Picasso, where you can find surprising examples of his teenage talent for realism.

- **Juan Gris** (1887–1927) The truest of the cubists, Gris had a palette more colorful than that of Picasso or France's Braque. He worked mostly in France, but **Madrid's Centro de Arte Reina Sofía** and the **Contemporary Art Museum in Palma de Majorca** hang some of his paintings.

- **Salvador Dalí** (1904–1989) The most famous surrealist was only briefly a member of that group (his anti-Marxist and pro-Franco position got him kicked out). Dalí's art used an intensely realistic technique to explore the very unreal worlds of dreams (nightmares, really) and paranoia in an attempt to investigate the Freudian depths of his own psyche. Some of his better works in Spain are at **Madrid's Centro de Arte Reina Sofía** and **Cadaqués's Perrot-Moore Museum,** but make sure to visit the quirky **Teatre Museu Dalí,** which he founded in his native Figueres.

- **Antoni Tàpies** (b. 1923) This abstract surrealist—Spain's most significant artist since the Civil War—founded his own museum, the **Fundació Antoni Tàpies,** in Barcelona.

ARCHITECTURE BASICS

There are a few points to keep in mind when considering a building's style, particularly for structures built before the 20th century. Very few buildings (especially churches) were actually built in only one style. Massive, expensive structures often took centuries to complete, during which time tastes would change and plans would be altered. While each architectural era has its own distinctive features, some elements, general floor plans, and terms are common to many, or may appear near the end of one era and continue through several later ones.

From the **Christian** Romanesque period on, most churches consist either of a single wide **aisle,** or a wide central **nave** flanked by two narrow aisles. The aisles are separated from the nave by a row of **columns,** or by square stacks of masonry called **piers,** usually connected by **arches.**

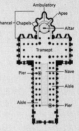

Church Floor Plan

This main nave/aisle assemblage is usually crossed by a perpendicular corridor called a **transept** near the far, east end of the church so that the floor plan looks like a **Latin cross** (shaped like a crucifix). The shorter, east arm of the nave is the holiest area, called the **chancel;** it often houses the stalls of the **choir** and the **altar.** If the far end of the chancel is rounded off, we call it an **apse.** An **ambulatory** is a curving corridor outside the altar and choir area, separating it from the ring of smaller chapels radiating off the chancel and apse.

Moorish & Mudéjar (8th–15th c.)

The Moors brought with them an Arabic architectural style that changed over the centuries but retained features that give their extant buildings, especially in Andalucía, an Eastern flair.

The early **Caliphate** style of Córdoba lasted from the 8th to the 11th century. It was replaced when the Caliphate fell by the simpler, more austerely religious **Almohad** style in Seville, in the 12th and 13th centuries. In their last stronghold of Granada, as they were being driven from most of Spain, the Moors constructed the Alhambra in the most sophisticated, ornately decorated style called **Nasrid** (13th–14th c.). After the Reconquest, Arab builders living

Alhambra, Granada

under Christian rule developed the **Mudéjar** style, embellishing churches and palaces with Moorish elements.

The Moors built three major structures: mosques, alcázares, and alcazabas. **Mosques,** Islamic religious buildings, were connected to minarets, tall towers from which the muezzin would call the people to prayer. **Alcázares** were palaces built with many small courtyards and gardens with fountains and greenery (the Arabs started as a desert people, so their version of paradise has an abundance of water). **Alcazabas** were fortresses built high atop hills and fortified as any defensive structure.

Identifiable Moorish features (with the name of the period when the feature first appeared) include:

- **Horseshoe arch (Caliphate)**   This arch describes more than 180 degrees of the circle's arc.

- **Ornamental brickwork (Caliphate)**   In relief alternating with stone.

- **Cupolas (Caliphate)**   These domes rest on arches, often dripping with coffered stuccoed decorations.

- **Geometric and plant-motif decorations (Caliphate)** The Koran forbids images of men or beasts, so the Moors used different ways to decorate their mosques and palaces.

- **Kufic script (Caliphate)**   Using another ingenious technique to get around the injunctions against imagery in art, artists turned religious passages from the Koran into elaborately swooping calligraphy.

- **Doors and arches (all periods)**   Surmounted by blind arcades.

- **Pointed arch (Almohad)**   Although horseshoe arches were still used during the Almohad period, they were often replaced by narrow pointy ones.

- **Artesonado ceilings (Almohad)**   These paneled wood ceilings were often painted and carved.

- **Azulejos (Almohad)** Patterns were created with these painted tiles.

  Mezquita-Catedral de Córdoba is the best-preserved building in the Caliphate style. Of the Almohad period, the best remaining example is **Seville's Giralda Tower,** a minaret but little altered when its accompanying mosque was converted into a cathedral; the mosque and tower at **Zaragosa's Palacio de la Aljafería** have survived from the era as well. The crowning achievement of the Nasrid—of all Spanish Moorish architecture—is **Granada's Alhambra** palace and the adjacent **Generalife** gardens. In **Madrid,** all that remains of Moorish architecture today are the modest foundations of a fort next to the Palacio Real and some wall fragments known as the *Muralla Arabe* on the Cuesta de la Vega slopes just below the Almudena cathedral, dating from its humble days as a village called Mayrit.

Romanesque (8th–13th c.)

As the Reconquest freed the north of Spain, a pilgrimage route sprang up along the coast to Santiago de Compostela. French and Italian pilgrims and Cistercian monks traveling the route brought the European Romanesque with them, sprinkling the way with small churches, and leaving a mighty cathedral at the trail's end.

The Romanesque took its inspiration and rounded arches from ancient Rome (hence the name). Romanesque architects concentrated on building large churches with wide aisles to accommodate the pilgrims. But to support the weight of all that masonry, the walls had to be thick and solid (meaning they could be pierced only by few and rather small windows) resting on huge piers, giving Romanesque churches a dark, somber, mysterious, and often oppressive feeling. Identifiable features of the Romanesque include:

- **Rounded arches** These load-bearing architectural devices allowed architects to open up wide naves and spaces, channeling all the weight of the stone walls and ceiling across the curve of the arch and down into the ground via the columns or pilasters.

- **Thick walls**
- **Infrequent and small windows**
- **Huge piers**

Although the great **Catedral de Santiago de Compostela,** the masterpiece of the style, has many baroque accretions, the floor plan is solidly Romanesque. Other good examples include **Sanguesa's Iglesia de Santa María** and **Iglesia de Santiago.**

Catedral de Santiago de Compostela

Gothic (13th–16th c.)

By the late 12th century, engineering developments freed church architecture from the heavy, thick walls of Romanesque structures and allowed ceilings to soar, walls to thin, and windows to proliferate. Spain imported the style (and often the masons and architects) from its birthplace in France.

Instead of dark, somber, unadorned Romanesque interiors that forced the eyes of the faithful toward the altar, where the priest stood droning on in unintelligible Latin, the Gothic interior enticed the churchgoers' gaze upward to high ceilings filled with light. The priests still conducted Mass in Latin, but now peasants could "read" the Gothic comic books of stained-glass windows.

The French style eventually developed into a genuine Spanish idiom, the elaborate, late-15th-century **Isabelline style,** named after the Catholic queen.

Identifiable features of the Gothic include:

- **Pointed arches** The most significant development of the Gothic era was the discovery that pointed arches could carry far more weight than rounded ones.

- **Cross vaults** Instead of being flat, the square patch of ceiling between four columns arches up to a point in the center, creating four sail shapes, sort of like the underside of a pyramid. The X separating these four sails is often reinforced with ridges called **ribbing.** As the Gothic progressed, four-sided cross

Cross Vault

vaults became six- or eight-sided, as architects played with the angles.

- **Tracery** These lacy webs of carved stone grace the pointy ends of windows and sometimes the spans of ceiling vaults.

- **Flying buttresses** These free-standing exterior pillars connected by graceful, thin arms of stone help channel the weight of the building and its roof out and down into the ground. To help counter the cross forces involved in this engineering sleight of hand, the piers of buttresses were often topped by heavy pinnacles or statues.

Cross Section of Gothic Church

- **Stained glass** Because pointy arches can carry more weight than rounded ones, windows could be larger and more numerous. They were often filled with Bible stories and symbolism written in the colorful patterns of stained glass.

The French style of Gothic was energetically pursued in Spain in the early to mid–13th century, first in adapting the Romanesque **Catedral de Santa María** in **Burgos,** then in **Catedral de Toledo** and **Catedral de León.**

Fourteenth- and 15th-century Gothic cathedrals include those at **Avila, Segovia, Pamplona, Barcelona,** and **Girona** (the last a peculiar aisle-less Catalán plan, although the interior is now baroque). The best of the **Isabelline style** can be seen in **Valladolid** in the facades of **Iglesia de San Pablo** and the **Colegio San Gregorio.**

Renaissance (16th c.)

As in painting, the rules of Renaissance architecture stressed proportion, order, classical inspiration, and mathematical precision to create unified, balanced structures based on Italian models. The earliest—and most Spanish—Renaissance style (really a transitional form from Gothic) was marked by facades done in an almost Moorish intricacy and was called **Plateresque,** for it was said to resemble the work of silversmiths *(plateros)*. Some identifiable Renaissance features include:

Catedral de Barcelona

• **A sense of proportion**

• **A reliance on symmetry**

• **The use of classical orders**   This specified three different column capitals, with plain Doric capitals, scrolled Ionic capitals, or leafy Corinthian capitals.

The best of the **Plateresque** decorates the facades of **Salamanca's Convento de San Esteban** and **Universidad.**

Charles V's **Summer Palace,** built amid **Granada's** Moorish **Alhambra,** is the greatest High Renaissance building in Spain.

The most monumentally classical of Renaissance structures was Phillip II's **El Escorial** monastery outside Madrid, designed by Juan de Herrera (1530–1597), who also started Valladolid's Cathedral in 1580, although the exterior was later finished in flamboyant baroque style.

Real Monasterio de San Lorenzo de El Escorial

Baroque (17th–18th c.)

The overall effect of the baroque is to lighten the appearance of structures and add movement of line and vibrancy to the static look of the classical Renaissance. At the beginning of this period, however, the classicism of Juan de Herrera continued to dominate, making the Spanish baroque more austere and simple than contemporary European versions. But soon the Churriguera family of architects and their contemporaries gave rise to the overly ornate, sumptuously decorated **Churriguesque** style.

Identifiable features of the baroque include:

- **Classical architecture rewritten with curves**   The baroque is similar to Renaissance, but many of the right angles and ruler-straight lines are exchanged for curves of complex geometry and an interplay of concave and convex surfaces.

- **Multiplying forms**   To create a rich, busy effect, the baroque loved to pile up its elements, such as columns, pediments (a low-pitched, triangular feature above a window, door, or pavilion), or porticoes (a projecting pavilion).

- **Churriguesque decorations**   The style was characterized by a proliferation of statues, curves, carvings, and twisty columns stacked into pyramids.

   Madrid's Plaza Mayor is the classic example of the restrained Herrera-style early baroque. A later form—verging on neoclassical—appears in Churriguera's 18th-century **Real Academia de Bellas Artes.** Other Churriguesque masterpieces include **Granada's Monasterio Cartuja** and **Salamanca's Plaza Mayor.** The baroque was largely used to embellish existing buildings, such as the fine, ornate facade on **Santiago de Compostela's Cathedral.**

Neoclassical (18th–19th c.)

By the mid–18th century, as a backlash against baroque excesses, Bourbon architects turned to the austere simplicity and grandeur of the Classical Age, and inaugurated neoclassicism. Their work was inspired by the rediscovery of Italy's Pompeii and other ancient sites. **Identifiable neoclassical features include:**

- **Mathematical proportion and symmetry** These classical ideals, first rediscovered during the Renaissance, are the hallmark of every classically styled era.

- **Reinterpreting ancient architecture** Features of temples and other buildings of ancient Greece and Rome, such as classical orders, colonnaded porticoes, and pediments, were adapted to new structures.

- **Monumental** The neoclassical never did anything small.

The primary neoclassical architect, **Ventura Rodríguez** (1717–1785), designed the facade of **Pamplona's Cathedral** and **Madrid**'s grand boulevard of the **Paseo del Prado.** On that boulevard is one of Spain's best neoclassical buildings, the **Museo del Prado.**

Museo del Prado

Modernisme & Modern (20th c.)

In Barcelona, architects such as **Lluís Doménech i Montaner** (1850–1923) and the great master **Antoni Gaudí** (1852–1926) developed an appealing, idiosyncratic form of Art Nouveau, called *modernisme*. This Catalán variant took a playful stab at building with undulating lines and colorful, broken tile mosaics.

During the long Franco years, architecture languished as utilitarian and bland, but in the late 1990s American Frank Gehry (b. 1929) gave a wake-up call to Spanish architecture with his curvaceous, gleaming silver **Guggenheim Museum** in **Bilbao.** Identifiable features of modernism include:

- **An emphasis on the uniqueness of craft** Like Art Nouveau practitioners in other countries, Spanish artists and architects rebelled against the era of mass production.

- **A use of organic motifs** Asymmetrical, curvaceous designs were often based on plants and flowers.

- **A variety of mediums** Wrought iron, stained glass, tile, and hand-painted wallpaper were some of the most-popular materials.

The best of modernisme is in **Barcelona,** including **Gaudí's apartment buildings** along Passeig de Gràcia and his massive unfinished cathedral, **La Sagrada Família.**

Francoist utilitarianism, meanwhile, is personified in **Madrid** by the bland self-contained **Edificio España,** built by the Otamendi brothers in 1953, and the 32-story **Torre de Madrid,** which appeared 4 years later. Both of them overlook the Plaza España, contrasting with the romantic statues of Cervantes, Don Quixote, and Sancho Panza below.

Madrid's Upper Castellana has the best examples of the city's futuristic Tokyo-cum–New York style architecture: the 1988 **Torre Picasso** designed by Minoru Yamasaki in the **AZCA** business development—the highest building in Madrid to date—and the slanting twin **Torres KIO,** also known as the Puerta de Europa, which were built in Plaza Castilla by a Kuwaiti consortium.

FAMOUS SPANIARDS

Authors & Writers   Three great writers dominated Spain's **Golden Age of Literature** which lasted from 1500 to 1681: novelist **Miguel de Cervantes** swept the world with *Don Quixote,* and playwrights **Tirso de Molina** and the hyper-prolific **Lope de Vega** (total output 1,500 works) satirized the social mores of their era.

The **Generation of '98** (who emerged after the loss of Cuba in 1898 during the American-Spanish War) revived the arts of criticism and intellectual analysis. Their leading members included philosophers and essayists **Miguel de Unamuno** and **José Ortega y Gasset,** and novelist **Pío Baroja,** whose terse but highly readable style was admired by Hemingway. **Perez Galdós,** meanwhile, wrote social chronicles comparable with those of Dickens and Balzac.

Rulers   Spain's most powerful leader was **Philip II** (1556–1598), a bureaucratic king who presided over the world's largest empire. During the last century, dictator **General Francisco Franco** (1892–1975) ruled the country from 1939 to 1975, after his Nationalist forces overthrew the Republican democracy in the 1936–1939 Civil War.

Classical Musicians   Three major **composers** stand out. **Isaac Albeñiz**—a child prodigy who played in piano concerts at the age of 4—with his *Iberia* suite; **Manuel de Falla,** an ascetic Andaluz from Cádiz, with his *Three Cornered Hat* ballet; and **Enrique Granados** with his lively *Goyescas.* (See also "Spanish Classical Composers" in chapter 10.) The most talented **musician** of modern times was cellist **Pablo (Pau) Casals.** Spain also boasts today's leading **opera singer, Placido Domingo.**

GENERAL INFORMATION

Best all-round site for information on Spain is **www.sispain.org**, which lists more than 1,000 websites covering a variety of topics ranging from institutions, law, and finance to music, sports, and entertainment. You can also find lots of great information at **www.okspain.org**, **www.red2000.com**, and **www.cyberspain.com**.

HISTORIC TIMELINE

11th century B.C.   Phoenicians settle Spain's coasts.

650 B.C.   Greeks colonize the east.

600 B.C.   Celts cross the Pyrenees and settle in Spain.

6th–3rd century B.C.   Carthaginians make Cartagena in the south-east their colonial capital, driving out the Greeks.

218–201 B.C.   Second Punic War: Rome defeats Carthage.

2nd century B.C.–A.D. 2nd century   Rome controls most of Iberia; Christianity spreads.

5th century   Vandals, then Visigoths, invade Spain.

8th–9th century   Moors conquer most of Spain, and found Mayrit on original site of Madrid.

10th century   Madrid occupied by Christian king Ramiro II.

1202   Madrid officially given town status.

1214   More than half of Iberia is regained by Catholics.

1339   First parliament (Cortes) held in Madrid by Alfonso XI.

1469   Ferdinand of Aragón marries Isabella of Castile.

1492   Catholic monarchs seize Granada, the last Moorish stronghold; Columbus lands in the New World.

1519   Cortés conquers Mexico; Charles I is crowned Holy Roman Emperor as Charles V.

1556   Philip II inherits throne; launches Counter-Reformation.

1561   Phillip II establishes Madrid as Spain's capital.

1588   England defeats Spanish Armada.

1600   Phillip II moves capital to Valladolid (restored to Madrid in 1606).

1700   Philip V becomes king; War of Spanish Succession follows, in wake of the death of the last Habsburg King, Charles II.

1713   Treaty of Utrecht ends war; Spain's colonies reduced.

1734   Madrid's Moorish Alcazar fortress burnt down; Royal Palace completed on same site 30 years later.

1759   Charles III ascends throne.

1808   Napoleon places brother Joseph on the Spanish throne.

1813   Wellington drives French out of Spain; monarchy is restored.

1876   Spain becomes a constitutional monarchy.

1898   Spain loses Puerto Rico, Cuba, and the Philippines to U.S.

1921   Launching of Madrid metro.

1923   Primo de Rivera forms military directorate.

1930   Right-wing dictatorship ends; Primo de Rivera exiled.

1931   King Alfonso XIII abdicates; Second Republic is born.

1933–1935   Falange party formed.

1936–1939   Civil War between governing Popular Front and Gen. Francisco Franco's Nationalists; Franco seizes Madrid.

1939   Franco establishes 36-year dictatorship.

1941   Spain is neutral in World War II, but Franco favors Germany.

1955   Spain joins the United Nations.

1969   Franco names Juan Carlos as his successor.

1975   Franco dies and Juan Carlos becomes king.

1976   *El País,* Spain's first great democratic newspaper, launched.

1978   New democratic constitution initiates reforms.

*1981   Right-wing coup attempt in Madrid fails.

1982   Socialists gain power after 43 years of right-wing rule.

1986   Spain joins the European Community (now the EU).

1992   Barcelona hosts Summer Olympics; Seville hosts EXPO '92.

1996   A conservative party defeats Socialist party, ending 13-year rule. José María Aznar is chosen prime minister.

1998   The Guggenheim Bilbao opens; Madrid's Teatro Real reopens; Real Madrid wins record seventh European Cup.

2001   Spain becomes economic powerhouse in Latin America.

2002   Spain adopts the euro as its national currency.

2003   Basque terrorists, after a brief, self-proclaimed "amnesty," continue a campaign against the government.

2004   Al Qua'ida strikes Spanish trains in the deadliest terrorist attack in Europe since WWII. Three days later a Socialist government is elected. Rodriguez Zapatero is the new Prime Minister.

2005   Gay marriage becomes legal in Spain.

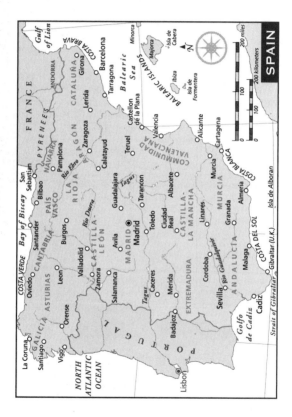

DICTIONARY KEY

n	noun	*m*	masculine
v	verb	*f*	feminine
adj	adjective	*s*	singular
prep	preposition	*pl*	plural
adv	adverb		

All verbs are listed in infinitive (to + verb) form, cross-referenced to the appropriate conjugations page. Adjectives are listed first in masculine singular form, followed by the feminine ending. *For food terms, see the Menu Reader (p103) and Grocery section (p112) in Chapter 4, Dining.*

ENGLISH—SPANISH

A

able, to be able to (can) *v poder* **p31**

above *adj arriba*

accept, to accept *v aceptar* **p22**

> **Do you accept credit cards?**
> *¿Acepta tarjetas de crédito?*

accident *n el accidente m*

> **I've had an accident.** *He tenido un accidente.*

account *n la cuenta f*

> **I'd like to transfer to / from my checking / savings account.** *Quiero transferir a / de mi cuenta corriente / de ahorros.*

acne *n el acné m*

across *prep a través de, al otro lado de*

> **across the street** *al otro lado de la calle*

actual *adj verdadero -a*

adapter plug *n el enchufe adaptador m*

address *n la dirección f*

> **What's the address?**
> *¿Cuál es la dirección?*

admission fee *n el precio de entrada m*

in advance *por adelantado*

African-American *adj afroamericano -a*

afternoon *n la tarde f*

> **in the afternoon** *por la tarde*

age *n la edad f*

> **What's your age?** *¿Cuántos años tiene?*

agency *n la agencia / la compañía f*

> **car rental agency** *la compañía de alquiler de coches*

agnostic *adj agnóstico -a*

air conditioning *n el aire acondicionado m*

> **Would you lower / raise the air conditioning?** *¿Puede bajar / subir el aire acondicionado?*

airport *n el aeropuerto m*

I need a ride to the airport.
Necesito ir al aeropuerto.

How far is it from the airport? *¿A qué distancia está del aeropuerto?*

airsickness bag n *la bolsa para mareos* f

aisle (in store) n *el pasillo* m

Which aisle is it in? *¿En qué pasillo está?*

alarm clock n *el despertador* m

alcohol n *el alcohol* m

Do you serve alcohol? *¿Sirven alcohol?*

I'd like nonalcoholic beer. *Quiero una cerveza sin alcohol.*

all n *todo* m

all adj *todo -a*

all of the time *todo el tiempo*

That's all, thank you. *Eso es todo, gracias.*

allergic adj *alérgico -a*

I'm allergic to ____. *Soy alérgico -a a a ____.* See and for common allergens.

altitude n *la altitud* f

aluminum n *el aluminio* m

ambulance n *la ambulancia* f

American adj *estadounidense*

amount n *la cantidad* f

angry adj *enojado -a*

animal n *el animal* m

another adj *otro -a* ,

answer n *la contestación, la repuesta* f

answer, to answer (phone call, question) v *contestar* p22

Answer me, please. *Contéstame por favor.*

antibiotic n *el antibiótico* m

I need an antibiotic. *Necesito un antibiótico.*

antihistamine n *el antihistamínico* m

anxious adj *ansioso -a*

any adj *cualquier, cualquiera*

anything n *cualquier cosa*

anywhere adv *dondequiera, cualquier lugar*

April n *abril*

appointment n *la cita* f

Do I need an appointment? *¿Necesito una cita?*

are v See **be, to be.** p27, 28

Argentinian adj *argentino -a*

arm n *el brazo* m

arrive, to arrive v *llegar* p22

arrival(s) n *las llegadas* f

art n *el arte* m

exhibit of art *exhibición de arte* See p148 for art types.

art adj *de arte*

art museum *museo de arte*

artist n *el* / *la artista* m f

Asian adj *asiático -a*

ask for (request) v *pedir* p32

ask a question v *preguntar* p22

aspirin n *la aspirina* f

assist v *ayudar* p22

ENGLISH—SPANISH

assistance n la asistencia f
asthma n el asma f
  I have asthma. *Tengo asma.*
atheist adj ateo -a
ATM n el cajero automático m
  I'm looking for an ATM.
  Estoy buscando un cajero automático.
attend v asistir p23
audio adj audio, auditivo
August n agosto
aunt n la tía f
Australia n Australia
Australian adj australiano -a
autumn n el otoño m
available adj disponible

B

baby n el / la bebé m / f
baby adj de bebés, para bebés
  Do you sell baby food?
  ¿Venden comida para bebés?
babysitter n la niñera f
  Do you have babysitters who speak English? *¿Tiene niñeras que hablen inglés?*
back n la espalda f
  My back hurts. *Me duele la espalda.*
back rub n el masaje de espalda m
backed up (toilet) adj tapado -a
  The toilet is backed up. *El váter está atascado.*
bag n la bolsa f, el bolso m

My bag was stolen. *Me robaron el bolso.*
  I lost my bag. *Perdí el bolso.*
bag v empacar p22
baggage n el equipaje m
baggage adj de equipaje
  baggage claim reclamo de equipaje
bait n el cebo m
balance (on bank account) n el saldo m
balance v balancear p22
balcony n el balcón m
ball (sport) n la pelota f
ballroom dancing n el baile de salón m
band (musical) n la banda f
band-aid n la tirita f
bandage n la venda f
bandage (dressing) vendaje
bank n el banco m
  Can you help me find a bank? *¿Puede ayudarme a encontrar un banco?*
bar n el bar m
barber n el barbero m
bass (instrument) n el contrabajo m
bath n el baño m
bathroom (restroom) n el baño / el aseo m
  Where is the nearest public bathroom? *¿Dónde hay un baño?*
bathtub n la bañera f

bathe, to bathe oneself v *bañarse* **p22, 35**

battery (for flashlight) n *la pila f*

battery (for car) n *la batería f*

bee n *la abeja f*

   I was stung by a bee. *Me picó una abeja.*

be, to be (temporary state, condition, mood) v *estar* **p27**

be, to be (permanent quality) v *ser* **p28**

beach n *la playa*

beard n *barba f*

beautiful adj *precioso* (thing) *guapísimo -a* (person)

bed n *la cama f*

beer n *la cerveza f*

   beer on tap *cerveza de barril*

begin v *comenzar* **p31**

behave v *comportar* **p22**

behind adv *detrás*

below adv *de / abajo*

belt n *el cinturón m*

   conveyor belt *cinta transportadora*

berth n *el camarote m*

best *mejor*

bet, to bet v *apostar* **p35** (like *jugar*)

better *mejor*

big adj *grande*

bilingual adj *bilingüe*

bill (currency) n *el billete m*

bill v *facturar* **p22**

biography n *la biografía f*

biracial adj *biracial*

bird n *el pájaro m*

birth control n *los anticonceptivos m* ,

birth control adj *anticonceptivo -a* ,

   I'm out of birth control pills. *Se me acabaron las píldoras anticonceptivas.*

   I need more birth control pills. *Necesito más píldoras anticonceptivas.*

bit (small amount) n *un poco m*

black adj *negro -a*

blanket n *la manta f*

bleach n *la lejía f*

   to bleach (one's hair) v *teñirse de rubio*

blind adj *ciego -a*

block v *bloquear* **p22**

blond(e) adj *rubio -a*

blouse n *la blusa f*

blue adj *azul*

blurry adj *borroso -a*

board n *bordo*

   on board *a bordo*

board v *abordar* **p22**

boarding pass n *la tarjeta de embarque f*

boat n *el barco m*

Bolivian adj *boliviano -a*

bomb n *la bomba f*

book n *el libro m*

bookstore n *la librería f*

boss n *el jefe m, la jefa f*

bottle n la botella f

> **May I heat this (baby) bottle someplace?** ¿Puedo calentar esta botella en algún lugar?

box (seat) n el palco m
box office n la taquilla f
boy n el niño m
boyfriend n el novio m
braid n la trenza f
braille, American n el braille americano m
brake n el freno m

> **emergency brake** el freno de mano

brake v frenar p22
brandy n el brandy m
bread n el pan m
break v romper p22
breakfast n el desayuno m

> **What time is breakfast?** ¿A qué hora sirven el desayuno?

bridge (across a river, dental) n el puente m
briefcase n el maletín m
bright adj brillante
broadband n la banda ancha f
bronze adj bronze (color)
brother n el hermano m
brown adj café, castaño -a, moreno -a, pardo -a
brunette n de cabello oscuro f
Buddhist n el budista m, la budista f
budget n el presupuesto m
buffet n el bufé m

bug n el insecto m, el bicho m
bull n el toro m
bullfight n la corrida de toros f
bullfighter n el torero m
burn v quemar p22

> **Can I burn a CD here?** ¿Puedo quemar un CD aquí?

bus n el autobús m

> **Where is the bus stop?** ¿Dónde está la parada de autobuses?
>
> **Which bus goes to ____?** ¿Qué autobús va hacia ____?

business n el negocio m
business adj de negocios

> **business center** centro de negocios

busy adj concurrido -a (restaurant), ocupado -a (phone)
butter n la mantequilla f
buy, to buy v comprar p22

C

café n el café m

> **Internet café** cibercafé

call, to call v llamar (shout) llamar por teléfono (phone) p22
camp, to camp v acampar p22
camper n el campista m
camping adj para acampar

> **Do we need a camping permit?** ¿Necesitamos un permiso para acampar?

campsite n el campamento m

can n la lata f

can (able to) v poder p31

Canada n Canadá

Canadian adj canadiense

cancel, to cancel v cancelar p22

My flight was canceled. *Han cancelado mi vuelo.*

canvas n el lienzo m (for painting), la lona f (material)

cappuccino n el (café) capuchino m

car n el auto m

car rental agency *compañía de alquiler de coches*

I need a rental car. *Necesito alquilar un coche.*

card n la tarjeta f

Do you accept credit cards? *¿Aceptan tarjetas de crédito?*

May I have your business card? *¿Me puede dar su tarjeta de presentación?*

car seat (child's safety seat) n el asiento para niños m

Do you rent car seats for children? *¿Alquilan asientos para niños con el coche?*

carsickness n el mareo m

cash n efectivo m

cash only *efectivo solamente*

cash, to cash v cobrar p30

to cash out (gambling) *cobrar el dinero*

cashmere n la cachemira f

casino n el casino m

cat n el gato m, la gata f

Catholic adj católico -a

cavity (tooth cavity) n la carie f

I think I have a cavity. *Creo que tengo una carie.*

CD n el CD m, el disco compacto m

CD player n el reproductor de discos compactos m

celebrate, to celebrate v móvil p22

cell phone n el teléfono móvil m

centimeter n el centímetro m

chamber music n la música de cámara f

change (money) n el cambio m

I'd like change, please. *Quiero cambio, por favor.*

This isn't the correct change. *No me ha dado el cambio correcto.*

change (to change money, clothes) v cambiar p22

changing room n el vestuario m (in a gym) / el probador m (in a store)

charge, to charge (money) v cobrar p22

charge, to charge (a battery) v recargar p22

charmed adj encantado -a

charred (meat) adj muy bien hecho

charter, to charter v fletar p22

cheap *adj* barato -a

check *n* el cheque *m*

Do you accept travelers' checks? ¿Aceptan cheques de viajero?

check, to check *v* verificar p22

checked (pattern) *adj* a cuadros

check-in *n* el registro (hotel), la facturación (airport)

What time is check-in? ¿A qué hora es el registro (hotel), la facturación (airport)?

check-out *n* la salida *f*

check-out time la hora de salida

What time is check-out? ¿A que hora es la salida del hotel?

check out, to check out *v* despedirse p32, 35 (like pedir)

cheese *n* el queso *m*

chicken *n* el pollo (food) *m*

child *n* el niño *m*, la niña *f*

children *n* los niños *m*

Are children allowed? ¿Se admiten niños?

Do you have children's programs? ¿Tienen actividades para niños?

Do you have a children's menu? ¿Tienen un menú para niños?

Chinese *adj* chino -a

chiropractor *n* el quiropráctico *m*

church *n* la iglesia *f*

cigar *n* el cigarro *m*

cigarette *n* el cigarrillo *m*

a pack of cigarettes un paquete de cigarrillos

cinema *n* el cine *m*

city *n* la ciudad *f*

claim *n* el reclamación *m*

I'd like to file a claim. Quiero presentar una reclamación.

clarinet *n* el clarinete *m*

class *n* la clase *f*

business class clase de negocios

economy class clase turista

first class primera clase

classical (music) *adj* clásico -a

clean *adj* limpio -a

clean, to clean *v* limpiar p22

Please clean the room today. Por favor limpie la habitación.

clear *v* aclarar p22

clear *adj* claro -a

climbing *n* el alpinismo *m*

climb, to climb *v* escalar, subir p22, 23

to climb a mountain escalar una montaña

to climb stairs subir las escaleras

close, to close *v* cerrar p31 (like comenzar)

close (near) cerca, cercano

closed *adj* cerrado -a

cloudy adj nublado -a

clover n el trébol m

go clubbing, to go clubbing v salir de marcha p25

coat n el abrigo m

coffee n el café m

iced coffee café con hielo

cognac n el coñac m

coin n la moneda f

cold n el catarro m

I have a cold. Tengo un catarro.

cold adj frío -a

I'm cold. Tengo frío.

It's cold out. Hace frío.

collect adj a cobro revertido

I'd like to place a collect call. Quiero hacer una llamada a cobro revertido.

collect, to collect v recolectar p22

college n la universidad f

Colombian adj colombiano -a

color n el color m

color v colorear p22

computer n el ordenador m

concert n el concierto m

condition n la condición f

in good / bad condition en buena / mala condición

condom n el condón m

Do you have a condom? ¿Tienes un condón?

not without a condom no sin un condón

confirm, to confirm v confirmar p22

I'd like to confirm my reservation. Quiero confirmar mi reserva.

confused adj confundido -a

congested adj congestionado -a

connection speed n la velocidad de conexión f

constipated adj estreñido -a

I'm constipated. Estoy estreñido -a.

contact lens n la lentilla f

I lost my contact lens. He perdido una lentilla.

continue, to continue v continuar p22

convertible n el descapotable m

cook, to cook v cocinar p22

I'd like a room where I can cook. Quiero una habitación con cocinar.

cookie n la galleta f

copper adj cobre

corner n la esquina f

on the corner en la esquina

correct v corregir p23

correct adj correcto -a

Am I on the correct train? ¿Estoy en el tren correcto?

cost, to cost v costar p35 (like jugar)

How much does it cost? ¿Cuánto cuesta?

Costa Rican adj costarricense

costume n el disfraz m

cotton n el algodón m

cough *n la tos f*

cough *v toser* **p23**

counter *n la barra* **(in bar)** *f, el mostrador* **(in kitchen)** *m, la ventomillo* **(in bank)** *f*

country-and-western (music) *n la música country f*

court (legal) *n el tribunal m*

court (sport) *n la cancha f*

courteous *adj cortés*

cousin *n el primo m, la prima f*

cover charge (in bar) *n la entrada f*

cow *n la vaca f*

crack (in glass object) *n la grieta f*

craftsperson *n el artesano m, la artesana f*

cream *n la crema f*

credit card *n la tarjeta de crédito f*

Do you accept credit cards? *¿Aceptan tarjetas de crédito?*

crib *n la cuna f*

crown (dental) *n la corona f*

curb *n el bordillo de la acera m*

curl *n el rizo m*

curly *adj rizado -a*

currency exchange *n el cambio de moneda m, la case de cambio* **(place)** *f*

Where is the nearest currency exchange? *¿Dónde está la casa de cambio más cercana?*

current (water) *n la corriente f*

customs *n aduana f*

cut (wound) *n el corte m, la cortadura f*

I have a bad cut. *Tengo una cortadura seria.*

cut, to cut *v cortar* **p22**

cybercafé *n el cibercafé m*

Where can I find a cyber-café? *¿Dónde puedo encontrar un cibercafé?*

D

damaged *adj dañado -a*

Damn! *expletive ¡Maldita sea!*

dance *v bailar* **p22**

danger *n el peligro m*

dark *n la oscuridad f*

dark *adj oscuro -a*

daughter *n la hija f*

day *n el día m*

the day before yesterday *anteayer*

these last few days *estos últimos días*

dawn *n la madrugada m*

at dawn *al amanecer*

deaf *adj sordo -a*

deal (bargain) *n la ganga f*

What a great deal! *¡Qué ganga!*

deal (cards) *v repartir* **p23**

Deal me in. *Dame cartas.*

December *n diciembre*

declined *adj rechazado -a*

Was my credit card declined? *¿Ha sido rechazada mi tarjeta?*

declare v declarar **p22**

I have nothing to declare. No tengo nada que declarar.

deep adj profundo -a

delay n el retraso m

How long is the flight delay? ¿Cuánto retraso llevo el vuelo?

How long is the delay? ¿Cuánto retraso tiene?

delighted adj encantado -a

democracy n la democracia f

dent v abollar **p22**

He / She dented the car. Él / Ella abolló el coche.

dentist n el dentista m

dentures n la dentadura postiza f

denture plate prótesis dental

departure n la salida f

designer n el diseñador m, la diseñadora f

dessert n el postre m

dessert menu el menú de postres

destination n el destino m

diabetic adj diabético -a

dial (a phone) v marcar **p22**

dial direct marcar directo

diaper n el pañal m

Where can I change a diaper? ¿Dónde puedo cambiar un pañal?

diarrhea n la diarrea f

dictionary n el diccionario m

different (other) adj diferente

difficult adj difícil

dinner n la cena f

directory assistance (phone) n el servicio de información telefónica f

disability n la discapacidad f

disappear v desaparecer **p33** (like conocer)

disco n el disco m

disconnected adj desconectado -a

Operator, I was disconnected. Operadora, se me ha cortado la llamada.

discount n el descuento m

Do I qualify for a discount? ¿Tengo derecho a un descuento?

dish n el plato m

dive v bucear **p22**

scuba dive buceo con escafandra

divorced adj divorciado -a

dizzy adj mareado -a

do, to do v hacer **p30**

doctor n el doctor m, la doctora f, el médico m f

doctor's office n la consulta del médico m

dog n el perro m

service dog perro de servicio

dollar n el dólar m

door n la puerta f

double adj doble

double bed cama doble

double vision visión doble

down adj abajo

download v descargar **p22**

downtown n el centro de la ciudad m

dozen n la docena f

drain n el desagüe m

drama n la obra dramática m

drawing (work of art) n el dibujo m

dress (garment) n el vestido m

dress (general attire) n la vestimenta f

What's the dress code? ¿Cuál es el código de vestimenta?

dress v vestirse p32 (like pedir), 35

Should I dress up for that affair? ¿Debería ponerte elegante para la ocasión?

dressing (salad) n el aderezo m

dried adj secado -a

drink n la bebida / una copa f

I'd like a drink. Quiero una copa.

drink, to drink v beber p23

drip v gotear p22

drive v conducir p22

driver n el chofer m

driving range n el campo de práctica m

drum n el tambor m

dry adj seco -a

This towel isn't dry. Esta toalla no está seca.

dry, to dry v secar p22

I need to dry my clothes. Necesito secarme la ropa.

dry cleaner n la tintorería f

dry cleaning n la limpieza en seco f

duck n el pato m

duty-free adj libre de impuestos

duty-free shop n la tienda libre de impuestos f

DVD n el DVD m

Do the rooms have DVD players? ¿Las habitaciones tienen DVD?

Where can I rent DVDs or videos? ¿Dónde puedo alquilar DVD o vídeos?

E

early adj temprano -a

It's early. Es temprano.

eat v comer p23

to eat out comer afuera

economy n la economía f

Ecuadorian adj ecuatoriano -a

editor n el editor m, la editora f

educator n el / la docente f

eight n ocho m

eighteen n dieciocho m

eighth n octavo m

eighty n ochenta m

election n la elección f

electrical hookup n la conexión eléctrica f

elevator n el ascensor m

eleven n once m

e-mail n el e-mail m

May I have your e-mail address? ¿Me puede dar su dirección de e-mail?

e-mail message mensaje de e-mail

e-mail, to send e-mail *v* enviar un e-mail **p22**

embarrassed *adj* avergonzado -a

embassy *n* la embajada *f*

emergency *n* la emergencia *f*

emergency brake *n* el freno de mano *m*

emergency exit *n* la salida de emergencia *f*

employee *n* el empleado *m*, la empleada *f*

employer *n* el empleador *m*

engine *n* el motor *m*

engineer *n* el ingeniero *m*, la ingeniera *f*

England *n* Inglaterra

English *n, adj* el inglés *m*, la inglesa *f*

Do you speak English? ¿Habla inglés?

enjoy, to enjoy *v* disfrutar **p22**

enter, to enter *v* entrar **p22**

Do not enter. Prohibida la entrada.

enthusiastic *adj* entusiasmado -a

entrance *n* la entrada *f*

envelope *n* el sobre *m*

environment *n* el medio ambiente *m*

escalator *n* la escalera mecánica *f*

espresso *n* el café solo *m*

exchange rate *n* la tasa de cambio *f*

What is the exchange rate for US / Canadian dollars? ¿Cuál es la tasa de cambio de dólares estadounidenses / canadienses?

excuse (pardon) *v* excusar, perdonar **p22**

Excuse me. Perdone.

exhausted *adj* agotado -a

exhibit *n* la exhibición *f*

exit *n* la salida *f*

not an exit no es una salida

exit *v* salir **p23** (I leave salgo)

expensive *adj* caro -a

explain *v* explicar **p22**

express *adj* expreso -a

express check-in facturación rápida

extra (additional) *adj* adicional / más

extra-large *adj* extra grande

eye *n* el ojo *m*

eyebrow *n* la ceja *f*

eyeglasses *n* las gafas *f*

eyelash *n* la pestaña *f*

F

fabric *n* la tela *f*

face *n* la cara *f*

faint *v* desmayar **p22**

fall (season) *n* el otoño *m*

fall *v* caer **p23** (I fall caigo)

family *n* la familia *f*

fan *n* el abanico *m*

far lejos

How far is it to _____? ¿A qué distancia está _____?

fare n la tarifa f

fast adj rápido -a ,

fat adj gordo -a

father n el padre m

faucet n el grifo m

fault n la culpa f

I'm at fault. Es mi culpa.
It was his fault. Fue su
culpa.

fax n el fax m

February n febrero

fee n el honorario m

female n la hembra f

fiancé(e) n el prometido m,
la prometida f

fifteen adj quince m

fifth adj quinto -a m

fifty adj cincuenta m

find v encontrar, hallar **p22**

fine (for traffic violation) n la
multa f

fine bien

I'm fine. Estoy bien.

fire! ¡Fuego!

first adj primero -a

fishing pole n la caña de
pescar f

fitness center n el gimnasio m

fit (clothes) v entallado **p22, 35**

Does this look like it fits?
¿Esto parece que me
entalla?

fitting room n el probador m

five adj cinco

flight n el vuelo m

Where do domestic flights
arrive / depart? ¿Dónde
llegan / De dónde salen los
vuelos nacionales?

Where do international flights
arrive / depart? ¿Dónde llegan / De dónde salen los vuelos internacionales?

What time does this flight
leave? ¿A qué hora sale
este vuelo?

flight attendant auxilior de
vuelo

floor n el piso m

ground floor planta baja
second floor primera planta

*Note that in Spanish, the
second floor is called the first,
the third is the second, etc.*

flower n la flor f

flush (gambling) n la escalera f

flush, to flush v tirar de la
cadena **p22**

This toilet won't flush. El
váter no funciona.

flute n la flauta f

food n la comida f

**foot (body part, measure-
ment)** n el pie m

forehead n la frente f

formula n la fórmula f

Do you sell infants' for-
mula? ¿Venden fórmula
para bebés?

forty adj cuarenta

forward adj hacia adelante

four adj cuatro

fourteen adj catorce

fourth adj cuarto -a

one-fourth un cuarto

fragile adj frágil

freckle n la peca f

French adj francés

fresh adj fresco -a

Friday n el viernes m

friend n el amigo m la amiga f

front adj delantero -a, enfrente de

front desk la recepción

fruit n la fruta f

fruit juice n el zumo de fruta m

full, to be full (after a meal) adj lleno -a

Full house! n ¡Full house!

fuse n el fusible m

G

gallon n el galón m

garlic n el ajo m

gas n el combustible m, la gasolina f

gas gauge indicador de combustible

out of gas quedarse sin combustible

gate (at airport) n la puerta de embarque f

German adj alemán, alemana

gift n el regalo m

gin n la ginebra f

girl n la chica f, la muchacha f

girlfriend n la novia f

give, to give v dar p22 (I give doy)

glass n la copa f

Do you have it by the glass? ¿Lo sirven por copa?

I'd like a glass please. Quiero una copa por favor.

glasses (eye) n las gafas f

I need new glasses. Necesito gafas nuevas.

glove n el guante m

go, to go v ir p25

goal (sport) n el gol m

goalie n el portero m

gold adj oro

golf n el golf m

golf, to go golfing v jugar al golf p35

good adj bueno -a

goodbye n adiós m

grade (school) n el curso m

gram n el gramo m

grandfather n el abuelo m

grandmother n la abuela f

grandparents n los abuelos m

grape n la uva f

gray adj gris

great adj fenomenal / magnífico -a

Greek adj griego -a

Greek Orthodox adj ortodoxo griego

green adj verde

groceries n los comestibles m la compra f

group n el grupo m

grow, to grow (get larger) v crecer (grow up) criarse p23

Where did you grow up? ¿Dónde te criaste?

guard n el guardia m

security guard guardia de seguridad

Guatemalan adj guatemalteco -a

guest n el invitado m, la invitada f

guide (of tours) n el / la guía m f

guide (publication) n la guía f

guide, to guide v guiar p22

guided tour n la visita guiada f

guitar n la guitarra f

gym n el gimnasio m

gynecologist n el ginecólogo m, la ginecóloga f

H

hair n el pelo m, el cabello m

haircut n el corte de pelo m

I need a haircut. Necesito cortarme el pelo.

How much is a haircut? ¿Cuánto cuesta cortarse el pelo?

hairdresser n el peluquero m, la peluquera f

hair dryer n el secador de pelo f

half n la mitad f

one-half medio

hallway n el pasillo m

hand n la mano f

handicapped-accessible adj accesible para personas con discapacidad

handle, to handle v manejar p22

handsome (good-looking) adj guapo -a

hangout (hot spot) n un local / bar muy frecuentado m

hang out (to relax) v pasar el rato p22

hang up (to end a phone call) v colgar p35 (like jugar)

hanger n la percha f

happy adj alegre

hard adj difícil (difficult), duro -a (firm)

hat n el sombrero m, el gorro m

have v tener p29

hazel adj color avellana

headache n el dolor de cabeza m

headlights n los faros delanteros m

headphones n los cascos m

hear v escuchar p22

hearing-impaired adj con discapacidad auditiva

heart n el corazón m

heart attack n el ataque cardiaco m, el ataque al corazón m

hectare n la hectárea f

hello n hola

Help! n ¡Socorro!

help, to help v ayudar p22

hen n la gallina f

her adj de ella

herb n la hierba f

here n aquí

high adj alto -a

highlights (hair) n los reflejos m

highway n la autopista f

hike n la caminata f

to hike v hacer senderismo **p22**

him pron él

Hindu adj hindú

hip-hop n hip-hop

his adj de él

historical adj histórico -a

history n la historia f

hobby n el pasatiempo m

hold, to hold v sujetar **p22**

> **to hold hands** cogerse de la mano
>
> **Would you hold this for me?** ¿Me lo puedes sujetar?

hold, to hold (to pause) v esperar **p22**

> **Hold on a minute!** ¡Espera un minuto!
>
> **I'll hold.** Espero.

hold, to hold (gambling) v quedar **p22**

holiday n el día festivo m

home n el hogar m, la residencia f

homemaker n la ama de casa f

Honduran adj hondureño -a

horn n la bocina f

horse n el caballo m

hostel n el hostal m

hot adj caliente

hot chocolate n el chocolate caliente m

hotel n el hotel m

> **Do you have a list of local hotels?** ¿Tiene una lista de hoteles locales?

hour n la hora f

hours (at museum) n el horario m

how adv cómo, cuánto (how much), cuántos (how many)

humid adj húmedo -a

hundred n cien m, cientos m

hurry v apresurarse **p22, 35**

> **I'm in a hurry.** Tengo prisa.
>
> **Hurry, please!** ¡Apresúrate por favor!

hurt, to hurt v herir **p31** (like querer)

> **Ouch! That hurts!** ¡Ay! ¡Eso duele!

husband n el marido m

I

I pron yo

ice n el hielo m

identification n el carné de identidad f

inch n la pulgada f

indigestion n la indigestión f

inexpensive adj económico -a, barato -a

infant n el bebé m

> **Are infants allowed?** ¿Se admiten bebés?

information n la información f

information booth n el puesto de información m, la caseta de información f

injury n la lesión l la herida f

insect repellent n el repelente para insectos m

inside adj dentro

insult v insultar **p22**

insurance *n* el seguro *m*

intercourse (sexual) *n* el coito *m*

interest rate *n* la tasa de interés *f*

intermission *n* el descanso *m*

Internet *n* Internet *m*

  High-speed Internet *Internet de alta velocidad*

  Do you have Internet access? ¿Tienen acceso a Internet?

  Where can I find an Internet café? ¿Dónde puedo encontrar un ciber-café?

interpreter *n* el / la intérprete *m f*

  I need an interpreter. *Necesito un intérprete.*

introduce, to introduce *v* introducir **p33** (like conocer)

  I'd like to introduce you to _____. *Quiero presentarle a _____.*

Ireland *n* Irlanda

Irish *adj* irlandés, irlandesa

is *v* See be (to be). **p27, 28**

Italian *adj* italiano -a

J

jacket *n* la chaqueta *f*

January *n* enero

Japanese *adj* japonés / japonesa

jazz *n* el jazz *m*

Jewish *adj* judío -a

jog, to run *v* hacer footing **p22**

juice *n* el zumo *m*

June *n* junio

July *n* julio

K

keep, to keep *v* guardar **p22**

kid *n* el niño *m*

  Are kids allowed? ¿Se permiten niños?

  Do you have kids' programs? ¿Tienen actividades para niños?

  Do you have a kids' menu? ¿Tienen un menú para niños?

kilo *n* el kilo *m*

kilometer *n* el kilómetro *m*

kind *n* el tipo *m*, la clase *F* (type)

  What kind of _____ is it? ¿Qué clase de _____ es?

kiss *n* el beso *m*

kitchen *n* la cocina *f*

know, to know (something) *v* saber **p33**

know, to know (someone) *v* conocer **p33**

kosher *adj* kósher

L

to be lactose-intolerant *v* tener intolerancia a la lactosa

land, to land *v* aterrizar **p22**

landscape *n* el paisaje *m*

language *n* el lenguaje *m*

laptop *n* el ordenador portátil *m*

large *adj grande*
last, to last *v durar* **p22**
last *adv último -a*
late *adj tarde*
  Please don't be late. *Por favor no llegues tarde.*
later *adv luego, más tarde*
  See you later. *Te veo luego.*
laundry *n la lavandería f*
lavender *adj lavanda*
law *n la ley f*
lawyer *n el abogado f*
least *n al menos f*
least *adj mínimo*
leather *n el cuero m*
leave, to leave (depart) *v salir* **p23 (I leave** *salgo***)**
left *adj izquierdo -a*
  on the left *a la izquierda*
leg *n la pierna f*
lemonade *n la limonada f*
less *adj menos*
lesson *n la lección f*
license (to drive) *n carné de conducir f*
life preserver *n el salvavidas m*
light *n (lamp) la luz f*
light (for cigarette) *n el fuego m*
  May I offer you a light? *¿Puedo ofrecerte fuego?*
lighter (cigarette) *n el mechero m*
like, desire *v gustar* **(to please) p34**

I would like ____. *Me gustaría ____.*
like, to like *v gustar* **(to please) p34**
  I like this place. *Me gusta este sitio.*
limo *n la limosina f*
liquor *n el licor m*
liter *n el litro m*
little *adj pequeño -a (size), poco -a (amount)*
live, to live *v vivir* **p23**
  Where do you live? *¿Dónde vives?*
living *n la vida f*
  What do you do for a living? *¿En qué trabajos? / ¿A qué te dedicas?*
local *adj local*
lock *n el candado m*
lock, to lock *v cerrar con llave* **p31 (like** *comenzar***)**
  I can't lock the door. *No puedo cerrar la puerta con llave.*
  I'm locked out. *Me he quedado a fuera sin llaves.*
locker *n el casillero m, la taquilla f*
  storage locker *consigna*
  locker room *vestuario*
long *adv mucho tiempo, bastante*
  For how long? *¿Por cuánto tiempo?*
long *adj largo -a*
look, to look *v (to observe) mirar* **p22**

I'm just looking. *Sólo estoy mirando.*

Look here! *¡Mira esto!*

look, to look *v* (to appear) *ver* p23 (I see *veo*)

How does this look? *¿Cómo me queda?*

look for, to look for (to search) *v buscar* p22

I'm looking for a porter. *Estoy buscando un portero.*

loose *adj suelto -a*

lose, to lose *v perder* p31 (like *querer*)

I lost my passport. *He perdido el pasaporte.*

I lost my wallet. *He perdido la cartera.*

I'm lost. *Estoy perdido -a.*

lost. *See* **lose** *perdido -a*

loud *adj ruidoso -a*

loudly *adv ruidosamente*

lounge *n el salón m*

lounge, to lounge *v relajarse* p22, 35

love *n el amor m*

love, to love *v amar* p22, *querer* p31

  to love (family) *querer*

  to love (a friend) *querer*

  to love (a lover) *amar*

  to make love *hacer el amor*

low *adj bajo -a*

lunch *n el almuerzo m*

luggage *n el equipaje m*

Where do I report lost luggage? *¿A dónde me dirijo para informar de pérdida de equipajes?*

Where is the lost luggage claim? *¿Dónde está el reclamo de equipaje?*

M

machine *n la máquina f*

made of *adj hecho de*

magazine *n la revista f*

maid (hotel) *n la camarera f*

maiden *adj soltera*

  That's my maiden name. *Ese es mi apellido de soltera.*

mail *n el correo m*

  air mail *correo aéreo*

  registered mail *correo certificado*

mail *v enviar* p22

make, to make *v hacer* p30

makeup *n el maquillaje m*

make up, to make up (apologize) *v hacer las paces* p30

make up, to make up (apply cosmetics) *v maquillar* p22

male *n el varón m*

male *adj masculino*

mall *n el centro comercial m*

man *n el hombre m*

manager *n el / la gerente m f*

manual (instruction booklet) *n el manual m*

many *adj muchos -as*

map *n el mapa m*

March (month) *n marzo*

market n el mercado m
  flea market el mercadillo m
  open-air market mercado al
  aire libre
married adj casado -a
marry, to marry v casarse
  p22, 35
massage, to massage v dar
  un masaje p22
match (sport) n el partido m
match n la cerilla f
  book of matches librito de
  cerillas
match, to match v igualar,
  hacer juego p22, 30
  **Does this ____ match my
  outfit?** ¿Este ____ hace
  juego con mi vestido?
May (month) n mayo
may v aux poder p31
  May I ____? ¿Puedo ____?
maybe talvez
meal n la comida f
meat n la carne f
meatball n la albóndiga f
medication n el medica-
  mento m, el fármaco m
medium (size) adj mediano -a
medium rare (meat) adj en su
  punto
medium well (meat) adj
  medio hecho
member n el miembro m
menu n el menú m
  May I see a menu? ¿Puedo
  ver un menú?
  children's menu menú para
  niños

  diabetic menu menú para
  diabéticos
  kosher menu menú kósher
metal detector n el detector
  de metales m
meter n el metro m
Mexican adj mexicano -a
middle adj de en medio
midnight n la medianoche f
mile n la milla f
military n el ejército m, los
  militares m
milk n la leche f
milliliter n el mililitro m
millimeter n el milímetro m
minute n el minuto m
  in a minute en un minuto
miss, to miss (a flight) v
  perder p31 (like querer)
missing adj perdido -a,
  ausente, desaparecido -a
mistake n el error m
moderately priced adj de
  precio moderado
Monday n el lunes m
money n el dinero m
  money transfer transferencia de dinero
month n el mes m
morning n la mañana f
  in the morning por la
  mañana
mosque n la mezquita f
mother n la madre f
mother, to mother v cuidar
  p22
motorcycle n la motocicleta f

mountain n la montaña f
  mountain climbing alpinismo
mouse n el ratón m
mouth n la boca f
move, to move v mover **p23**
movie n la película f
much n mucho m, gran cantidad f
mug, to mug (someone) v asaltar **p22**
  mugged adj asaltado -a
museum n el museo m
music n la música f
  live music música en vivo
musician n el músico m, la musica f
muslim adj musulmán
mustache n el bigote m
mystery (novel) n la novela de misterio f

N

name n el nombre m
  My name is ___. Me llamo ___.
  What's your name? ¿Cómo te llamas?
napkin n la servilleta f
narrow adj estrecho -a
nationality n la nacionalidad f
nausea n la náusea f
near adj cercano -a
nearby adj cercano -a
neat (tidy) adj ordenado -a
need, to need v necesitar **p22**

neighbor n el vecino m, la vecina f
nephew n el sobrino m
network n la red f
new adj nuevo -a
newspaper n el periódico m
newsstand n el quiosco m
New Zealand n Nueva Zelanda
New Zealander adj neozelandés, neozelandesa
next prep próximo, al lado
  next to al lado de
  the next station la próxima estación
Nicaraguan adj nicaragüense
nice adj agradable, simpático
niece n la sobrina f
night n la noche f
  at night de noche
  per night por noche
nightclub n la discoteca f
nine adj nueve
nineteen adj diecinueve
ninety adj noventa
ninth adj noveno -a
no adv no
noisy adj ruidoso -a
none n el ninguno
nonsmoking adj de no fumadores
  nonsmoking area zona para no fumadores
  nonsmoking room habitación para no fumadores
noon n el mediodía m

nose n la nariz f
novel n la novela f
November n noviembre
now adv ahora
number n el número m

> **Which room number?** ¿Cuál es el número de la habitación?
> **May I have your phone number?** ¿Me puede dar su número de teléfono?

nurse n la enfermera f
nurse v amamantar p22

> **Do you have a place where I can nurse?** ¿Tienen un lugar dónde pueda amamantar a mi hijo -a?

nursery n la guardería f

> **Do you have a nursery?** ¿Tienen una guardería?

nut n la nuez f

O

o'clock adv en punto

> **two o'clock** dos en punto

October n octubre
offer, to offer v ofrecer p33 (like conocer)
officer n el oficial m, la oficial f
oil n el aceite m
okay adv de acuerdo, vale
old adj viejo -a
olive n la aceituna f
one adj uno -a
one way (street) adj (calle) de sentido único

open (business) adj abierto -a

> **Are you open?** ¿Está abierto?

opera n la ópera f
operator (phone) n el operador m, la operadora f
optometrist n el oculista m
orange (color) adj naranjo -a
orange juice n el zumo de naranja m
order, to order (demand) v exigir p23 (I demand exijo)
order, to order (request) v pedir p32
organic adj orgánico -a
outside n afuera
overcooked adj sobrecocido -a
overheat, to overheat v sobrecalentarse p31 (like comenzar), 35

> **The car overheated.** El auto se ha recalentado.

overflowing adv desbordante
oxygen tank n el tanque de oxígeno m

P

package n el paquete m
pacifier n el chupete m
page, to page (someone) v mandar a llamar p22
paint, to paint v pintar p22
painting n el cuadro m
pale adj pálido -a
Panamanian adj panameño -a

paper n el papel
parade n el desfile m
Paraguayan adj paraguayo -a
parent n el padre m
park n el parque m
park, to park v aparcar **p22**
  no parking prohibido aparcar
  parking fee tarifa de estacionamiento
  parking garage aparcamiento
partner n el compañero m, la compañera f
party n el partido m
party n la fiesta f
  political party partido político
pass, to pass v pasar **p22**
  I'll pass. Paso.
passenger n el pasajero m, la pasajera f
passport n el pasaporte m
  I've lost my passport. He perdido el pasaporte.
pay, to pay v pagar **p22**
peanut n el cacahuete m
pedestrian adj peatonal
pediatrician n el pediatra m, la pediatra f
  Can you recommend a pediatrician? ¿Me puede recomendar un pediatra?
permit n el permiso m
  Do we need a permit? ¿Necesitamos un permiso?
permit, to permit v permitir **p23**
Peruvian adj peruano -a

phone n el teléfono m
  May I have your phone number? ¿Me puede dar su número de teléfono?
  Where can I find a public phone? ¿Dónde hay una cabina de teléfono?
  phone operator operadora
  Do you sell prepaid phones? ¿Venden teléfonos prepagados?
phone adj telefónico -a
  Do you have a phone directory? ¿Tiene un listín de teléfonos / una guía telefónico?
phone call n la llamada f
  I need to make a collect phone call. Necesito hacer una llamada a cobro revertidos.
  an international phone call una llamada internacional
photocopy, to photocopy v fotocopiar **p22**
piano n el piano m
pillow n la almohada f
  down pillow almohada de plumas
pink adj rosado -a
pint n una caña f
pizza n la pizza f
place, to place v colocar **p22**
plastic n el plástico m
play n la obra de teatro f
play, to play (a game) v jugar **p35**

play, to play (an instrument) v tocar **p22**

playground n el patio de recreo, el parque infantil m

Do you have a playground? ¿Tienen un parque infantil?

please (polite entreaty) adv por favor

please, to be pleasing to v agradar **p22**

pleasure n el placer m

It's a pleasure. Es un placer.

plug n el enchufe m

plug, to plug v enchufar **p22**

point, to point v señalar, apuntar **p22**

Would you point me in the direction of____? ¿Me puede indicar cómo llegar a ____?

police n la policía f

police station n la comisaría f

pool n la piscina f

pool (the game) n el billar m

pop music n la música pop f

popular adj popular

port (beverage) n el oporto m

port (for ship) n el puerto

porter n el portero m, la portera f

portion n la porción f

portrait n el retrato m

postcard n la postal f

post office n la oficina de correos f

Where is the post office? ¿Dónde está la oficina de correos?

poultry n las aves de corral f pl

pound n la libra f

prefer, to prefer v preferir **p31** (like querer)

pregnant adj embarazada

prepared adj preparado -a

prescription n la receta f

price n el precio m

print, to print v imprimir **p23**

problem n el problema m

process, to process v procesar **p22**

product n el producto m

professional adj profesional

program n el programa m

May I have a program? ¿Me puede dar un programa?

Protestant n protestante m

publisher n la editorial f

Puerto Rican adj puertorriqueño -a m / f

pull, to pull v tirar de **p22**

pump n la bomba f

purple adj morado -a

purse n el bolso m

push, to push v empujar **p22**

put, to put v poner **p23** (I put pongo)

Q

quarter adj un cuarto

one-quarter un cuarto

quiet adj tranquilo -a

R

rabbit n el conejo m

radio n la radio f

satellite radio radio satelita

rain, to rain v llover **p31** (like poder)

Is it supposed to rain? ¿Va a llover?

rainy adj lluvioso -a

It's rainy. Está lluvioso.

ramp, wheelchair n la rampa para las sillas de ruedas f

rare (meat) adj poco hecho

rate (for car rental, hotel) n la tarifa f

What's the rate per day? ¿Cuál es la tarifa por día?

What's the rate per week? ¿Cuál es la tarifa por semana?

rate plan (cell phone) n el plan de servicio m

read, to read v leer **p23**

really adv verdaderamente

receipt n el recibo m

receive, to receive v recibir **p23**

recommend, to recommend v recomendar **p31** (like comenzar)

red adj rojo -a

redhead n el pelirrojo m, la pelirroja f

reef n el arrecife m

refill (of prescription) n Dispensar de nuevo una receta

reggae adj reggae

relative (family) n el pariente m

remove, to remove v remover **p31** (like poder)

rent, to rent v alquilar **p22**

I'd like to rent a car. Quiero alquilar un coche.

repeat, to repeat v repetir **p32** (like pedir)

Would you please repeat that? ¿Puede repetir eso por favor?

reservation n la reserva f

I'd like to make a reservation for ____. Quiero reservar un / una ____. See p7 for numbers.

restaurant n el restaurante m

Where can I find a good restaurant? ¿Dónde puedo encontrar un buen restaurante?

restroom n el baño m

Do you have a public restroom? ¿Tienen baños?

return, to return (to a place) v regresar **p22**

return, to return (something to a store) v devolver (**p31**, like poder)

ride, to ride v correr **p23**

right adj derecho -a

It is on the right. Está a mano derecha.

Turn right at the corner. Gire a la derecha en la esquina.

rights n pl los derechos m

civil rights *derechos civiles*

river *n el río m*

road *n la carretera f*

road closed sign *n el letrero de carretera cerrada m*

rob, to rob *v robar* **p22**

I've been robbed. *Me han robado.*

rock and roll *n el rock and roll*

rock climbing *n la escalada en roca f*

rocks (ice) *n el hielo m*

I'd like it on the rocks. *Con hielo, por favor.*

romance (novel) *n la novela romántica f*

romantic *adj romántico -a*

room (hotel) *n la habitación f*

room for one / two *habitación para uno / dos*

room service *servicio de habitaciones*

rope *n la cuerda f*

rose *n la rosa f*

royal flush *n la escalera real f*

rum *n el ron m*

run, to run *v correr* **p23**

S

sad *adj triste*

safe (for storing valuables) *n la caja fuerte*

Do the rooms have safes? *¿Las habitaciones tienen caja fuerte?*

safe (secure) *adj seguro -a*

Is this area safe? *¿Es segura esta zona?*

sail *n la vela f*

sail, to sail *v zarpar* **p22**

When do we sail? *¿Cuándo zarpamos?*

salad *n la ensalada f*

salesperson *n el vendedor m, la vendedora f*

salt *n la sal f*

Is that low-salt? *¿Eso es bajo en sal?*

Salvadorian *adj salvadoreño -a*

satellite *n el satélite m*

satellite radio *radio satelital*

satellite tracking *navegación por satélite*

Saturday *n el sábado m*

sauce *n la salsa f*

say, to say *v decir* (**p32**, like *pedir*) (I say *digo*)

scan, to scan *v* (document) *escanear* **p22**

schedule *n el itinerario m*

school *n el colegio m*

scooter *n la vespa f*

Scottish *adj escocés*

scratched *adj rayado -a*

scratched surface *superficie rayada*

scuba dive, to scuba dive *v bucear con escafandra* **p22**

sculpture *n la escultura f*

seafood *n el marisco m*

search *n la búsqueda f*

hand search *inspección manual*

search, to search v buscar
p22

seasick adj mareado -a
  I am seasick. Estoy
    mareado -a.
seasickness pill n la pastilla
  para el mareo f
seat n el asiento m
  child seat asiento para niños
second adj segundo -a
security n la seguridad f
  security checkpoint el con-
    trol de seguridad
  security guard guardia de
    seguridad
sedan n el sedán m
see, to see v ver p23 (I see veo)
  May I see it? ¿Puedo verlo?
self-serve adj auto servicio
sell, to sell v vender p23
seltzer n el sifón m
send, to send v enviar p22
separated (marital status)
  adj separado -a
September n el septiembre m
serve, to serve v servir p32
  (like pedir)
service n el servicio m
  out of service fuera de ser-
    vicio
services (religious) n el oficio
  religioso m
service charge n el recargo m
seven adj siete
seventy adj setenta
seventeen adj diecisiete
seventh adj séptimo -a
sew, to sew v coser p23

sex (gender) n el sexo m
sex, to have (intercourse) v
  tener relaciones sexuales
  p29
shallow adj poco profundo -a
sheet (bed linen) n la sábana f
shellfish n el crustáceo m
ship n el barco m
ship, to ship v enviar p22
  How much to ship this to
    _____? ¿Cuánto cuesta
    enviar esto a _____?
shipwreck n el naufragio m
shirt n la camisa f
shoe n el zapato m
shop n la tienda f
shop v comprar p22
  I'm shopping for mens'
    clothes. Estoy comprando
    ropa de hombres.
  I'm shopping for womens'
    clothes. Estoy comprando
    ropa de mujer.
  I'm shopping for childrens'
    clothes. Estoy comprando
    ropa para niños.
short adj corto -a
shorts n los pantalones cortos m
shot (liquor) n el trago m
shout v gritar p22
show (performance) n el
  espectáculo m, la función f
  What time is the show? ¿A
    qué hora comienza el
    espectáculo?

show, to show v mostrar **p35** (like *jugar*)

Would you show me? *¿Puede mostrarme?*

shower n la ducha f

Does it have a shower? *¿Tiene una ducha?*

shower, to shower v ducharse **p22, 35**

shrimp n la gamba f

shuttle bus n el autobús de enlace m

sick adj enfermo -a

I feel sick. *Me siento enfermo -a.*

side n el lado m

on the side (e.g., salad dressing) *a un lado*

sidewalk n la acera f

sightseeing n las visitas turísticas m

sightseeing bus n el autobús de turistas m

sign, to sign v firmar **p22**

Where do I sign? *¿Dónde firmo?*

silk n la seda f

silver adj plato -a

sing, to sing v cantar **p22**

single (unmarried) adj soltero -a

Are you single? *¿Eres soltero -a?*

single (one) adj sencillo -a, individual

single bed *cama individual*

sink n el fregadero (kitchen) m, el lavabo (bathroom) m

sister n la hermana f

sit, to sit v sentarse **p31, 35** (like *comenzar*)

six adj seis

sixteen adj dieciséis

sixty adj sesenta

size (clothing, shoes) n la talla f

skin n la piel f

sleeping berth n el camarote para dormir m

slow adj lento -a

slow, to slow v reducir la velocidad **p33** (like *conocer*)

Slow down! *¡Vaya más despacio!*

slow(ly) adv lentamente, despacio

Speak more slowly. *Hable más despacio.*

slum n el barrio marginal m

small adj pequeño -a

smell, to smell v oler **p31** (like *poder*)

smoke, to smoke v fumar **p22**

smoking n fumar m **p37**

smoking area *zona de fumadores*

No Smoking *Prohibido fumar*

snack n el bocadillo m

Snake eyes! n *¡Ojos de serpiente!, ¡Par de ases!*

snorkel n el tubo de respiración m

soap n el jabón m

sock n el calcetín m

soda n el refresco m

diet soda *refresco light*

soft adj suave

software n el software m

sold out adj agotado -a

some adj algún, alguno -a

someone n alguien

something n algo m

son n el hijo m

song n la canción f

sorry adj apenado -a

I'm sorry. Lo siento.

soup n la sopa f

spa n el balneario m

Spain n España

Spanish adj español -a

spare tire n la rueda de recambio f

speak, to speak v hablar p22

Do you speak English? ¿Habla inglés?

Would you speak louder, please? ¿Podría hablar más alto, por favor?

Would you speak slower, please? ¿Podría hablar más despacio, por favor?

special (featured meal) n el especial m

specify, to specify v especificar p22

speed limit n el límite de velocidad m

What's the speed limit? ¿Cuál es el límite de velocidad?

speedometer n el velocímetro m

spell, to spell v deletrear p22

How do you spell that? ¿Cómo se deletrea eso?

spice n la especie f

spill, to spill v derramar p22

split (gambling) n la división f

sports n los deportes m

spring (season) n la primavera f

stadium n el estadio m

staff (employees) n el personal m

stamp (postage) n el sello m

stair n la escalera f

Where are the stairs? ¿Dónde están las escaleras?

Are there many stairs? ¿Hay muchas escaleras?

stand, to stand v pararse p22, 35

start, to start (commence) v comenzar p31

start, to start (a car) v encender p31 (like querer)

state n el estado m

station n la estación f

Where is the nearest____? ¿Dónde está ____ más cercana?

gas station la gasolinera

bus station la estación de autobuses

subway station la estación de metro

train station la estación de tren

stay, to stay v quedarse p22, 35

We'll be staying for ____ nights. Me quedaré por ____ noches. Numbers, p7.

steakhouse n el asador m

steal, to steal v robar p22

stolen adj robado -a

stop n la parada f

Is this my stop? ¿Ésta es mi parada?

I missed my stop. Perdí mi parada.

stop, to stop v detener p29 (like *tener*)

Please stop. Por favor deténgase.

STOP (traffic sign) PARE

Stop, thief! ¡Detente, ladrón!

store n la tienda f

straight adj recto -a, derecho -a, liso (hair)

straight ahead todo recto

straight (drink) sencillo

Go straight. (giving directions) Siga derecho.

straight (gambling) n la escalera f

street n la calle f

across the street al otro lado de la calle

down the street calle abajo

Which street? ¿En qué calle?

How many more streets? ¿Cuántas calles más?

stressed adj estresado -a

striped adj a rayas

stroller n el cochecito para niños / bebés m

Do you rent baby strollers? ¿Alquilan cochecitos para bebés?

substitution n la sustitución f

suburb n la zona residencial en las afueras de una ciudad f

subway n el metro m

subway line línea de metro

subway station parada de metro

Which subway do I take for _____? ¿Qué línea tomo para ir a _____?

subtitle n el subtítulo m

suitcase n la maleta f

suite n la suite f

summer n el verano m

sun n el sol m

sunburn n la quemadura de sol f

I have a bad sunburn. Tengo una quemadura de sol mala.

Sunday n domingo m

sunglasses n las gafas de sol f

sunny adj soleado -a

It's sunny out. Hace sol.

sunroof n el techo corredizo m

sunscreen n el protector solar m

Do you have sunscreen SPF _____? ¿Tienen protector solar factor _____? See numbers p7.

supermarket n el supermercado m

surf v hacer surf p22

surfboard n la tabla de surf f

suspiciously adv sospechosamente

swallow, to swallow v *tragar* p22

sweater n *el jersey* m

swim, to swim v *nadar* p22

Can one swim here?
¿Puedo nadar aquí?

swimsuit n *el bañador* m

swim trunks n *el bañador* m

symphony n *la sinfonía* f

T

table n *la mesa* f

table for two *una esa para dos*

tailor n *el sastre* m

Can you recommend a good tailor? *¿Puede recomendar un buen sastre?*

take, to take v *tomar, llevar* p22

Take me to the station.
Lléveme a la estación.

How much to take me to ____? *¿Cuánto cuesta llevarme a ____?*

takeout menu n *el menú para llevar* m

talk, to talk v *hablar* p22

tall adj *alto -a*

tanned adj *bronceado -a*

taste (flavor) n *el sabor* m

taste (discernment) el *gusto* m

taste, to taste v *probar* p35 (like *jugar*)

tax n *el impuesto* m

value-added tax (VAT) *impuesto al valor agregado (IVA)*

taxi n *el taxi* m

Taxi! *¡Taxi!*

Would you call me a taxi? *¿Me puede llamar un taxi?*

tea n *el té* m

team n *el equipo* m

Techno n *la música techno* f

television n *el televisor* m

temple n *el templo* m

ten adj *diez*

tennis n *el tenis* m

tennis court *cancha de tenis*

tent n *la tienda de campaña* f

tenth adj *décimo -a*

terminal n (airport) *la terminal* m

Thank you. *Gracias.*

that (near) adj *ese / eso / esa*

that (far away) adj *aquel / aquello / aquella*

theater n *el teatro* m

them (m/f) *ellos / ellas*

there (demonstrative) adv *ahí* (nearby), *allí* (far)

Is / Are there ? *¿Hay ?*

over there *allí*

these adj *éstos -as*

thick adj *grueso -a, espeso -a*

thin adj *delgado -a, flaco -a, fino -a*

think v *pensar* p31 (like *comenzar*)

third adj *tercero -a*

thirteen adj *trece*

thirty adj *treinta*

this adj *este, esto, esta*

those adj *aquellos -as, esos -as*

thousand *mil*

three *tres*

Thursday *n el jueves m*

ticket *n el billete m*

  ticket counter *mostrador de venta de billetes*

  one-way ticket *billete de ida*

  round-trip ticket *billete de ida y vuelta*

tight *adj apretado -a*

time *n el tiempo m*

  Is it on time? *¿Llegará a la hora prevista?*

  At what time? *¿A qué hora?*

  What time is it? *¿Qué hora es?*

timetable *n (train) el itinerario m*

tip (gratuity) *la propina f*

tire *n la llanta f*

  I have a flat tire. *Tengo una rueda desinflada.*

tired *adj cansado -a*

today *adv hoy*

toilet *n el váter, el retrete m*

  The toilet is overflowing. *El váter se está desbordando.*

  The toilet is backed up. *El váter está atascado.*

toilet paper *n el papel higiénico m*

  You're out of toilet paper. *No hay papel higiénico.*

toiletries *n los artículos de tocador m*

toll *n el peaje m*

tomorrow *n mañana*

ton *n la tonelada f*

too (excessively) *adv demasiado -a*

too (also) *adv también*

tooth *n el diente m*

  I lost my tooth. *Perdí mi diente.*

toothache *n el dolor de muelas m*

  I have a toothache. *Tengo dolor de muelas.*

total *n el total m*

  What is the total? *¿Cuál es el total?*

tour *n la excursión / la visita f*

  Are guided tours available? *¿Tienen visitas?*

  Are audio tours available? *¿Tienen audioguías?*

towel *n la toalla f*

  May we have more towels? *¿Me puede dar más toallas?*

toy *n el juguete m*

  toy store *n la juguetería f*

  Do you have any toys for the children? *¿Tiene juguetes para niños?*

traffic *n el tráfico m*

  How's traffic? *¿Cómo está el tráfico?*

  traffic rules *normas de circulación*

trail *n el sendero m*

  Are there trails? *¿Hay senderos?*

train n el tren m
> **express train** tren expreso
> **local train** tren local
> **Does the train go to ____?**
> *¿El tren va a _____?*
> **May I have a train schedule?** *¿Me puede dar un itinerario de trenes?*
> **Where is the train station?**
> *¿Dónde está la estación del tren?*

train, to train v entrenar **p22**

transfer, to transfer v transferir **p31** (like querer)
> **I need to transfer funds.**
> *Necesito transferir fondos.*

transmission n la transmisión f
> **automatic transmission**
> *transmisión automática*
> **standard transmission**
> *transmisión manual*

travel, to travel v viajar **p22**

travelers' check n el cheque de viajero m
> **Do you cash travelers' checks?** *¿Cambian cheques de viaje?*

trim, to trim (hair) v cortar (el pelo) **p22**

trip n el viaje m

triple adj triple

trumpet n la trompeta f

trunk n el baúl m **(luggage)**, el maletero m **(in car)**

try, to try (attempt) v intentar **p22**, tratar **p22**

try, to try on (clothing) v medir **p32** (like pedir)

try, to try (food) v probar **p35** (like jugar)

Tuesday n el martes m

turkey n el pavo m

turn, to turn v girar **p22**
> **to turn left / right** gire a la izquierda / derecha
> **to turn off / on** encender / apagar **p22**

twelve adj doce

twenty adj veinte

twine n la cuerda f

two adj dos

U

umbrella (beach) n la sombrilla f, **(rain)** el paraguas m

uncle n el tío m

undercooked adj crudo -a

understand, to understand v entender **p31** (like querer)
> **I don't understand.** No entiendo.
> **Do you understand?**
> *¿Entiendes?*

underwear n la ropa interior f

university n la universidad f

up adv arriba / hacia arriba

update, to update v actualizar **p22**

upgrade n mejora de categoría f

upload, to upload v cargar **p22**

upscale adj de lujo

Uruguayan adj uruguayo -a

us pron nosotros -as

USB port n el puerto USB m

use, to use v usar **p22**

V

vacation n las vacaciónes m

on vacation de vacaciones

to go on vacation irse de vacaciones

vacancy n la habitación libre f

van n la furgoneta f

VCR n el grabador de vídeo m

Do the rooms have VCRs? ¿Las habitaciones tienen grabador de vídeo?

vegetables n las verduras f

vegetarian n el vegetariano m, la vegetariana f

vending machine n la máquina expendedora f

Venezuelan adj venezolano -a

version n la versión f

very muy

video n el vídeo m

Where can I rent videos or DVDs? ¿Dónde puedo alquilar vídeos o DVD?

view n las vistas f

beach view vistas a la playa

city view vistas a la ciudad

vineyard n el viñedo m

vinyl n el vinilo m

violin n el violín m

visa n el visado m

Do I need a visa? ¿Necesito un visado?

vision n la visión f

visit, to visit v visitar **p22**

visually-impaired adj con discapacidad visual

vodka n el vodka m

voucher n el vale m

W

wait, to wait v esperar **p22**

Please wait. Por favor espere.

How long is the wait? ¿Cuánto tiempo tengo que esperar?

waiter n el camarero f

waiting area n la zona de espera f

wake-up call n el servicio despertador m

wallet n la cartera f

I lost my wallet. He perdido la cartera.

Someone stole my wallet. Alguien me robó la cartera.

walk, to walk v caminar **p22**

walker (ambulatory device) n el andador m

walkway n el pasillo, el paso, m, la pasarela f

moving walkway el pasillo mecánico

want, to want v querer **p31**

war n la guerra f

warm adj caliente

watch, to watch v observar **p22**

water n el agua m
Is the water potable? ¿El agua es potable?
Is there running water? ¿Hay agua corriente?
wave, to wave v saludar con la mano **(hello)**, decir adiós con la mano **(goodbye)** p22
waxing n la depilación con cera f
weapon n el arma m
wear, to wear v usar p22
weather forecast n el pronóstico del tiempo m
Wednesday n el miércoles m
week n la semana f
this week esta semana
last week la semana pasada
next week la próxima semana
weigh v pesar p22
I weigh _____. Yo peso _____.
It weighs _____. Pesa _____. See for numbers.
weights n las pesas f
welcome adv bienvenido
You're welcome. (at a place) Está bienvenido. **(after "Thank You)** De nada.
well adv bien
well done (meat) bien hecho
well done (task) bien hecho
I don't feel well. No me siento bien.
western adj occidental, de vaqueros (pelicula)

whale n la ballena f
what adv qué
What sort of _____? ¿Qué clase de _____?
What time is _____? ¿A qué hora es _____?
wheelchair n la silla de ruedas f
wheelchair access acceso para sillas de ruedas
wheelchair ramp rampa para sillas de ruedas
power wheelchair silla de ruedas eléctricas
wheeled (luggage) adj con ruedas
when adv cuándo
where adv dónde
Where is it? ¿Dónde está?
which adv cuál
Which one? ¿Cuál?
white adj blanco -a
who adv quién
whose adj de quién
wide adj ancho -a
widow, widower n la viuda f, el viudo m
wife n la mujer f
wi-fi n la red inalámbrica f
window n la ventana f, la ventanilla f
drop-off window ventanilla de entregas
pickup window ventanilla de recogido

windshield n el parabrisas m

windshield wiper n el limpia-parabrisas m

windsurf, to windsurf v practicar windsurf **p22**

windy adj ventoso -a

wine n el vino m

winter n el invierno m

wiper n el limpiaparabrisas m

with prep con

withdraw v retirar **p22**

I need to withdraw money. Necesito retirar dinero.

without prep sin

woman n la mujer f

work, to work v trabajar, funcionar **p22**

This doesn't work. Esto no funciona.

workout n el ejercicio m

worse peor

worst lo peor

write, to write v escribir **p23**

Would you write that down for me? ¿Me lo puede escribir?

writer n el escritor m

X

x-ray machine n la máquina de rayos X f

Y

yellow adj amarillo -a

Yes. adv Sí.

yesterday n ayer m

the day before yesterday anteayer

yield sign n la señal de ceda el paso f

you pron usted, tú, ustedes, vosotros -as

you (singular, informal) tú
you (singular, formal) usted
you (plural informal) vosotros -as (rare)
you (plural formal) ustedes

your, yours adj suyo -a, tuyo -a

young adj joven

Z

zoo n el zoológico m

A

abajo *down adv*

el abanico *m fan (hand-held) n*

la abeja *f bee n*

abierto -a *open (business) adj*

el / la abogado *m lawyer n*

la abolladura *f dent n*

abordar *to board v* **p22**

el abrigo *m coat n*

abril *m April n*

la abuela *f grandmother n*

el abuelo *m grandfather n*

acampar *to camp v* **p22**

el accidente *m accident n*

el aceite *m oil n*

la aceituna *f olive n*

aceptar *to accept v* **p22**

  Se aceptan tarjetas de crédito. *Credit cards accepted.*

la acera *f sidewalk n*

aclarar *to clear v* **p22**

el acné *m acne n*

actual *current / now adj*

actualizar *to update v* **p22**

De acuerdo. / Vale. *Okay. adj adv*

el adaptador *m adapter plug n*

adelante *forward adj*

el adelanto *m advance n*

adentro *inside adj*

el aderezo *m dressing (salad) n*

adicional *extra adj*

adiós *m goodbye n*

la aduana *f customs n*

el aeropuerto *m airport n*

afroamericano -a *African American adj*

afro, africano *afro adj*

afuera *outside n*

la agencia *f agency n*

la agencia de crédito *f credit bureau n*

agnóstico -a *m f agnostic n adj*

agosto *m August n*

agotado -a *exhausted (person) adj, sold out (thing) adj*

  (estar) agotado -a *(to be) exhausted*

agradable *nice adj*

agradar *to please v, to be pleasing to v* **p22**

el agua *m water n*

  el agua caliente *hot water*

  el agua frío *cold water*

el águila *m eagle n*

ahí *there (nearby) adv (demonstrative)*

ahora *now adv*

el aire acondicionado *m air conditioning n*

el ajo *m garlic n*

la albóndiga *f meatball n*

el alcohol *m alcohol n*

alegre *happy adj*

el alemán *m*, **la alemana** *f German n adj*

la alergia *f allergy n*

alérgico -a *allergic adj*

  Soy alérgico -a _____. *I'm allergic to _____.*

algo m *something* n

el algodón m *cotton* n

alguien *someone* n

algún, alguno -a *some* adj

allá *over there* adv

allí *there (far)* adv (demonstrative)

la almohada f *pillow* n

　la almohada de plumas
　down pillow

el almuerzo m *lunch* n

alquilar *to rent* v **p22**

el alpinismo m *mountain climbing* n

alto -a *high, tall* adj

　más alto *higher*
　lo más alto *highest*

la altitud f *altitude* n

el aluminio m *aluminum* n

amable *kind (nice)* adj

el ama de casa m *homemaker* n

amamantar *to breastfeed* v **p22**

el amanecer m *dawn* n

　al amanecer *at dawn*

amar *to love* v **p22**

amarillo -a *yellow* adj

la ambulancia f *ambulance* n

americano -a *American* adj

el / la amigo -a m f *friend* n

el amor m *love* n

ancho -a *wide* adj

el andador m *walker (ambulatory device)* n

el animal m *animal* n

ansioso -a *anxious* adj

el antibiótico m *antibiotic* n

　Necesito un antibiótico.
　I need an antibiotic.

los anticonceptivos m pl *birth control* n

　Estoy usando anticonceptivos. *I'm on birth control.*

anticonceptivo -a *birth control* adj

　Se me acabaron las pastillas anticonceptivas. *I'm out of birth control pills.*

el antihistamínico m *antihistamine* n

el año m *year* n

　¿Cuántos años tiene?
　What's your age?

apagar *to turn off (lights)* v **p22**

el aparcamiento *parking* n

aparcar *to park* v **p22**

　prohibido aparcar *no parking*

el apellido m *last name* n

　Me quedé con mi apellido de soltera. *I kept my maiden name.*

apenado -a *sorry* adj

　Lo siento. *I'm sorry.*

apostar *to bet* v **p35** (like *jugar*)

apresurarse *to hurry* v **p22, 35**

　¡Apresúrate por favor!
　Hurry, please!

apretado -a *tight* adj

la apuesta f *bet* n

　Igualo tu apuesta. *I'll see your bet.*

apuntar to point v **p22**

aquellos / aquellas those adj pl

aquí here adv

argentino -a Argentinian adj

el arma m weapon n

el arrecife m reef n

arriba up adv

el arte m art n

  la exhibición de arte art exhibit

  de arte art adj

  el museo de arte art museum

el / la artesano -a m f craftsperson / artisan n

los artículos de tocador m toiletries n

el / la artista m f artist n

el asador steakhouse

asaltar to mug (assault) v **p22**

  asaltado mugged

el aseo m bathroom, restroom n, bath n

  ¿Tienen aseos? Do you have a public restroom?

asiático -a Asian adj

el asiento m seat n

la asistencia f assistance n

asistir to attend v **p23**

el asma f asthma n

  Tengo asma. I have asthma.

la aspirina f aspirin n

el asunto m matter, affair n

  No te metas en mis asuntos. Mind your own business.

el ataque cardiaco m, **el ataque al corazón** m heart attack n

el atasco f traffic jam n

ateo -a atheist adj

aterrizar to land v **p22**

el ático de lujo m penthouse n

los audífonos m headphones n

el audio m audio n

audio -a, auditivo -a audio adj

ausente missing adj

Australia m Australia n

australiano -a Australian adj

el automóvil m car n

el autobús m bus n

  la parada de autobús bus stop

  el autobús de enlace shuttle bus

  el autobús de turistas sightseeing bus

la autopista f highway n

de auto servicio self-serve adj

avergonzado -a embarrassed adj

las aves de corral f pl poultry n

¡Ay! Ouch! interj

ayer yesterday adv

  anteayer the day before yesterday

ayuda f help n

¡Ayuda! Help!

ayudar to help v **p22**

azul blue adj

B

bailes de salón *m* ballroom
dancing *n*

bailar to dance *v* **p22**

bajo -a low *adj*

más bajo lower

lo más bajo lowest

balancear to balance *v* **p22**

el balcón *m* balcony *n*

el balneario *m* spa *n*

bancario -a bank *adj*

la cuenta bancaria bank
account

la tarjeta bancaria bank card

el banco *m* bank *n*

la banda *f* band *n*

banda ancha *f* broadband *n*

el bañador *m* swimsuit *n*

bañarse to bathe *v* **p22, 35**

la bañera *f* bathtub *n*

el baño *m* bathroom, restroom, bath *n*

el baño de caballeros men's
restroom

el baño de damas women's
restroom

el bar *f* bar *n*

el bar piano piano bar

un bar para solteros singles
bar

barato cheap, inexpensive
adj

más barato cheaper

lo más barato cheapest

el barbero *m* barber *n*

el barco *m* boat, ship *n*

el barrio *m* neighborhood *n*

el barrio marginal *m* slum *n*

la batería *f* battery (for car) *n*

el batido *m* milk shake *n*

el baúl *m* trunk (luggage) *n*

el / la bebé *m f* baby *n*

de bebés, para bebés for
babies *adj*

cochecitos para bebés baby
strollers

comida para bebés baby
food

beber to drink *v* **p23**

la bebida *f* drink *n*

el beso *m* kiss *n*

bien okay, well *adv*, fine *adj*

¿Está bien? Are you okay?

Estoy bien. I'm fine.

bienvenido -a welcome *adj*

Está bienvenido. You're
welcome here.

bilingüe bilingual *adj*

el billar *m* pool (the game) *n*

el billete *m* bill (currency) *n*

el billete *m* ticket *n*

el billete de ida one-way
ticket

el billete de ida y vuelta
round-trip ticket

el mostrador de billetes
ticket counter

birracial biracial *adj*

blanco -a white, off-white
adj

el bloque *m* block *n*

bloquear to block *v* **p22**

la blusa *f* blouse *n*

la boca *f mouth n*
el bocadillo *m snack n*
la bocina *f horn n*
boliviano -a *Bolivian adj*
la bolsa *f* / **el bolso** *m bag n*
el bolso *m purse n*
la bomba *f bomb, pump n*
el bordillo de la acera *m curb n*
el bordo *m board n*
  a bordo *on board*
borroso -a *blurry adj*
la botella *f bottle n*
el braille americano *m braille (American) n*
brandy *m brandy n*
el brazo *m arm n*
brillante *bright adj*
bronceado -a *tanned adj*
bronce (color de) *bronze (color) adj*
bucear *to dive v p22*
  bucear con tubo *to snorkel v*
  bucear con escafandra *to scuba dive v*
  Buceo con escafandra. *I scuba dive.*
el budista *m,* **la budista** *f Buddhist n*
bueno -a *good adj*
  buenos días *good morning*
  buenas noches *good evening*
  buenas noches *good night*
  buenas tardes *good afternoon*
el bufé *m buffet n*
  de tipo bufé *buffet-style adj*

el burro *m donkey n*
buscar *to look for (to search) v p22*
la búsqueda *f search n*
la butaca *f seat n*
  la butaca de patio *orchestra seat*

C

el caballo *m horse n*
el cabello *m hair n*
la cabra *f goat n*
el cacahuete *m peanut n*
el cachemir *m cashmere n*
caer *to fall v p23 (I fall* **caigo***)*
café (color) *brown adj*
el café *m café n, coffee n*
  el café con hielo *iced coffee*
  el café solo *espresso*
  el café expreso *espresso*
  el cibercafé *Internet café*
la caja fuerte *safe (for storing valuables) n*
el cajero automático *m ATM n*
el calcetín *f sock n*
caliente *hot adj, warm adj*
callado -a *quiet adj*
la calle *f street n*
  calle abajo *down the street*
  al cruzar la calle *across the street*
la cama *f bed n*
la camarera de habitación *f maid (hotel) n*
el camarero *m waiter n*
el camarote *m berth n*

cambiar to change (money) v / to change (clothes) v **p22**

el cambio m change (money) n

la casa de cambio m currency exchange n

caminar to walk v **p22**

la caminata f walk n

la camisa f shirt n

el campamento m campsite n

el campista m camper n

el campo de práctica m driving range n

Canadá m Canada n

canadiense Canadian adj

cancelar to cancel v **p22**

la cancha f court (sport) n

la canción f song n

el candado m lock n

cansado -a tired adj

cantar to sing v **p22**

la cantidad f amount n

la caña f pint n

la caña de pescar f fishing pole n

el (café) capuchino m cappuccino n

la cara f face n

cargar to upload v **p22**

el cargo por servicio m service charge n

la carie f cavity (tooth cavity) n

la carne f meat n

el carné de conducir m driver's license n

el carné de identidad m identification n

caro -a expensive adj

la carretera f road n

la cartera f purse n, wallet n

He perdido la cartera. I lost my wallet.

Alguien me robó la cartera. Someone stole my wallet.

casado -a married adj

casarse to marry v **p22, 35**

los cascos m headphones n

el casillero m locker n

el casino m casino n

el catarro m cold (illness) n

el católico m, **la católica** f Catholic n adj

catorce fourteen adj

el CD m, **el disco compacto** m CD n

el cebo m bait n

la ceja f eyebrow n

celebrar to celebrate v **p22**

la cena f dinner n

el centímetro m centimeter n

el centro comercial m mall n

el centro de la ciudad m downtown n

cerca close, near adj

más cerca closer

lo más cerca closest

cercano -a near, nearby adj

más cercano nearer (comparative)

lo más cercano nearest (superlative)

la cerilla m match (fire) n

el cerdo m pig, pork n

cerrado -a closed adj

la cerradura f lock n

cerrar to close v **p31** (like comenzar)

cerrar con llave to lock v p31
(like *comenzar*)

la cerveza f *beer* n

cerveza de barril *beer on tap, draft beer*

la chaqueta f *jacket* n

el cheque m *check* n

el cheque de viajero m *travelers' check* n

la chica f *girl* n

chino -a *Chinese adj*

el chocolate caliente m *hot chocolate* n

el chofer m *driver* n

el chupete m *pacifier* n

el cibercafé m *Internet café* n

ciego -a *blind adj*

cien m *one hundred* n, *adj*

cientos m *hundreds*

el cigarrillo m *cigarette* n

el paquete de cigarrillos *pack of cigarettes*

el cigarro m *cigar* n

cinco *five* n *adj*

cincuenta m *fifty* n *adj*

el cine m *cinema* n

la cinta de correr f *treadmill* n

la cinta transportadora f *conveyor belt* n

el cinturón m *belt* n

el cisne m *swan* n

la cita f *appointment* n

la ciudad f *city* n

el clarinete m *clarinet* n

claro -a *clear adj*

la clase f *kind (type)* n

¿Qué clase es? *What kind is it?*

la clase f *class* n

la clase de negocios *business class*

la clase turista *economy class*

la primera clase *first class*

clásico -a *classical (music) adj*

cobrar to cash v p30

cobrar to charge (money) v p22

cobrar el dinero to cash out (gambling) p30

cobre (color de) *copper adj*

a cobro revertido *collect adj*

el cochecito para niños / bebés m *stroller* n

la cocina f *kitchen* n

la cocina pequeña f *kitchenette* n

cocinar to cook v p22

el coche m *car* n

el coche cama m *sleeping car* n

cogerse de la mano to hold hands v

el coito m *intercourse (sexual)* n

el colegio m *school* n

el colegio de primaria *primary school*

colgar hang up (to end a phone call) v p35 (like *jugar*)

colocar to place v p22

colombiano -a *Colombian adj*

el color *m* color *n*

colorear to color *v* p22

color hueso off-white *adj*

el combustible *m* gas *n*

el indicador de combustible *gas gauge*

sin combustible out of gas

comenzar to begin *v*, to start (commence) *v* p31

comer to eat *v* p23

comer afuera to eat out

los comestibles *m* groceries *n*

la comida *f* food *n*

la comida *f* meal *n*

la comida para diabéticos *diabetic meal*

la comida kósher *kosher meal*

la comida vegetariana *vegetarian meal*

la comisaría *f* police station *n*

cómo how *adv*

el compañero *m*, la compañera *f* partner *n*

la compañía de alquiler de coches *f* car rental agency

compensar to make up (compensate) *v* p22

comportar to behave *v* p22

comprar to shop *v* p22

comprobar to check *v* p22

con with *prep*

el concierto *m* concert *n*

concurrido busy (restaurant) *adj*

la condición *f* condition *n*

en buena / mala condición *in good / bad condition*

el condón *m* condom *n*

¿Tienes un condón? *Do you have a condom?*

no sin un condón *not without a condom*

conducir to drive *v* p22

el conejo *m* rabbit *n*

la conexión eléctrica *f* electrical hookup *n*

la confirmación *f* confirmation *n*

confirmar to confirm *v* p22

confundido -a confused *adj*

la congestión *f* congestion (sinus) *n*

congestionado -a congested *adj*

conocer to know (someone) *v* p33

la consola de juegos *f* game console *n*

la consulta del médico *m* doctor's office *n*

el contacto de emergencia *m* emergency contact *n*

la contestación *f* answer *n*

Necesito una contestación. *I need an answer.*

contestar to answer (phone call) *v*, to answer (a question) *v* p22

Contésteme por favor. *Answer me, please.*

continuar to continue *v* p22

el contrabajo *m* bass (instrument) *n*

la contraseña *f* password *n*

el **coñac** m cognac n

la **copa** f glass (drinking) / a drink n

¿Lo tienen por la copa? *Do you have it by the glass?*

Quisiera una copa por favor. *I'd like a glass / a drink please.*

la **copa incluida** complimentary drink

el **corazón** m heart n

la **corona** f crown (dental) n

correcto -a correct adj

corregir to correct v p23

el **correo** m mail n / post office n

correo aéreo air mail

correo certificado certified / registered mail

correo urgente express mail

¿Dónde está la oficina de correos? *Where is the post office?*

correr to ride v / to run v p23

la **corrida de toros** f bullfight n

la **corriente** f current (water) n

la **corsigna** f storage locker n

cortar to cut, to trim (hair) v p22

el **corte** m cut (wound), incision n

el **corte de pelo** m haircut n

cortés courteous adj

corto -a short adj

coser to sew v p23

costarricense Costa Rican n adj

costar to cost v p35 (like jugar)

cuánto how (much) adv

¿Cuánto? *How much?*

¿Por cuánto tiempo? *For how long?*

¿Cuánto tiempo tardará esto? *How long will this take?*

cuántos how (many) adv

country (la música) f country-and-western adj

crecer to grow (get larger) v p23

la **crema** f cream n

criarse to grow up v p22

¿Dónde te criaste? *Where did you grow up?*

crudo -a undercooked adj

a cuadros checked (pattern) adj

cuál which adv

cualquier -a any adj

cualquier cosa anything n

cualquier lugar anywhere adv

cuándo when adv

cuarenta forty n adj

cuarto -a fourth n adj

un cuarto one quarter, one fourth

el **cuarto de galón** m quart n

cuatro four n adj

el **cubismo** m Cubism n

la **cuenta** f account n

la **cuerda** f rope, twine n

el **cuero** m leather n

cuidar to mother v, to take care of (someone) p22

culpa f *fault* n
> **Es mi culpa.** *I'm at fault.*
> **Fue su culpa.** *It was his fault.*

la cuna f *crib* n
el curso m *grade (school)* n

D

dañado -a *damaged* adj
dar *to give* v **p25** *ir*
dar un masaje *to give a massage* v **p22**
debajo *below* adj
décimo -a *tenth* adj
decir *to say* v **p32** (like *pedir*) (*I say* **digo**)
declarar *to declare* v **p22**
delantero -a *front* adj
deletrear *to spell* v **p22**
> **¿Cómo se deletrea eso?** *How do you spell that?*

delgado -a *thin (slender)* adj
demasiado -a *too (excessively)* adv
la democracia f *democracy* n
De nada. *You're welcome.*
la dentadura f *dentures, denture plate* n
el dentista m *dentist* n
la depilación con cera f *waxing* n
los deportes m pl *sports* n
derecho -a *right* adj, *straight* adv
> **Está a mano derecha.** *It is on the right.*

> **Gire a la derecha en la esquina.** *Turn right at the corner.*
> **Siga derecho.** *Go straight. (giving directions)*

los derechos m pl *rights* n pl
> **los derechos civiles** *civil rights*

derramar *to spill* v **p22**
desacelerar *to slow down* v **p22**
el desagüe m *drain* n
desaparecer *to disappear* v **p33** *conocer*
el desayuno m *breakfast* n
el descanso m *intermission* n
el descapotable m *convertible* n
la descarga f *download* n
descargar *to download* v **p22**
desconectar *to disconnect* v **p22**
el descuento m *discount* n
> **el descuento para niños** *children's discount*
> **el descuento para personas mayores de 65 años** *senior discount*
> **el descuento de estudiantes** *student discount*

el desfile m *parade* n
desmayarse *to faint* v **p22**
despedirse v *to check out (of hotel)* **p32, 25** (like *pedir*)
el despertador m *alarm clock* n
el destino m *destination* n
el detector de metales m *metal detector* n

detener to stop v p29

   Deténgase por favor. Please stop.

   ¡Detente ladrón! Stop, thief!

detrás behind adj

devolver to return (something) v p31 poder

el día m day n

   estos últimos días these last few days

diabético -a diabetic adj

el día festivo m holiday n

la diarrea f diarrhea n

dibujar m drawing (activity) v p22

el dibujo m drawing (work of art) n

el diccionario m dictionary n

diciembre m December n

diecinueve nineteen n adj

dieciocho eighteen n adj

dieciséis sixteen n adj

diecisiete seventeen n adj

el diente m tooth n

diez ten n adj

diferente different (other) adj

difícil difficult adj

el dinero m money n

   la transferencia de dinero money transfer

la dirección f address, direction n

   ¿Cuál es la dirección? What's the address?

   dirección particular (de casa) home address

la discapacidad f disability n

   la persona con discapacidad f disabled person n

   con discapacidad auditiva hearing-impaired adj

la discoteca m nightclub n

el diseñador m, **la diseñadora** f designer n

el disfraz m costume n

disfrutar to enjoy v p22

disponible available adj

la división f split (gambling) n

divorciado -a divorced adj

doble double adj

doce twelve n adj

la docena f dozen n

el doctor m / **la doctora** f doctor n

el dólar m dollar n

doler to hurt (to feel painful) v p31 (like poder)

   ¡Ay! ¡Eso duele! Ouch! That hurts!

el dolor de cabeza m headache n

el dolor de muelas m toothache n

   Tengo dolor de muelas. I have a toothache.

el domingo m Sunday n

dónde where adv

   ¿Dónde está? Where is it?

dondequiera anywhere adv

dorado -a golden (color) adj

dos two n adj

   ¡Dos unos! Snake eyes! (gambling) n

la ducha f shower n

ducharse to shower v **p22, 35**

durar to last v **p22**

duro hard (firm) adj

el DVD m DVD n

E

la economía f economy n

económico -a, barato -a inexpensive adj

ecuatoriano -a Ecuadorian adj

la edad f age n

  ¿Qué edad tienes? What's your age?

el editor m, **la editora** f editor, publisher n

el educador m, **la educadora** f educator n

efectivo m cash n

  efectivo solamente cash only

el ejercicio m workout n

el ejército m the military n

él him pron

de él his adj

la elección f election n

el elefante m elephant n

el ascensor m elevator n

ella f she pron

de ella hers adj

ellos / ellas them pron pl

el e-mail m e-mail n

  ¿Me puede dar su dirección de e-mail? May I have your e-mail address?

  el mensaje de e-mail e-mail message

la embajada f embassy n

embarazada pregnant adj

embarcar to ship v **p22**

la emergencia f emergency n

el empleado m, **la empleada** f employee n

el empleador m employer n

empujar to push v **p22**

encantado -a charmed adj

encender to start (a car) v, to turn on v **p31** querer

enchufar to plug v **p22**

el enchufe m plug n

encontrar to find v **p35** (like jugar)

enero m January n

enfadado -a angry adj

la enfermera f nurse n

enfermo -a sick adj

la ensalada f salad n

en su punto medium rare (meat) adj

entallar to fit (clothes) v **p22**

entender to understand v **p23**

  No entiendo. I don't understand.

  ¿Entiende? Do you understand?

la entrada f entrance / cover charge (in bar) n

entrar to enter v **p22**

  No entre. Do not enter.

  Prohibida la entrada. Entry forbidden. / Do not enter.

entrenar to train v **p22**

entusiasmado -a enthusiastic adj

enviar *to send v* **p22**

enviar un e-mail *to send an e-mail v* **p22**

el equipaje *m baggage, luggage n*

pérdida de equipajes *lost baggage*

de equipaje *baggage adj*

reclamo de equipaje *baggage claim*

el equipo *m team / equipment n*

el error *m mistake n*

la escalada *f climbing n*

la escalada en roca *rock climbing*

para escalar *climbing adj*

el equipo para escalar *climbing gear*

escalar, subir *to climb v* **p22, 23**

escalar una montaña *to climb a mountain*

subir las escaleras *to climb stairs*

la escalera *f stair / flush, straight (gambling) n*

la escalera real *royal flush*

la escalera mecánica *f escalator n*

escanear *to scan (document) v* **p22**

escocés *Scottish adj*

escribir *to write v* **p23**

¿Me lo puede escribir? *Would you write that down for me?*

el escritor *m writer n*

escuchar *to listen v* **p22**

la escultura *f sculpture n*

ese / eso / esa *that (near) adj*

esos / esas *those (near) adj pl*

la espalda *f back n*

español *Spanish n adj*

el especial *m special (featured meal) n*

la especie *f spice n*

especificar *to specify v* **p22**

el espectáculo *m show (performance) n*

la espera *f wait n*

esperar *to hold (to pause) v, to wait v* **p22**

espeso -a *thick adj*

la esquina *f corner n*

en la esquina *on the corner*

la estación *f station n*

¿Dónde está la gasolinera más cercana? *Where is the nearest gas station?*

el estadio *m stadium n*

el estado *m state n*

estadounidense *American adj*

estar *to be (temporary state, condition, mood) v* **p27**

este / esta *this adj*

esto *this n*

éstos / éstas *these n adj pl*

estrecho -a *narrow adj*

estreñido -a *constipated adj*

estresado -a *stressed adj*

la excursión *f tour n*

la exhibición *f exhibit n*

explicar *to explain v* **p22**

expreso *express adj*

extra grande *extra-large adj*

F

la facultad de derecho *law
    school*
la facultad de medicina *med-
    ical school*
la facturación *f check-in n*
la facturación electrónica
    electronic check-in
la facturación en la acera
    curbside check-in
la facturación rapida
    express check-in
pagar la factura *to check
    out (of hotel) v* **p23, 25**
facturar *to bill v* **p22**
la familia *f family n*
el fármaco *m medication n*
los faros delanteros *m pl
    headlights n pl*
el fax *m fax n*
febrero *m February n*
¡Fenomenal! *Great! interj*
el festival *m festival n*
fino -a *fine adj*
firmar *to sign v* **p22**
Firme aquí. *Sign here.*
la flauta *f flute n*
fletar *to charter (transporta-
    tion) v* **p22**
fleteado *charter adj*
la flor *f flower n*
el formato *m format n*
la fórmula *f formula n*
fotocopiar *to photocopy v*
    p22
frágil *fragile adj*
francés *m*, francesa *f French adj*

el fregadero *m sink n*
frenar *to brake v* **p22**
el freno *m brake n*
la frente *f forehead n*
del frente *front adj*
fresco *fresh adj*
frío -a *cold adj*
la fruta *f fruit n*
el fuego *m fire, light (for a
    cigarette) n*
¿Puedo ofrecerte fuego?
    May I offer you a light?
las fuerzas armadas *f pl
    armed forces n pl*
¡Full! *Full! n*
fumar *to smoke v* **p22**
el fumar *m smoking n*
la zona para fumadores
    smoking area
prohibido fumar *no smoking*
la función *f show (perform-
    ance) n*
funcionar *to work v* **p22**
la furgoneta *f van n*
el fusible *m fuse n*

G

las gafas *f pl glasses (specta-
    cles) n*
las gafas de sol *f pl sun-
    glasses n*
la galleta *f cookie n*
el galón *m gallon n*
la gamba *m shrimp n*
la ganga *f deal (bargain) n*
la gasolina *f gas n*
el gato *m*, la gata *f cat n*

el / la **gerente** *m f manager n*

el **gimnasio** *m gym n*

la **ginebra** *f gin n*

el **ginecólogo** *m,* la **ginecóloga** *f gynecologist n*

girar *to turn v* **p22**

Gire a la izquierda / derecha. *Turn left / right.*

el **gol** *m goal (sport) n*

el **golf** *m golf n*

el **campo de golf** *golf course*

gordo -a *fat adj*

el **gorro** *m hat n*

gotear *to drip v* **p22**

el **grabador de vídeo** *f VCR n*

gracias *thank you*

el **gramo** *m gram n*

gran cantidad *f a lot n*

grande *big, large adj*

más grande *bigger, larger*

lo más grande *biggest, largest*

griego -a *Greek adj*

la **grieta** *f crack (in glass object) n*

el **grifo** *m faucet n*

gris *gray adj*

gritar *to shout v* **p22**

grueso -a *thick adj*

el **grupo** *m group n*

el **guante** *m glove n*

guapísimo -a *beautiful adj*

guapo *handsome adj*

guardar *to keep v* **p22**

la **guardería** *f nursery n*

el **guardia** *m guard n*

el **guardia de seguridad** *security guard*

guatemalteco -a *Guatemalan adj*

la **guerra** *f war n*

la **guía** *f guide (publication) n*

el / la **guía** *m f guide (of tours) n*

guiar *to guide v* **p22**

la **guitarra** *f guitar n*

gustar *to please v* **p34**

el **gusto** *m taste (discernment) n*

H

la **habitación** *f room (hotel) n*

habitaciones libres *m vacancy n*

no hay habitaciones *no vacancy*

hablar *to speak v, to talk v* **p22**

Se habla inglés aquí. *English spoken here.*

hacer *to do v, to make v* **p30**

hacer footing *jogging n*

hacer juego *to match v* **p30**

hacer las paces *to make up (apologize) v* **p30**

hacer surf *to surf v* **p22**

hacia *toward prep*

hacia adelante *forward adv*

¿Hay _____? *Is / Are there _____?*

hecho de *made of adj*

la **hectárea** *f hectare n*

la hermana *f sister n*
el hermano *m brother n*
el hielo *m ice n*
la máquina de hielo *ice machine*
con hielo *on the rocks (drink)*
la hierba *f herb n*
la hija *f daughter n*
el hijo *m son n*
el hindú *m,* la hindú *f Hindu n*
hip-hop *hip-hop n*
la historia *f history n*
histórico -a *historical adj*
el hogar *m home n*
la hoja del limpiaparabrisas *f wiper blade n*
hola *hello n*
el hombre *m man n*
hondureño -a *Honduran adj*
el honorario *m fee n*
la hora *f hour n, time n*
el horario *m hours (at museum) n*
el hostal *f hostel n*
la hostería con cama y desayuno *f bed-and-breakfast (B & B) n*
el hotel *m hotel n*
hoy *today n*
húmedo -a *humid adj*

I
la iglesia *f church n*
igualar *to match v p22*
el impresionismo *m Impressionism n*

imprimir *to print v p23*
el impuesto *m tax n*
impuesto al valor agregado (IVA) *value-added tax (VAT)*
la indigestión *f indigestion n*
la información *f information n*
la infusión *f herbal tea n*
el ingeniero *m,* la ingeniera *f engineer n*
Inglaterra *f England n*
inglés *m,* inglesa *f English adj*
el insecto *m bug n*
la inspección manual *f hand search n*
el instituto *m high school n*
insultar *to insult v p22*
intentar *to try (attempt) v p22*
Internet *m Internet n*
¿Dónde puedo encontrar un cibercafé? *Where can I find an Internet café?*
el / la intérprete *m f interpreter n*
(tener) intolerancia a la lactosa *lactose-intolerant adj*
el invierno *m winter n*
el invitado *m /* la invitada *f guest n*
ir *to go v p25*
ir a las discotecas *to go clubbing v p25*
ir de compras *to shop v p25*
Irlanda *f Ireland n*
irlandés *m,* irlandesa *f Irish adj*

italiano -a *Italian adj*
el itinerario *m schedule n, timetable (train) n*
izquierdo -a *left adj*

J

el jabón *m soap n*
japonés *m,* **japonesa** *f Japanese adj*
el jazz *m jazz n*
el jefe *m,* **la jefa** *f boss n*
el jersey *m sweater n*
joven *young adj*
judío -a *Jewish adj*
el jueves *m Thursday n*
jugar al golf *to go golfing v p35*
jugar *to play (a game) v p22*
el juguete *m toy n*
la juguetería *f toy store n*
julio *m July n*
junio *m June n*

K

el kilo *m kilo n*
el kilómetro *m kilometer n*
kósher *kosher adj*

L

el lado *m side n*
a un lado *on the side (e.g., salad dressing)*
al lado de *next to prep*
largo *long adj*
más largo *longer*
lo más largo *longest*

la lata *f can n*
el lavabo *m bathroom sink n*
lavanda *lavender adj*
la lavandería *f laundry n*
la lección *f lesson n*
la leche *f milk n*
leer *to read v p23*
la lejía *f bleach n*
lejos *far adj*
más lejos *farther*
lo más lejos *farthest*
el lenguaje *m language n*
lentamente *slowly adv*
la lentilla *f contact lens n*
lento -a *slow adj*
la lesión *f injury n*
el letrero de carretera cerrada *m road closed sign n*
la ley *f law n*
la libra *f pound n*
libre de impuestos *duty-free adj*
la librería *f bookstore n*
el libro *m book n*
la licencia *f license n*
el licor *m liqueur, liquor n*
el límite de velocidad *m speed limit n*
la limonada *f lemonade n*
el limpiaparabrisas *m windshield wiper n*
limpiar *to clean v p22*
la limpieza en seco *f dry cleaning n*
limpio -a *clean, neat (tidy) adj*
la limusina *f limo n*

(pelo) liso *straight (hair)* adj
el litro m *liter* n
la llamada de despertar f
wake-up call n
la llamada telefónica f *phone
call* n
la llamada a cobro revertido
collect phone call
la llamada internacional
international phone call
la llamada de larga distancia *long-distance phone
call*
llamar *to call (shout)* v p22
llamar por teléfono *to call
(to phone)* v p22
la llanta f *tire* n
las llegadas f pl *arrivals* n
llegar *to arrive* v p22
lleno -a *full* adj
llevar *to take* v p22
llover *to rain* v p31 poder
lluvioso -a *rainy* adj
local *local* adj
el local *club, bar* n
un local muy frecuentado m
hangout (hot spot) n
la lona f *canvas (fabric)* n
luego, más tarde *later* adv
Hasta luego. *See you later.*
las luces delanteras m *head-
light* n
de lujo *upscale* adj
el lunar m *mole (facial feature)* n
el lunes m *Monday* n

la luz f *light (lamp)* n
la luz indicadora *light (on
car dashboard)*
la luz de freno *brake light*
la luz de aviso del motor
check engine light
la luz de aviso del aceite *oil
light*

M
la madre f *mother* n
¡Maldita sea! *Damn! expletive*
la maleta f *suitcase* n
el maletero m *trunk (of car)*
n
el maletín m *briefcase* n
la mamá f *mom* n, *mommy* n
mandar a llamar *to page
(someone)* v p22
manejar *to handle* v p22
Manejar con cuidado.
Handle with care .
la mano f *hand* n
la manta f *blanket* n
la mantequilla f *butter* n
el manual m *manual (instruction booklet)* n
el mañana m *tomorrow* n adv
la mañana f *morning* n
en la mañana *in the morning*
el mapa m *map* n
el mapa a bordo *onboard
map*
el maquillaje m *makeup* n
maquillar *to make up (apply
cosmetics)* v p22

la **máquina** f machine n

la **máquina de rayos X** x-ray machine

la **máquina expendedora** vending machine

marcar to dial (a phone number) v **p22**

marcar directo to dial direct

mareado -a dizzy adj / seasick adj

el **mareo por viajar en coche** m carsickness n

el **marido** m husband n

el **marisco** m seafood n

el **martes** m Tuesday n

marzo m March (month) n

más more, extra adj

el **masaje de espalda** m back rub n

masculino male adj

la **matrícula** f automobile license plate n

mayo m May (month) n

el **mechero** m lighter (cigarette) n

mediano -a medium adj (size)

la **medianoche** f midnight adv

las **medias** f pl stockings n

la **medicina** f the field of medicine n

medio -a half adj, one-half adj / una

media libra half-pound

en **medio** middle adj

medio hecho medium well (meat) adj

el **medioambiente** m environment n

el **mediodía** m noon n

medir to measure v **p32** pedir

mejor better. See good

el / la / lo mejor best. See good

mejor categoría f upgrade n

menos See **poco**

al menos f at least n

el **menú** m menu n

el **menú para niños** children's menu

el **menú para diabéticos** diabetic menu

el **menú de comida para llevar** takeout menu

el **mercadillo** m flea market n

el **mercado** m market n

el **mercado al aire libre** open-air market

el **mes** m month n

la **mesa** f table n

meter bolsas to bag v **p22**

el **metro** m subway n / meter n

la **línea de metro** subway line

la **estación de metro** subway station

¿Qué línea tomo para ____? Which subway do I take for ____?

mexicano -a Mexican adj

la **mezquita** f mosque n

el **miembro** m member n

el **miércoles** m Wednesday n

mil *thousand n adj*
el mililitro *m milliliter n*
el milímetro *m millimeter n*
la milla *f mile n*
el minibar *m minibar n*
el mínimo *least. See little*
el minuto *m minute n*
en un minuto *in a minute*
mirar *to look (observe) v* **p22**
¡Mira aquí! *Look here!*
la mitad *f half n*
la moneda *f coin, currency n*
la montaña *f mountain n*
morado -a *purple adj*
el mostrador *m counter (in bar) n*
mostrar *to show v* **p35** *(like jugar)*
¿Puede mostrarme? *Would you show me?*
el motor *m engine n*
mover *to move v* **p31** *(like poder)*
la muchacha *f girl n*
mucho -a *much adj*
muchos -as *many adj*
la mujer *f woman / wife n*
la multa *f fine (for traffic violation) n*
el museo *m museum n*
la música *f music n*
la música pop *pop music*
la música disco *m disco music n*
la música techno *m techno n (music)*
el musical *m musical (music genre) n*
musical *musical adj*

el músico *m musician n*
el musulmán *m,* **la musulmana** *f Muslim n adj*
muy *very*
muy bien hecho -a *charred (meat) adj*

N

la nacionalidad *f nationality n*
nadar *to swim v* **p22**
Prohibido nadar. *Swimming prohibited.*
la naranja *orange n*
naranja *orange (color) adj*
la nariz *f nose n*
el naufragio *m shipwreck n*
la náusea *f nausea n*
necesitar *to need v* **p22**
el negocio *m business n*
de negocios *business adj*
el centro de negocios *business center*
negro -a *black adj*
neozelandés *m,* **neozelandesa** *f New Zealander n*
nicaragüense, nicaragüeña *Nicaraguan adj*
ninguno -a *none n*
la niña *f little girl n*
la niñera *f babysitter n*
el niño *m boy n, kid n*
los niños *m pl children n pl*
no *no adj adv*
la noche *f night n*
anoche *last night*

de noche *at night*

por noche *per night*

de no fumar *nonsmoking adj*

la seccion de no fumadores *nonsmoking area*

el coche para no fumadores *nonsmoking car*

la habitación para no fumadores *nonsmoking room*

el nombre *m name n*

Me llamo ___. *My name is ___.*

¿Cómo se llama? *What's your name?*

el primer nombre *first name*

las normas de circulación *f pl traffic rules n pl*

nosotros -as *we, us pron pl*

la novela *f novel n*

la novela de misterio *mystery novel*

la novela de romance *romance novel*

noveno -a *ninth n adj*

noventa *ninety n adj*

la novia *f girlfriend n*

noviembre *m November n*

el novio *m boyfriend n*

nublado -a *cloudy adj*

Nueva Zelanda *f New Zealand n*

nueve *nine n adj*

nuevo -a *new adj*

la nuez *f nut (food) n*

el número *m number n*

O

la obra dramática *m drama n*

la obra de teatro *f play n*

observar *to watch v p22*

occidental *western adj*

ochenta *m eighty n adj*

ocho *m eight n adj*

octavo *m eighth n adj*

tres octavos *three eighths*

octubre *m October n*

el / la oculista *m f optometrist n*

ocupado -a *busy adj (phone line), occupied adj*

el oficial *m officer n*

el oficio religioso *m service (religious) n*

ofrecer *to offer v p33 (like conocer)*

oír *to hear v*

el ojo *m eye n*

oler *to smell v p23*

once *eleven n adj*

la onza *f ounce n*

la ópera *f opera n*

el operador *m,* **la operadora** *f operator (phone) n*

el oporto *m port (beverage) n*

el ordenador *m computer n*

el ordenador portátil *m laptop n*

orgánico -a *organic adj*

el órgano *m organ n*

el oro *m gold n*

ortodoxo griego *Greek Orthodox adj*

la oscuridad *f darkness n*

oscuro -a *dark adj*

el otoño *m autumn (fall season) n*

otro -a *another adj*

P

el padre *m father, parent n*

pagar *to pay v* **p22**

el paisaje *m landscape (painting), scenery n*

el pájaro *m bird n*

el pájaro carpintero *m woodpecker n*

el palco *m box (seat) n*

pálido -a *pale adj*

el pan *m bread n*

panameño -a *Panamanian adj*

el pantalón *m pair of pants n*

los pantalones cortos *shorts*

el pañal *m diaper n*

el pañal de tela *cloth diaper*

el pañal desechable *disposable diaper*

el papel *paper n*

el plato de papel *paper plate*

la servilleta de papel *paper napkin*

el papel higiénico *m toilet paper n*

el paquete *m package n*

el parabrisas *m windshield n*

la parada *f stop n*

la parada del autobús *bus stop*

paraguayo -a *Paraguayan adj*

¡Par de ases! *Snake eyes! n*

PARE *STOP (traffic sign)*

el pariente *m,* la pariente *f relative n*

el parque *m park n*

el parque infantil *playground (in park)*

particular / de casa *home adj*

el número de teléfono particular (de casa) *home telephone number*

el partido *m match (sport) n*

el partido político *m political party n*

el pasajero *m,* la pasajera *f passenger n*

el pasaporte *m passport n*

pasar *to pass (gambling) v* **p22**

pasar el rato *to hang out (relax) v* **p22**

el pasatiempo *m hobby n*

el pasillo *m aisle (in store) / hallway, walkway n*

el pasillo mecánico *moving walkway*

el patio de recreo *m playground (in a school) n*

el pato *m duck n*

el pavo *m turkey n*

el peaje *m toll n*

peatonal *pedestrian adj*

la zona peatonal y de compras *pedestrian shopping district*

la peca *f freckle n*

el pedagogo *m,* la pedagoga *f educator n*

el / la pediatra *pediatrician n*

pedir *to order, request, demand v* **p32**

la película *f movie n*

el peligro *m danger n*

el pelirrojo *m,* **la pelirroja** *f redhead n adj*

el pelo *m hair n*

de pelo oscuro *brunette adj*

la pelota *f ball (sport) n*

el peluquero *m,* **la peluquera** *f hairdresser n*

el pensamiento *m thought n*

pensar *v to think* **p31** *(like comenzar)*

pensión *room and board n*

peor *worse. See bad*

lo peor *worst. See bad*

pequeño -a *small adj, short adj, little adj*

más pequeño *smaller, littler*
lo mas pequeño *smallest, littlest*

la percha *f hanger n*

perder *to lose v / to miss (a flight) v* **p31** *(like querer)*

perdido -a *missing adj, lost adj*

perdonar *to excuse (pardon) v* **p22**

Perdone. *Excuse me.*

el periódico *m newspaper n*

la permanente *f permanent (hair) n*

el permiso *m permit n*

permitir *to permit v* **p23**

el perro *m dog n*

el perro de servicio *service dog*

la persona *f person n*

la persona con discapacidad visual *visually-impaired person*

el personal *m staff (employees) n*

el peruano *m,* **la peruana** *f Peruvian n adj*

pesar *to weigh v* **p22**

las pesas *f pl weights n*

la pestaña *f eyelash n*

el piano *m piano n*

el pie *m foot (body part), foot (unit of measurement) n*

la piel *f skin n*

la pierna *f leg n*

la pila *f battery (for flashlight) n*

la píldora *f pill n*

la píldora para el mareo *seasickness pill*

pintar *to paint v* **p22**

la pintura *f painting n*

la piscina *f pool (swimming) n*

la pizza *f pizza n*

el placer *m pleasure n*

Es un placer. *It's a pleasure.*

el plan de servicio *m rate plan (cell phone) n*

¿Tiene un plan de servicio? *Do you have a rate plan?*

la planta *m floor n*

la primera planta *ground floor, first floor*

el plástico *m plastic n*

la plata *f silver (color) n*

plateado -a *silver adj*

el plato *m* dish *n*

la playa *f* beach *n*

poco -a *little adj*

un poco *m* bit (small amount) *n*

poco hecho *rare (meat) adj*

poco profundo -a *shallow adj*

poder *to be able to (can) v, may v aux* **p31**

¿Puedo ____? *May I ____?*

la policía *f* police *n*

el pollo *m* chicken *n*

poner *to put (gambling) v* **p23** (*I put* pongo)

¡Ponlo en rojo / negro! *Put it on red / black!*

ponerse de pie *to stand v* **p22, 35**

popular *popular adj*

por adelantado *in advance adv*

la porción *f* portion (of food) *n*

por favor *please (polite entreaty) adv*

el portero *m*, la portera *f* goalie *n*, porter *n*

la postal *f* postcard *n*

la postiza *f* dentures *n*

el postre *m* dessert *n*

el menú de postres *dessert menu*

el precio *m* price *n*

el precio de entrada *admission fee*

de precio moderado *moderately priced*

preferentemente *preferably adv*

preferir *to prefer v* **p31** (like querer)

preguntar *to ask v* **p22**

preparado -a *prepared adj*

presentar *to introduce v* **p22**

Quiero presentarle a ____. *I'd like to introduce you to ____.*

presupuestar *to budget v* **p22**

el presupuesto *m* budget *n*

la primavera *f* spring (season) *n*

primero -a *first adj*

el primo *m*, la prima *f* cousin *n*

el probador *m* fitting room *n*

probar *to taste, to try (food or clothes) v* **p35** (like jugar)

el problema *m* problem *n*

procesar *to process (a transaction) v* **p22**

el producto *m* product *n*

profesional *professional adj*

profundo -a *deep adj*

el programa *m* program *n*

el prometido *m*, la prometida *f* fiancé(e) *n*

el pronóstico del tiempo *m* weather forecast *n*

la propina *f* tip (gratuity) *n*

propina incluida *tip included*

el protector solar *m* sunscreen *n*

la prótesis dental *f* dentures *n*

protestante *Protestant n adj*
próximo -a *next adj*
   la próxima estación *the next station*
el puente *m bridge (across a river) n / bridge (dental structure) n*
la puerta *f door n*
   la puerta de embarque *gate (at airport)*
el puerto *port (for ship mooring) n*
el puerto USB *m USB port n*
puertorriqueño -a *Puerto Rican adj*
el puesto / punto de información *m information booth n*
la pulgada *f inch n*
en punto *o'clock adv*
   dos en punto *two o'clock*
la puntuación *f exam score n*

Q
qué *what adv*
   ¿Qué tal? *What's up?*
quedar *to hold (gambling) v* **p22**
quedarse *to stay v* **p22, 35**
la quemadura de sol *f sunburn n*
quemar *to burn v* **p22**
querer *to want v* **p31**
el queso *m cheese n*
quién *who adv*
   ¿De quién es ____? *Whose is ____?*

quince *m fifteen n adj*
el quinto *m fifth n adj*
el quiosco *m newsstand n*
el quiropráctico *m chiropractor n*

R
la radio *m radio n*
   la radio satelital *satellite radio*
la rampa para sillas de ruedas *f wheelchair ramp n*
rápido -a *fast adj*
el rasguño *m scratch (on a person) n*
el ratón *m mouse n*
rayado -a *scratched adj*
rayar *to scratch v* **p22**
a rayas *striped adj*
el rayazo *m scratch n*
el rayón *m scratch (on paint, furniture, or a record) n*
recargar *to charge (a battery) v* **p22**
la recepción *f front desk n*
la receta *f prescription n*
   dispensar de nuevo una receta *m refill (of prescription) n*
rechazado -a *declined adj*
   Su tarjeta de crédito ha sido rechazada. *Your credit card was declined.*
recibir *to receive v* **p23**
el recibo *m receipt n*
la reclamación *m claim n*
recocido -a *overcooked adj*

recolectar *to collect v* **p22**

recomendar *to recommend v* **p31** (like *comenzar*)

recto -a *straight adj*

la red *f network n*

la red inalámbrica *f wi-fi n*

reducir la velocidad *to slow v* **p33** *conocer*

¡Vaya más despacio! *Slow down!*

los reflejos *m pl highlights (hair) n*

el refresco *m soda n*

el refresco bajo en calorías *diet soda*

el regalo *m gift n*

el reggae *m reggae n*

regresar *to return (to a place) v* **p22**

relajarse *to relax v* **p22, 35**

el reloj *m clock n, watch n*

remover *to remove v* **p23, 31** *poder*

repartir *to deal (cards) v* **p23**

Déme cartas. *Deal me in.*

el repelente para insectos *m insect repellent n*

repetir *to repeat v* **p23, 32** *pedir*

¿Puede repetir eso por favor? *Would you please repeat that?*

el reproductor de discos compactos *m CD player n*

la reserva *m reservation n*

el restaurante *m restaurant n*

retirar *to withdraw v* **p22**

el retiro *m withdrawal n*

el retraso *m delay n*

el retrato *m portrait n*

la revista *f magazine n*

el río *m river n*

rizado -a *curly adj*

el rizo *m curl n*

robado -a *stolen adj*

robar *to rob, to steal v* **p22**

la roca *f rock n*

el rock and roll *m rock and roll n*

rojo -a *red adj*

romántico -a *romantic adj*

romper *to break v* **p23**

el ron *m rum n*

la ropa interior *f underwear n*

la rosa *f rose n*

rosa *pink adj*

el rubio *m,* **la rubia** *f blond(e) n adj*

la rueda de recambio *f spare tire n*

con ruedas *wheeled (luggage) adj*

ruidoso -a *loud, noisy adj* 77

S

el sábado *m Saturday n*

la sábana *f sheet (bed linen) n*

saber *to know (something) v* **p33**

el sabor *m taste, flavor n*

con sabor a chocolate *chocolate flavored*

la sal *f salt n*

bajo(s) en sal *low-salt*

la sala de degustación *m tasting room n*

la sala de espera *f waiting room n*

el saldo *m balance (on bank account) n*

la salida *f check-out / departure / exit n*

la hora de salida *check-out time*

no es una salida *not an exit*

la salida de emergencia *emergency exit*

salir *to leave (depart) v* **p23** (*I leave* **salgo**)

el salón *m lounge n*

la salsa *f sauce n*

salvadoreño -a *Salvadoran n adj*

el salvavidas *m life preserver n*

el sastre *m tailor n*

el satélite *m satellite n*

la radio satelital *satellite radio*

navegación por satélite *satellite tracking*

secado -a *dried adj*

el secador *m hair dryer n*

secar *to dry v* **p22**

seco -a *dry adj*

la seda *f silk n*

el sedán *m sedan n*

segundo -a *second adj*

la seguridad *f security n*

el punto de control de seguridad *security checkpoint*

el guardia de seguridad *security guard*

el seguro *m insurance n*

el seguro contra daños materiales *collision insurance*

el seguro de responsabilidad civil *liability insurance*

seguro -a *safe (secure) adj*

seis *six n adj*

el sello *f stamp (postage) n*

la semana *f week n*

esta semana *this week*

la semana pasada *last week*

la próxima semana *next week*

una semana *one week*

dentro de una semana *a week from now*

sencillo -a *single n adj / simple adj*

el senderismo *hiking n*

el sendero *m trail n*

sentar *to sit v* **p31** (like *comenzar*)

de sentido único *one way (traffic sign)*

señalar *to point v* **p22**

la señal de ceda el paso *f yield sign n*

separado -a *separated (marital status) adj*

septiembre *m September n*

séptimo -a *seventh n adj*

ser *to be (permanent quality) v* **p28**

ser socio -a *f membership n*

el servicio *m service n*

fuera de servicio *out of service*

el servicio de información telefónica *m directory assistance*

la servilleta *f napkin n*

servir *to serve v* p32 (like *pedir*)

sesenta *sixty n adj*

setenta *seventy n adj*

el sexo *m sex (gender) n*

sí *yes adv*

siete *seven n adj*

el sifón *m seltzer water n*

la silla de ruedas *f wheelchair n*

el acceso para sillas de ruedas *wheelchair access*
rampa para sillas de ruedas *wheelchair ramp*
la silla de ruedas eléctrica *power wheelchair*

sin *without prep*

la sinfonía *f symphony n*

sobre *above adj*

el sobre *m envelope n*

sobrecalentar *to overheat v* p31 (like *comenzar*)

la sobrina *f niece n*

el sobrino *m nephew n*

el socialismo *m socialism n*

el software *m software n*

el sol *m sun n*

solo *alone, straight up (drink) adj*

soleado *sunny adj*

soltero -a *single (unmarried) adj*

¿Eres soltero / soltera? *Are you single?*

el sombrero *m hat n*

la sombrilla *f beach umbrella n*

la sopa *f soup n*

sordo -a *deaf adj*

sospechosamente *suspiciously adv*

suave *soft adj*

el subtítulo *m subtitle n*

suelto -a *loose adj*

la suite *f suite n*

sujetar *to hold v* p22

el supermercado *m supermarket n*

la sustitución *f substitution n*

suyo -a *your, yours adj sing (formal)*

T

la taberna *f bar n*

la tabla de surf *f surfboard n*

el tablero *m game board n*

el tablón de anuncios *m notice board n*

la talla *f size (clothing, shoes) n*

también *too (also) adv*

el tambor *m drum n*

el tanque de oxígeno *m oxygen tank n*

la taquilla *f box office / gym locker n*

tarde *late adj*

Por favor no llegues tarde. *Please don't be late.*

la tarde *f afternoon n*

por la tarde *in the afternoon*

la tarifa *f* fare / rate *n*
la tarjeta *f* card *n*
  la tarjeta de crédito *credit card*
  ¿Aceptan tarjetas de crédito? *Do you accept credit cards?*
  la tarjeta de presentación *business card*
  la tarjeta de embarque *f boarding pass n*
la tasa de cambio *f* exchange rate *n*
la tasa de interés *f* interest rate *n*
el taxi *m* taxi *n*
  ¡Taxi! *Taxi!*
  la parada de taxi *taxi stand*
el té *m* tea *n*
  el té con leche y azúcar *tea with milk and sugar*
  el té con limón *tea with lemon*
el teatro *m* theater *n*
el teatro de la ópera *m* opera house *n*
el techo *m* roof *n*
  el techo corredizo *sunroof*
la tela *f* fabric *n*
telefónico *phone adj*
  el directorio telefónico *phone directory*
el teléfono *m* phone *n*
  el teléfono móvil *cell phone*
  ¿Me puede dar su número de teléfono? *May I have your phone number?*

el operador *m* / la operadora *f* de teléfono *phone operator*
teléfonos prepagados *prepaid phones*
la televisión *f* television *n*
  la televisión por cable *cable television*
  la televisión por satélite *satellite television*
el templo *m* temple *n*
temprano *early adj*
tener *to have v* p29
  tener relaciones sexuales *to have sex*
el tenis *m* tennis *n*
tercero -a *third n adj*
la terminal *f* terminal (airport) *n*
la tía *f* aunt *n*
el tiempo *m* time *n*
la tienda *f* shop, store *n*
  la tienda de campaña *f* tent *n*
la tintorería *f* dry cleaner *n*
el tío *m* uncle *n*
el tipo *m* kind (sort, type) *n*
tirar de *to pull v* p22
tirar de la cadena *to flush v* p22
la toalla *f* towel *n*
tocar *to touch / to play (an instrument) v* p22
todo -a *all adj*
  todo el tiempo *all the time*
  Eso es todo. *That's all.*
tomar *to take v* p22
la tonelada *f* ton *n*

el **torero** *m* bullfighter *n*

el **toro** *m* bull *n*

la **tos** *f* cough *n*

toser to cough *v* **p23**

el **total** *m* total *n*

¿Cuál es el total? *What is the total?*

trabajar to work *v* **p22**

Yo trabajo para ____. *I work for ____.*

¿En qué trabajas? / ¿A qué te dedicas? *What do you do for a living?*

el **tráfico** *m* traffic *n*

¿Cómo está el tráfico? *How's traffic?*

El tráfico está horrible. *Traffic is terrible.*

tragar to swallow *v* **p22**

el **trago** *m* shot (liquor) *n*

la **transacción** *f* transaction *n*

la **transferencia** *f* transfer *n*

la **transferencia de dinero** *money transfer, wire transfer*

transferir to transfer *v* **p31** querer

la **transmisión** *f* transmission *n*

la **transmisión automática** *automatic transmission*

la **transmisión manual** *standard transmission*

tratar to handle *v* **p22**

Tratar con cuidado. *Handle with care.*

trece thirteen *n adj*

treinta thirty *n adj*

el **tren** *m* train *n*

el **tren expreso** *express train*

el **tren local** *local train*

la **trenza** *f* braid *n*

tres three *n adj*

el **tribunal** *f* court (legal) *n*

triste sad *adj*

triple triple *adj*

la **trompeta** *f* trumpet *n*

tú you *pron sing (informal)*

el **tubo de respiración** *m* snorkel (breathing tube) *n*

tuyo -a your, yours *adj sing (informal)*

U

último -a last *adv*

la **universidad** *f* university *n*

uno one *n adj*

la **uva** *f* grape *n*

el **uruguayo** *m*, la **uruguaya** *f* Uruguayan *n*

usar to use *v* **p22**

usted you *pron sing (formal)*

ustedes you *pron pl (formal)*

V

la **vaca** *f* cow *n*

las **vacaciones** *f* vacation *n*

de vacaciones *on vacation*

ir de vacaciones *to go on vacation*

el **vale** *m* voucher *n*

el **vale para comida** *meal voucher*

el **vale para hospedaje** *room voucher*

de vaqueros *western adj (movie)*

el varón *m male (person) n*

el váter *m toilet n*

el vecino *m,* la vecina *f neighbor n*

el vegetariano *m,* la vegetariana *f vegetarian n adj*

el vehículo *m car n*

veinte *twenty n adj*

la vela *f sail n*

la velocidad de conexión *f connection speed n*

el velocímetro *m speedometer n*

el vendedor *m,* la vendedora *f salesperson n*

el vendedor callejero *m,* la vendedora callejera *f street vendor*

vender *to sell v* **p23**

venezolano -a *Venezuelan adj*

la ventana *f window n*

la ventanilla *f window n*

la ventanilla de entregas *drop-off window*

la ventanilla de recogida *pickup window*

ventoso -a *windy adj*

ver *to see v* **p23**

¿Puedo verlo? *May I see it?*

el verano *m summer n*

verdaderamente *really adj*

verde *green adj*

las verduras *m vegetables n*

verificar *to check v*

la verruga *f wart n*

verse *to look (appear) v* **p23, 35**

la versión *f version n*

la vespa *f motorcycle n*

el vestido *m dress (garment) n*

la vestimenta *f dress (general attire) n*

vestirse *to dress v* **p32** pedir **p35**

los vestuarios *m locker room n*

viajar *to travel v* **p22**

el viaje *m trip n*

la vida *f life n*

el vídeo *m video n*

viejo -a *old adj*

el viernes *m Friday n*

el vinilo *m vinyl n*

el vino *m wine n*

el viñedo *m vineyard n*

el violín *m violin n*

el visado *m visa n*

la visita guiada *f guided tour n*

visitar *to visit v* **p22**

visitar lugares de interés *m to sightsee v*

la vista *f view n / vision n*

vistas a la playa *beach view*

vistas a la ciudad *city view*

la viuda *f widow n*

el viudo *m widower n*

vivir *to live v* **p23**

¿Dónde vives? *Where do you live?*

el vodka *m vodka n*

vosotros -as *(Spain) you pron pl(informal)*
votar *to vote* **v p22**
el vuelo *m flight* **n**
  el / la auxiliar de vuelo *m f flight attendant* **n**
  vuelo charter *charter flight*

W
windsurf *to windsurf* **v**

Y
yo *I pron*

Z
el zapato *m shoe* **n**
zarpar *to sail* **v p22**
  ¿Cuándo zarpamos? *When do we sail?*
el zumo *m juice* **n**
  el zumo de fruta *m fruit juice* **n**
  el zumo de naranja *m orange juice* **n**

NOTES (LAS NOTAS)

NOTES (LAS NOTAS)